The Final Farewell

Celebrating
30 Years of Publishing
in India

The Final Farewell

Understanding Last Rites and Rituals Across India's Major Faiths

Minakshi Dewan

HarperCollins *Publishers* India

First published in India by HarperCollins *Publishers* 2023
4th Floor, Tower A, Building No. 10, DLF Cyber City,
DLF Phase II, Gurugram, Haryana – 122002
www.harpercollins.co.in

2 4 6 8 10 9 7 5 3 1

P-ISBN: 978-93-5699-478-2
E-ISBN: 978-93-5699-476-8

Typeset in 11/15.2 Adobe Garamond at
Manipal Technologies Limited, Manipal

Printed and bound at
Replika Press Pvt. Ltd.

My parents, Vijay and Nirmal Dewan, my guiding lights,
and
my daughter and husband, Kaavya and Sourabh, who inspire me every
day.

Contents

Introduction

Why do we need a book on last rites and rituals? This is the question I asked myself before embarking on this enriching yet challenging journey. Of course, every writer deals with this fundamental question before advancing with a non-fiction book project. However, I will explore the answer as I go along.

I lost my father in 2019, which is when I experienced these rites first-hand as a chief mourner, watching everything closely. Moreover, lighting the funeral pyre and immersing papa's ashes in the Ganges of Haridwar with my sister was an enriching journey. I didn't understand the meanings behind these rituals, but my conversations with specialists like the funeral pandit and the tirath purohit, while observing the crematorium staff, were exciting and intriguing.

I remember when I asked a funeral pandit about his work. He said, 'Didi, we only deal with death-work. Other pandits assist in shubh karya.' I wondered how funeral pandits are different. I remember Shambu, who tirelessly assisted in preparing the pyre and collecting the ashes. I remember his red eyes and the slur in his voice. I wondered why he was perpetually intoxicated. I was fascinated by the end-of-life rituals and the people who assisted in the thirteen-day journey.

It is all so humbling. When us humans thought they had triumphed over deadly epidemics, we were hit by a pandemic and the anguish of an enormous death toll. Amidst restrictions, people worldwide had to compromise when it came to the traditional end-of-life rituals aligned with deeply held customs and traditions while coping with the unexpected departure of loved ones.

Numerous stories illustrated how the performance of sacred last rites was affected by the pandemic, revealing the extent of the crisis. 'The cremations previously performed with utmost respect became a burden for families during the pandemic—*pehle insaan kandhe par aata tha* (once the family members carried the bier on the shoulders). During Covid, the corpses came wrapped in white plastic sacks instead of the traditional white cloth. The plastic-wrapped bodies were lifted straight from the ambulances and placed upon the pyre—the bier was missing. The only way to identify the deceased was through labels. The staff had to forgo many crucial rituals, bound by the government protocols,' recounted a crematorium supervisor of Nigambodh Ghat in Delhi during a conversation.

Moreover, in the absence of formal mourning and grieving avenues, people were left to their own devices—causing enormous distress and exacerbating the grief. 'Madam, no one was available to collect the corpses from the homes,' said a volunteer. At that time, the end-of-life rituals and their relevance became clear to many. Everyone started speaking about these ceremonies, bringing the death care work into the spotlight, and everything surrounding death grasped the human imagination.

The idea behind this book was conceived amidst the raging crisis when we saw countless deaths—compelling us to rethink/reimagine the end-of-life rituals and their relevance in human life. The aim was to develop a comprehensive and readable volume encapsulating and demystifying varied aspects of last rites and rituals—a daunting task that involved stringing various narratives and experiences together in one book.

This book doesn't just describe the practices of last rites and traditions among Hindus, Parsis, Muslims, Christians and Sikhs in the Indian subcontinent. Instead, it delves deeper into the meanings and interpretations behind end-of-life rituals through information I gathered by speaking to ritual specialists, researchers, death workers. Some of the things I mention come from my own experiences. So much of what was said and learnt has grown into the many stories gathered here.

As I started my research, my curiosity about death care workers like Shambhu led me to the ghats and kabristans of Delhi and Varanasi, each a theatre to lives, struggles and journeys I try to weave into words for you, dear reader. Despite challenges, how these workers tirelessly worked during the pandemic was heartwarming and inspiring. I recount conversing with a worker in South Delhi's crematorium, who told me, 'We fought the war against Corona—just like the army. The work was difficult (*jokhim ka kaam*), but we never stopped—we worked day and night. It is our dharam to serve people.' Through these candid conversations, I gathered how overlooked and important their work was.

My exchanges with the ritual specialists featured in this volume were equally insightful and exciting. It was delightful speaking to the tirath purohit, an enterprising practitioner I had met during papa's last rites in Haridwar. 'I am the purohit of Sunil Dutt, Dr Manmohan Singh and Virat Kohli,' he told me boisterously, naming a few well-known personalities from films, sports and politics among his clients. Similarly, talking to the humorous and fearless Parsi priest was equally amusing. At the beginning of the conversation, he told me, '*Pucho kya puchna hai, mujhe kisi se dar nahin lagta* (ask me whatever you want to ask, I am not afraid of anyone).' Priest Mirza is a revolutionary in his own right. When sky burials at Doongerwadi came under the scanner, he offered his community members cremation services. It was hilarious how he told me why he didn't want to be born as a priest in his next life. Moreover, these conversations led me to understand how these professions are transitioning in the current scenario, determining the future of last rites in India.

While performing papa's last rites, I confronted many difficult questions about such rituals. I was particularly inquisitive about their relationship with the environment. However, as I went deeper, I discovered many disturbing aspects. For example, I found how the Parsi funerary practice of dokhmenashini, or sky burial, was threatened because of the extinction of vultures.

Until I started working on this volume, I was unaware of India's professional funeral service scene, unlike in the West, where funeral directors became indispensable long ago. I always associated funerals in India with families coming together and organizing the funeral as we did for papa. However, while talking to funeral directors, I discovered how these services slowly took on a commercial tint. I remember a professional funeral service provider telling me, 'Outside India, these services are commonly available. However, the death sector is not professionalized in our country. Moreover, in the current times, families are growing smaller—one can't rely on relatives. Sometimes, people are not even aware of the closest crematorium.' I, therefore, thought it would be pertinent to discuss these emerging trends in the book.

While working on another section, I learned about death tourism in Varanasi. Intrigued by this concept, I started browsing through the websites. I discovered walking tours with themes like 'Death and Rebirth.' Then I heard stories about how these tourists and travel companies commenced walking tours to quench tourists' morbid fascination. Later, my curiosity took me to Varanasi's burning ghats and the Aghori Ashram, where I unravelled more.

And there was still so much to learn. Gender is an overarching theme I explore throughout the book. For instance, while exploring gender and mourning, I discovered mirasans of Punjab and oppari performers of Tamil Nadu. I found that hiring lower-caste women to perform mourning rituals/lamentations in India was common. I was aware of the professional women employed to sing laments and eulogies in Rajasthan, like the Rudaalis, but others were unexplored. Therefore, I take the opportunity of documenting these mourning traditions in the book before they are relegated to history.

Of course, it was not all gloomy. Can you imagine death being celebrated with music? Yes! Music has been an integral part of human existence in life and death worldwide. While talking to music composers in Tamil Nadu, I discovered parai and gaana music performed at funerals. In 2018, gaana artists, who were initially funeral singers, came together to form the *Casteless Collective* music band. Through interviews with performers and music composers, I delineate parai and gaana in their current avatar.

Inspired by my experience as the chief mourner during papa's last rites, I wanted to capture the involvement of women during death. So I wrote a lengthy post on social media inviting my friends to share their stories. Instead, I received an overwhelming response from many women who had actively participated in the last rites of their family members. These stories and anecdotes are an important part of this book.

While I was still disentangling the conversations with these women, someone approached me with a different story. Gunjan was distraught because her newborn daughter was not given a respectful farewell after her untimely death. Her compelling narrative led me to write a section on gender discrimination during the last rites.

Later, as I conversed with a friend, she suggested I look at women's portrayal during the last rites and rituals in cinema. So, since cinema is a popular media of mass consumption and plays a crucial role in moulding opinions, I started looking at films. In the process, I reviewed two recent films: *Ramprasad ki Tehrvi* and *Pagglait*. As a result, this book now holds candid interviews with the writers and directors of the films.

As I moved forward, I came across two documentary films that revealed discrimination in death. The documentary film *Six Feet Under* brings out stories of Dalit families from several districts of Kerala who have been forced to bury their loved ones in their homes and under public pathways. I realized the concept of caste remains pervasive even in the end-life rituals—following people to their graves and pyres. So I built a section based on eye-opening interviews with activists, filmmakers, victims and experts.

While exploring forms of discrimination surrounding death and related ceremonies, I could not ignore the Kinnar community. Everyone is intrigued by them, and more so, their last rites. I try to straighten out many misconceptions surrounding the community here.

As I said before, I started working on this book amidst the deadly second wave of Covid-19. I was intrigued by how this ongoing pandemic challenged our age-old beliefs and customs around death. However, discovering just how many members of the community came forward to help humanity deal with this crisis was heartwarming. Innumerable stories were floating around, waiting to be told. I learned how a volunteer converted his car into a make-shift ambulance/hearse to carry corpses of the individuals who succumbed to the deadly virus. Next, I understood how death care workers worked day and night during the emergency. I listened to stories of young women volunteers who conducted the last rites without informing their families. 'My aai was terrified. She told me working with an NGO is fine, but this work is unacceptable for girls,' said Nikita, a volunteer.

Finally, I learned how the aggrieved families coped with the sudden, heartbreaking loss of loved ones—compromising traditional rituals and condolence practices. 'It was the most traumatizing experience for my family. My mother was shocked—she went silent for two days. I felt helpless sitting here in the USA. I still feel numb many times,' Asha said while narrating her story.

In the absence of prayer meetings, I looked at how online initiatives helped relieve the families, balming their wounds without conventional grieving mechanisms. 'I was concerned about what was happening around me. Usually, when death occurs, there is a considerable grieving process that humans go through. But unfortunately, this was not happening during the Covid pandemic. So, people were carrying the grief within them. I understood that people needed help—they wanted to talk and vent. That's when I started The Katha Club, an online initiative,' said Smita, dance and movement therapist and personal counsellor from Mumbai, during our conversation.

India's diversity is highlighted in its various last rites and rituals. This book is my attempt to weave these disparate strands together because what I felt after this eye-opening journey was rewarding and deserves to be shared. No matter what one may believe in, all forms of life share that certainty of death, and so it deserves respect and care for all the stories it leaves behind for the living.

1

Antam Sanskar in Sikh Tradition

I

Interpreting Death

Death is a unique phenomenon that even science cannot fully comprehend. However, religious scriptures have elaborated on the philosophy of death and related rites and rituals. Based on my conversations with religious experts and interpretation of Gurbani, I have written this section, providing a glimpse of Sikh philosophy on death and related last rites and rituals.

According to Gurbani, death is inevitable, a law of nature. Guru Nanak, the first Sikh guru, said, we all enter this world with death as our written fate (SGGS: 876). Therefore, whosoever is born must die.

Furthermore, Gurbani teaches us that only the Supreme controls birth and death. He has the power to create and destroy, and none other can interfere. Similarly, Dr Manpreet Singh, a Sikh kathavachak,

1

reiterated—birth and death are not under human control, so we should leave them to supreme powers.

According to Gurbani, death is pre-ordained, and no one can foretell the time of its arrival. For instance, in the Guru Granth Sahib, there is a mention that the end does not ask the time, the date or the day of the week. Moreover, according to the holy scripture, death does not consider age or place and sometimes occurs unexpectedly. Therefore, some are destined to die in infancy, while others die of old age.

According to the sacred scripture, the soul is immortal. Therefore, physical death does not mean the death of the soul. It further elaborates how the soul of the gurmukh merges with the supreme just like a rain drop joins the ocean.

Furthermore, the Guru Granth Sahib also highlights that death cannot be apprehended apart from life. By contemplating both together, one can truly comprehend the phenomenon of life and death. An essential aspect of Guru Nanak's philosophy emphasized everyday life's values. Therefore, the guru preached attaining God while being part of the social world and earning one's living. Thus, the faith focuses on earthly duties, such as honouring God, performing charity and promoting justice.

Moreover, Sikh scriptures don't dwell on what happens after death. Instead, Gurbani teaches one to be unafraid of death and live one's life remembering God. According to the holy scripture, life is temporary— everyone has to leave this world sooner or later. Therefore, one should not think of hell or heaven. Instead, one should focus on being united with God.

In addition, Gurbani stresses on leading a life of gurmukh to free oneself from the cycle of birth and death. By extension, the scripture stresses that living the life of manmukh can impede a soul from attaining mukti. Therefore, a considerable part of the Guru Granth Sahib distinguishes between gurmukh and manmukh. Thus, throughout the

Guru Granth Sahib, Gurbani elaborates on the qualities of gurmukhs as spiritual beings who live by gurmat.

II
How to Approach Death: the Guru Granth Sahib

Gurbani also elaborates on how to approach the end. The scripture teaches us not to weep over death. 'We need to accept death as a reality and not fear it,' Dr Manpreet told me. Instead, one should submit to the will of the Lord and pray for the peace of the departed soul. According to Gurbani, one should not lose strength by grieving because the body is bound to perish. There is no denying that one feels pain upon the death of loved ones. However, the Sikh faith underlines that emotional attachments and doubts cause pain and suffering for the living and dead.

1.   Sing Alahunia: Remembering His Name

Guru Nanak advised against customary ritual mourning. Instead, he suggested remembering God and singing the alahunia of Guru Nanak as a replacement for the traditional dirges. In Guru Granth Sahib, there are Guru Nanak's five eulogies and four by Guru Amar Das (third Guru of the Sikhs) that advise Sikhs to rely on prayer, scriptures, and kirtan in discovering peace during grief. Besides, according to Guru Nanak, the sorrow of Separation from the supreme is genuine, and all the other expressions of grief are hollow and transitory.

2.   Anand: the Blissful Experience

In the Guru Granth Sahib, birth, marriage and death are viewed as blissful. Therefore, hymns of 'Anand Sahib' are recited during all the life-cycle events, both in happiness and sorrow. 'Anand Sahib' is one of the most celebrated hymns in the Gurbani, composed by Guru Amar Das, seeking God's grace and blessings and expressing delight at the union with God.

'The concept of death is anand in Sikhism. So if life is anand, then death is anand too,' explains Manpreet Singh.

The composition centres upon the experience of anand, resulting from the individual soul merging with the supreme soul—attained through simran or constant remembrance of God. Thus, anand is the soul's bliss, which does not diminish in adversity. On the contrary, it is a positive spiritual state of inner poise and composure in which one is freed from all suffering.

3. Ramkali Sadd—the Advice of Guru Amar Das

'The Ramkali Sadd', a six-stanza composition in the Guru Granth Sahib written by Baba Sundar in Ramkali Raga, informs the Sikh attitude toward physical death. It primarily depicts the event when Guru Amar Das receives a call from the Almighty on the completion of his sojourn in the world.

Baba Sundar, the great-grandson of Guru Amar Das, recaptures the guru's advice for his followers and family members. Guru Amar Das informs them not to weep, wail, or perform the customary mourning rite over his death. Since death is an opportunity for the individual soul to unite with the supreme soul, it is not a moment for lament. Therefore, 'Ramkali Sadd' highlights the importance of remembering God at the final departure instead of mourning.

According to 'Ramkali Sadd', one should surrender to the name of the Supreme Being. It states that the imperishable and immeasurable Lord can be realized only through simran. Therefore, when the call of death came, Guru Amar Das was immersed in the meditation of God's name.

In addition, the composition teaches how to achieve equanimity at one's departure. It summarizes the guru's commands in facing the sad moment of his end with calm serenity. One is instructed to rejoice in the Lord's will and remember his name because only that will help humans in their journey to the next world, not traditional funeral rituals.

Two stanzas, written in the first person, represent the guru's last advice to his followers and relations. 'The Sadd' is commonly recited after reading the Guru Granth Sahib as part of the obsequies. This philosophy broadly guides the Sikh end-life rites and rituals.

III
Funeral Rites in Rahit-Namas

I thought it would be interesting to trace the development of last rites and rituals among Sikhs. Harjot Oberoi in his book, *The Construction of Religious Boundaries: Culture, Identity and Diversity in the Sikh Religion,* maintains that the Sikhs possessed a fluid identity before the Khalsa transformation (Oberoi 1994, 63). The Khalsa tradition was created in 1699 by the Tenth Guru of Sikhism, Guru Gobind Singh.

With its formation, the Khalsa introduced new rituals related to birth, initiation and death, which endowed an individual with a new and unique identity to distinguish the Khalsa from the rest of civil society (Oberoi 1994, 63). With the declaration of the establishment of the Khalsa by Guru Gobind Singh, the Rahit was developed to include new obligations recorded in texts called Rahit-namas. Scholars consider rituals as a critical element in constructing religious identity. Therefore, it was crucial to consolidate the rites of passage to strengthen the Sikh identity through Rahit-namas.

In his book, Oberoi writes: 'Sometime in the 18th century, an extensive body of literature emerged known as the Rahit-namas or manuals of conduct. Although very little is known about their exact origin, the authorship, or the nature of their audience, one central theme of the literature is its repeated emphasis on purging the Sikh tradition of what were considered non-Sikh practices' (Oberoi 1994, 329).

According to historian W.H. McLeod, Rahit is the code of belief and conduct that all Khalsa members must obey. It is the manual of Rahit principles. Although, he states, the Rahit-namas might not be well-known to many members of the Sikh community. Nevertheless, the documents represented the normative standard of Sikh beliefs and behaviour. Besides, the manual may not share the views of an ordinary Sikh, nor do they describe the ordinary Sikh's way of life. Furthermore, as per him, most Sikhs will not have read a Rahit-nama and will be unaware of its contents. However, according to him the Rahit-namas theoretically provide the ideal standard for a Khalsa Sikh (McLeod 2003, 7).

Given the significance of Rahit-namas in Sikh literature, in the next part, I will broadly highlight the end-of-life rituals specified in different Rahit-namas of the eighteenth and nineteenth centuries. According to Harjot Oberoi, the mortuary rituals were the final set of rituals appropriated by the Khalsa Sikhs in the 18th century (Oberoi 1994, 65). Interestingly, the Rahit-namas dictated what was not to be followed during Sikh lamentation. Unfortunately, there is also a lack of consensus among historians on the dates and authorship of multiple Rahit-namas. Besides, each Rahit-nama may not describe the last rites in detail, but instead offer a glimpse of the funerary codes of conduct.

1.   Chaupa Singh's Rahit-nama

In this Rahit-nama, Hindu conventions were retained to some extent. However, at funerals, the head of the deceased Sikh must not be shaved, but the ashes should be deposited in the Ganga. Furthermore, a shraddh ceremony should be held on the anniversary of a father's death.

> The head of a deceased *Gursikh* must not be shaved, not even that of *Sahaj-dhari*. *Kirtan* (devotional singing) should be sung and charitable offerings distributed. There should be no

public lamentation. *Karah prasad* (sacred pudding) should be distributed after washing the corpse. *Katha* and *kirtan* should continue for as many days as the deceased's family can afford. The mourners should all be Sikhs. Spread a complete reading of the Granth Sahib over this period. After the funeral the ashes of the deceased should be deposited in the Ganga. On the anniversary of a father's death, hold a *shraddh* ceremony (McLeod 2003, 106).

2. Daya Singh's Rahit-nama

This Rahit-nama forbids the offerings to the ancestors, holding a shraddh ceremony like Hindus or worshipping at the cenotaph or tomb of a dead person. Furthermore, it lays stress on reading Sikh scriptures and distributing Karah prasad. The end-of-life rituals are described as follows:

When a Sikh dies, change his kachh, bathe him and tie on a turban. Read Japuji continuously. Prepare and distribute karah prasad to Sikhs. Do not weep when a Sikh dies. If a Khalsa dies without wearing a kachh, he cannot achieve spiritual liberation (McLeod 2003, 129).

3. Mukti-nama (Sakhi 8)

This Rahit-nama forbids following the Vedic traditions during the funeral ceremony. It also advises against the excessive display of grief. The funeral rites described in this Rahit-nama are:

Do not weep endlessly for a Sikh friend who had died. Prepare *karah prasad*, read Anand, and abandon all grieving for the deceased Sikh. Women should not beat their breasts, but instead, hear sacred hymns, read. The entire gathering of holy

people, both Brahmins and Sikhs, should be fed and given gifts.
Do not follow Vedic ceremony. Do not cremate the deceased
Sikh in accordance with it (McLeod 2003, 143).

4.   Prem Sumarag

This Rahit-nama also advises against excessive lamenting the death. It
additionally prescribes a widow's role after the death of her husband.
The Prem Sumarag, Chapter 7, describes death rites as follows:

> Do not cry, lament, or abjure sleeping on beds. Accept (His)
> *hukam* (divine order) as true and be resigned. A new pair
> of *kachh* should be put on the deceased's body after it has
> been washed. After dressing it, a sword should be placed on
> its right. There should be no wailing—God's will should be
> accepted without any sign of grief. The widow should adopt
> simplicity and restraint, think of the deceased as ever-present
> with her, and read the *Pothi* of *Shabad-Bani* (McLeod 2003).

Harjot Oberoi mentions that to encourage the acceptance of the
changed rituals, the Tat Khalsa popularised the last rites and rituals
through various publications and leading Sikh newspapers. 'The Tat
Khalsa were also unwilling to leave death alone. The environment of
the corpse was seen to have as much potential for communicating
communal identity as the body of a living person' (Oberoi 1994, 341).

We saw a lack of uniformity in the rites and rituals described
in different sources, but there is a significant consensus on some
aspects. Despite variation in modes, death rites are conceived as non-
Brahmanical. Along with this, the recitation of the Anand, performing
Ardas, and distribution of karah parshad are the standard features of
Sikh death rites. In addition, excessive mourning is discouraged in
the Rahit-namas.

IV
Cremation and Last Rites in the Current Times

Later, to provide an agreed Rahit-nama, the SGPC (Shiromani Gurdwara Parbandhak Committee) prepared a new manuscript with the expert team's assistance. Rehat Marayada is a document underlying the official Sikh Code of Conduct. The current version of Rehat was produced by involving several Sikh scholars and theologians of this century. The Rehat Marayada is authorized by the Akal Takht, the seat of supreme temporal authority for Sikhs. However, according to McLeod, the conformity of Rehat Marayada does not apply to all Sikhs. There are those who, in varying degrees, do not accept all that Sikh Rehat Marayada prescribes. However, the final obsequies, also denoted as 'Antam Sanskaar' described in Rehat Marayada, are mentioned in Article XIX.

As said before, the Sikh funeral service does not focus on the pain or grief of losing a loved one but treats it like a celebration of the soul. However, it is mentioned that the body of a dying or dead person must not be put on the floor, like in Vedic tradition. According to Guru Granth Sahib, the survivors must recite Waheguru (name of God). The gathering should not indulge in excessive grief but hear sacred hymns. Furthermore, according to the Sikh religion, both young and old should be cremated. However, it is specified that if arrangements for cremation cannot be made, one may immerse the body in flowing water and dispose of the body in any other manner. In the later part, I describe the last rites in more detail.

1. Preparations Before the Funeral

The close family members generally prepare the body for cremation. Before the funeral service, the deceased's body is washed and dressed by immediate family members. 'First, the body should be appropriately cleaned to eliminate any dirty contents,' said Atma Singh, a Granthi.

While that is done, it is advised that one should not remove Sikh Khalsa symbols such as comb, kaccha, karha, and kirpan. In addition, a Sikh man should be clothed in fresh garments and a turban, while the married woman, whose husband is alive, may be dressed in red clothes, indicating her marital status. After that, the body is covered with a shroud, usually a white sheet. However, decorating the arthi (bier) with flowers is not crucial during Sikh last rites. But the rituals should be carried out without excessive display of grief.

Next, the Antam Yatra Ardas (a prayer that follows the recitation of the banis) is offered while transferring the body on the arthi. Finally, after viewing the body, the visitors bid farewell to the deceased by joining the palms of their hands in the Sikh salutation before accompanying the mourners.

Generally, the family doesn't light the kitchen hearth when a death occurs. Instead, neighbours, friends and relatives bring food. Again, a custom is shared across religions in India.

In the end, the body is secured to an arthi by tying it with sutli (red cotton strands) while the face is left uncovered. Next, the body is draped with a shawl as a sign of respect by the wife's family members. Finally, the relatives, neighbours and friends follow the bier with heads covered to the shamshan bhoomi.

2. The Procession

Before taking the body for cremation, the 'Antim Hazri Ardas' is offered as a means of seeking permission from the Almighty on the dead person's final journey. Then, the arthi is lifted and carried on the shoulders of the male relatives or other male members. Traditionally, the arthi was taken by the chief mourners on their shoulders to the crematorium. However, nowadays, with longer distances, it's common to transfer the bier to a hearse van, accompanied by the mourners.

3. Lighting the Pyre

The Antam Sanskar, the last rites of the Sikhs, is performed by cremating the body through open-air burning or incineration in the electric crematorium. On reaching the cremation ground, the pyre is laid on a raised platform of wood logs and dried grass. First, the deceased is placed on the pyre. Then the Ardas called 'Angetha Sajna Ardas' before consigning the body to fire is offered. 'The son or any other relation or friend of the deceased should set fire to it' (Gulshan 2015, 241). However, it is nowhere mentioned in the texts that only sons can light the pyre, said Gyani Atma Singh, a Sikh Granthi (see Gulshan 2015, 241). 'When we bring up our sons and daughters equal, why can't daughters light the pyre? Even wives can light the pyre of the husband,' he said.

After consigning the body to fire, the accompanying members sit and listen to kirtan. Finally, the 'Kirtan Sohila' (the prayer sung at the close of the day) is recited when the pyre is fully aflame, and the Ardas is offered. On their way back, the congregation assembles at the Gurdwara Sahib, and the Granthi recites the 'Alahunia Ardas' and 'Anand Sahib Ardas'.

4. The Ashes

When the pyre is wholly burnt, the bulk of the ashes, including the burnt ones, are collected by the chief mourner—the ceremony is called phul chukna or angeetha sambhalna. Then, the remains of the deceased are accumulated in an earthen pot to be immersed in any flowing water. However, some Sikhs choose the river Sutlej at Kiratpur Sahib (a town in Punjab) for the immersion of ashes. Then, the Ardas is again recited while immersing the ashes in water. Among the Sikhs, constructing a monument in memory of the deceased is taboo.

5.   Bhog: the Funeral Service

After returning, an unbroken reading of the Guru Granth Sahib (Akhand Path) is commenced at home or in a nearby Gurudwara. Finally, the bhog and Antam Ardas are performed at the end of three, ten or thirteen days of mourning. Ideally, the Guru Granth Sahib reading should be concluded on the tenth day. However, if it cannot be completed on the tenth day, then another day may be appointed based on the convenience of the relatives. At the end of the uninterrupted reading of the Guru Granth Sahib and kirtan, the funeral service ends formally with Ardas (the petitionary prayers for the salvation of the departed soul). The Anand Sahib is generally recited before the Ardas. After the Ardas, the karah prasad is distributed among the sangat.

Infants and small children are not cremated. Instead, pravah is done for infants. According to Atma Singh, children's bodies are tender and sometimes not fully developed to undergo cremation and are immersed in water.

I have broadly described the last rites and rituals. However, at this juncture, it is crucial to distinguish between normative and operational practices. 'Normative beliefs and practices are those which are officially stated and prescribed or proscribed by the recognized religious authority, which can be a person, an organization or an official statement. Operative beliefs and practices, on the other hand, are those actually held by people' (McMullen 1989, 5).

Because of regional differences, end-of-life rituals may differ slightly. Gyani Atma Singh and Dr Manpreet Singh both confirmed the regional variations.

For instance, there may be slight variations in certain end-of-life rituals in the Punjabi districts of Malwa, Doaba and Majha. In some areas, for example, members break a pot before performing cremation. In other regions, mourners carry rice straw as part of the funeral procession. However, systematic research is required to investigate/document various regional practises.

2

Islamic Last Rites and Rituals

I
Conceptions of Death

Just like other religions, views around death occupy an important place in Islamic doctrine. For example, according to the Quran, the death of a human being signals the separation of the ruh (soul) from the badan (body) (Sultan 2003, 649). Furthermore, the body is believed to be destructible, whereas the spirit and soul are indestructible. Similarly, death is inevitable but occurs only with God's command with a timing predetermined by Allah (Sultan 2003, 649). Besides, Islamic scholars stress that death is unpredictable and can happen anytime. Therefore, Muslims should always be prepared for the inevitable.

Death, however, is the precise mechanism that signals a Resurrection process on the Day of Judgment, according to the Quran (Sultan 2003, 649). It is the day when an individual is finally judged by Allah for his actions. The process culminates in a person either admitted to Jannat

(Paradise) and beginning a new and eternally blissful life, or entering Jahannam (Hell), a life of physical and spiritual suffering and misery (Sultan 2003, 649).

'What is of interest, however, is that despite the fact that the Koran is the authoritative source of teachings for Muslims, details concerning body preparation, burial, mourning, and notions about what happens to an individual immediately after burial originate almost exclusively in pronouncements (Hadiths) made by Prophet Mohammed' (Sultan 2003, 650).

In the next part, I will elaborate on the last rites, rituals, and practices Muslims in India follow. But, here, I would like to say that some death traditions might vary by region.

II
Pre-Death Rituals

Among the Muslims, home is seen as a preferred place for dying. As previously stated, Muslims believe in the Day of Judgment and life after death. As a result, it is deemed critical to seek forgiveness for human transgressions before confronting God. The sick person should be visited by people, whether acquaintances or strangers, according to religious advice. The act is regarded as virtuous. As a result, a Muslim dying in a hospital may have a large number of visitors. Furthermore, administering zam zam (holy water) and reading Quranic verses when death is near is beneficial. However, artificially extending life is strongly opposed unless it results in a reasonable quality of life (Gatrad 1994).

After death, the deceased's face should ideally be turned towards Mecca, but in a hospital, it is deemed appropriate to turn it towards the right. Furthermore, the arms and legs should be straightened, and the mouth and eyes should be closed immediately after death (Gatrad 1994).

III
Body Preparation Rites

Islamic funerary rituals and rites place a high value on preserving the deceased's dignity and well-being. As a result, these principles are central to Muslim end-of-life rituals.

The corpse of any Muslim, young or old, is prepared for burial in the same manner. However, preparations should begin as soon as the death is confirmed. While talking to a Hafez, he explained the reason behind the immediate burial. He said, 'With death ruh (soul), the real thing is gone, and only the bare skeletal remains, which should be buried soon so that the deceased's further journey can be completed sooner.' Furthermore, quick burials protect the living from any sanitary issues that may arise from decomposition.

However, preparing a body for burial is a simple process. First, the body is ghusl (washed) to remove all impurities such as blood, urine, and faeces, particularly those that threaten the sanctity of a place that is needed for prayers. Death is regarded as impure, and washing enables the deceased to face God in a pure state. For example, when Prophet Muhammed died, his closest relatives washed him according to his wishes, as is still done today (Taylor 2000, 142). Muslim family members continue the tradition by lovingly performing the ritual in honour of the deceased.

Washing begins on the right side of the body for Muslims. Furthermore, because the body is to be washed an uneven number of times, the first wash is usually with plain water, the second with water and soap, and the final with water and camphor. Salt is sometimes added to water as a symbolic purifier. However, if there is a risk of infection spreading from sores or disease, one may simply pour water over the body a predetermined number of times (Taylor 2000,142). The washing ritual and other pre-burial body preparations are gender-specific. For example, only men are permitted to wash a man's body, whereas only women are permitted to cleanse a woman's body. The body is arranged in a sleeping position after washing. Furthermore, the dead person's arms are stretched straight along his or her sides, with closed eyelids. In addition, the big toes are tied together with a strip of cloth, and the mouth is similarly closed (Sultan 2003, 650).

The body is shrouded in a clean white cloth once the washing ritual begins. Many people who are about to die pre-arrange their shrouding fabric of choice, informing close relatives.

Prophet Muhammed was buried without a shirt or turban, dressed in three white garments. Many of his favourite garments were given to family members and close friends, who later used them as grave clothes when they died. In general, it is preferable to bury the dead in old clothes because the living require new ones (Taylor 2000, 143).

The sunnah (Islamic tradition) is to wrap a deceased man in three unstitched cloth pieces: an izar (wraparound), a qamis (shift), and a lifafa. The izar of a deceased person covers the body from head to toe. In comparison, the lifafa, which is slightly longer than izar, covers the entire body from the top of the head to the feet, confirmed Hafez Gulam Sarwar.

If the deceased is a woman, the sunnah is to envelop her in five pieces. There are also two additional pieces of clothing for women, namely a sarbandh (head cover) and a khirqa tied around her breasts, according to Hafez Gulam.

A woman's body is also covered with an extra sheet on top. Finally, the woman's hair is divided into two sections and placed on either breast. The shrouded body is then transferred to a cot or lightweight bed for transport to the burial site (Sultan 2003, 651).

However, it is preferable to bury the martyrs' bodies unwashed. For the martyrs, even the shrouding rituals are skipped. As a result, they must be buried unwashed and in the same clothing they were wearing when they died (Sultan 2003, 651).

Furthermore, for Muslims who do not have relatives or friends, the town's Muslim community elders cover the costs of ritual washing and funerals. A kabristan committee member also confirmed that they take responsibility for the burial of laavaris (unclaimed bodies).

IV
Funerary Rites

Women's participation in burial rites is minimal, in contrast to washing and preparation rituals. Although not prohibited, they are discouraged from attending burials or accompanying the deceased to their final resting place (Gatrad 1994, 522). Even if women accompany the dead in exceptional circumstances, they are not permitted to approach the grave once the rituals begin.

'The people carrying jinaza (funeral procession) should walk swiftly but not too fast. Moreover, during the jinaza, the crowd should silently say Allahu Akbar (God is great) throughout the procession,' confirmed Hafez Gulam.

Following arrival at the gravesite, a prayer for the dead (salat al-jinaza) is performed, which is usually led by an Imam or a devout male. Funeral prayer rituals, on the other hand, differ significantly from the regular prayer, which is held five times daily. Kneeling, bowing the head, and other prayer rituals, for example, are not permitted during funerals, other than raising the hands to the ears and pronouncing Allahu Akbar (Sultan 2003, 651).

The body is usually placed in front of the Imam, facing Mecca (qiblah). The males at the gravesite form two to three rows behind the Imam, who has been appointed by the aggrieved family to perform the prayer over the deceased body. 'And despite the existence of classic variations reported to have been offered by Prophet Mohammed, the prayer for the dead can be constituted to take any substantive or verbal form that asks for God's forgiveness of a deceased adult' (Sultan 2003, 651).

The grave is dug perpendicular to the qiblah, and the body should be placed in the grave on its right side, facing the qiblah, with the head supported by mud brick. Those lowering the body into the grave should recite *Bismillah Walla Millati Rasulilllah* (in the name of Allah and the faith of the Messenger of Allah). 'A woman's body should always remain (covered) in parda while placing her in the grave. *Yeh Sunnat tarika hai* (the Islamic way),' said Hafez Gulam.

The Islamic principles around death stress egalitarianism even in the last rites. Halevi describes it like this in his book:

> The principle of egalitarianism was also emphasized below ground, for all corpses were to be positioned sideways in the grave, lying on the right side and facing Mecca. As a result, all graves would be uniformly lined up in neat rows perpendicular to the *qibla* axis. And for the duration of this slumber between death and the resurrection, every Muslim would lie down facing Mecca. Were these ideals implemented, it would be impossible to distinguish the graves of men from those of women, those of the mighty from those of the poor, and those of saints from the rest of us (Halevi 2007).

Once in the grave, the body is covered with a layer of wood or stones to avoid direct contact between the body and the soil. 'Then, while reciting prayers three times, each mourner leaves three handfuls of soil to fill the grave. However, it is traditionally forbidden to erect a large monument or pukhta kabr (cemented structure) on the grave,' Gulam Hafez confirmed this. Pukhta kabr, he claimed, interfered with the recycling of kabrs. 'We dig open the kabr after three years of burial. Where will we find the land if we make cemented structures?' asked Jawadul Hasan, a kabristan management committee president.

However, neither the ritual wash nor the usual shrouding is necessary for unborn foetus. Besides, the rites and rituals like reading Janaze ki Namaz are not performed in such cases (Gatrad 1994, 521).

Finally, prayer is offered by the graveside in the direction of Mecca. The burial rites and rituals are concluded with a prayer, and the accompanying members depart from the gravesite.

Post-funeral last rites vary by community due to cultural influences. Some community members, for example, host a khana (funeral feast) for their friends and relatives on the fortieth day. According to Hafez Gulam, these elaborate rituals are not prescribed in the Hadiths. Duva (prayer) for the dead is suggested instead. Simultaneously, a charity for the deceased individual may be offered, with the reward going to the deceased member.

V
Expression of Mourning

The extended family network among Muslims provides excellent support for the bereaved. As a result of the physical proximity of family members, feelings of loneliness and isolation are less common. Furthermore, religion encourages the sharing of grief and provides a means of absolving it through rituals.

However, theological teachings call for restraint in excessive mourning following the death of a loved one. Crying and weeping, for example, are still acceptable forms of expression at the time of death, funeral and burial. However, violent expressions of emotion in response to death, such as wailing, shrieking, and tearing clothing, are not acceptable (Taylor 2000, 143 &144).

Weeping excessively is thought to torment the dead. However, Muslims in various societies exhibit varying responses and patterns of mourning following the death of a family member.

Mourning appears to be a gender-specific ritual. For example, unless a close relative dies, Muslim men rarely cry openly. Women, on the other hand, cry more frequently in public to express their grief.

VI
Post Burial Interrogation of the Corpse

According to Islamic doctrine, the wandering spirit returns to dwell within the body for an indefinite period after the burial rituals are completed. During this time, it is believed that the deceased member regains vision, hearing, and other mental faculties (Sultan 2003, 652).

'*Akhir ki pareshani duniya ke parashani se alag hai. Kabr ke aandar murde se farishte sawaal jawab karte hain* (The difficulties that the dead face inside the grave differ from the problems of this world. They have to face the interrogation of the angels inside the grave),' said Gulam.

It is said that the deceased Muslim meets two terrifying angels in the grave, Munkar and Nakir, who interrogate the dead and have bluish faces, huge teeth, green eyes, and wild hair (Halevi 2007). However, the descriptions of the angels' appearance vary slightly from one account to the next.

The experience is traditionally called the Anguish of the Grave, Punishment of the Tomb and Discipline in the Grave (Smith and Haddad 1981, 41& 46). These angels conduct a trial to probe the deceased's soundness of the Islamic faith by asking questions about the tenets of Islam. They ask the dead: 'Who is your Lord? What is your religion? Who is your Prophet?' Upon answering the questions right and having no sin on record, the grave transforms into a luxurious space, making the wait bearable until the final judgment. Besides, a cool breeze wafts in until God resurrects them from the grave. However, if the questions are answered wrongly, the person is bound to face the torture of the grave. As a result, the grave transforms into an oppressive, constricting space. Again, there are vivid descriptions of torture described in different places. For instance, the angels approach the dying person with various instruments of punishment like burning skewers and thorns that penetrate every hair and vein (Halevi 2007).

A door to the Garden also opens above the dead. Below, seventy-seven doors to hell open, and a hot wind blows into the grave as a reminder that God will resurrect the dead in the fire (Halevi 2007).

Many virtuous Muslims today still hold this belief. As a result, Muslims are frequently reminded in invocations, funeral prayers, sermons and popular literature to heed this punishment (Halevi 2007).

However, according to Islamic theology, some Muslim groups, including martyrs, are exempt from the torment of the grave. Furthermore, young children who have not reached the appropriate age and are presumed innocent of any sin are exempt from this questioning (Sultan 2003, 652).

VII
Judgement and Afterlife

As previously stated, Muslims believe in a final Day of Judgement on which all life ceases to exist and the judgement takes place. The day is described as dreadful, painful, and stormy.

The day is known by various names in the Quranic vocabulary, including the Day of Resurrection, and the Day of Judgement (Sultan 2003, 653).

The Quran describes the day's arrival signs (ala-mat). The heavenly blasts of the trumpet, for example, announces the resurrection and divine judgement. Because the arrival of this day is divine intervention, no one knows when it is.

On this day, every person is brought before Allah to be judged. An individual's good and evil deeds will be weighed against each other during judgement (Hisab or Reckoning).

Following the verdict, people will be divided into three groups. First, those on the left will go to hell. Those on the right will then enter Paradise, while those in front (ahead in terms of faith and good deeds) will be the first to experience the bliss of heaven.

The individuals are then forced to cross a narrow and treacherous bridge (sirat) over the fires of hell. For sinners, the bridge will resemble a strand of hair, the edge of a sword, and be hotter than fire. Without God's intervention (which may or may not occur for whatever reason), they will be cast into hell for a period of purgation before being admitted to Paradise (Sultan 2003, 654).

The Quran contains detailed descriptions of the afterlife in Hell and Heaven. Afterlife in Paradise is eternal and often described as delightful and full of pleasure. The 'Gardens of Delight' are arranged hierarchically in Paradise. Among the inhabitants of heaven, there are different levels of holiness, and only the most deserving can advance to the higher gardens. However, the highest level is reserved for great saints and martyrs who ascend directly without trial or judgement on the Day of Resurrection (Taylor 2000,155).

Furthermore, Paradise is described in the Quran as a place full of pleasures with four rivers of pure water, milk, wine and honey (Taylor 2000,156). It is blissful, with no room for hatred, anguish, or exhaustion. It is described as a magnificent, peaceful, and shaded area with unusual golden and silver trees (Taylor 2000,157).

The Quran, on the other hand, describes hell as a terrifying place with seven layers, 'each descending on an abode of increased torment' (Smith and Haddad 1981, 85). Those who are fated to it will live forever, subjected to unending torture at the hands of angels tasked with punishing them. Indeed, this particular religious and folkloric presentation explains why many Muslims are afraid of death. As a result, they obey God's commands and strive to live up to Islamic principles (Sultan 2003, 654).

3

Last Rites in Zoroastrianism

I
Background

Zoroastrianism is one of the world's oldest religions, based on the teachings of the prophet Zoroaster. It was practised in Iran for at least three thousand years and was a significant religion in pre-Islamic Iran. However, after the Arabs defeated the Sasanian Empire, it became a minority community in Iran, India and around (Daruwalla 2016-2017). During this period, many Zoroastrians faced religious and political persecution from Islamic forces (Stepaniants 2002). According to a Zoroastrian epic, a small group of community emigrated from the Sasanian empire to Gujarat, where they sought asylum, to avoid religious persecution during the Islamic conquests (Chaubey et al. 2017). In India, they became known as Parsis after migrating (Daruwalla 2016-2017). Over centuries, a thriving community of bankers, industrialists, traders and engineers grew along India's western coast. In India, they adhere to their religious and cultural practises, including their unique funerary rituals. Unlike other religions, many Parsi corpses are left at the dakhmas (Towers of Silence) for scavenging birds.

II
The Impurity of the Body After Death—Zoroastrian Beliefs

The ancient Zoroastrian funeral ceremonies serve two purposes. The first step is to isolate the dead body, which is thought to be the source of impurity. The second step is to properly lay it while respectfully separating it from the immortal soul (Zekov 2012). The ceremonies and Zoroastrian ideas of sanitation, segregation, purification and cleanliness are described in *Vendidad*, the nineteenth book of Avesta. According to the Zoroastrian faith, a body after death is possessed by a demon (nasu) that defiles it. Contact between the dead matter and other substances such as earth, water, and fire is therefore strictly forbidden in the faith (Zykov 2016).

Furthermore, Zoroastrian laws prohibit any contact between the dead and living beings, not even allowing relatives of the deceased to touch the dead after a certain point. Instead, corpse-bearers (nasu-Salars), who control the nasu, carry the body to the dakhma after death. The pallbearers are considered contaminated until they take a purifying bath, nahn, with taro to clean themselves (Zykov 2016). The Zoroastrian funerary rites and customs revolve around these purification and sanitation beliefs.

III
Soul After Death: Zoroastrian Beliefs

According to Zoroastrianism, humans are made up of gaetha (physical) and mainyu (spiritual) existence. Furthermore, all living things have an urvan (soul) that does not perish after death. Although the soul is no longer connected to the body after the final breath, it is immortal. It remains close to the body for three days and nights after death, before departing. During this time, family members pray for the deceased and perform acts of charity on their behalf (Taylor 2000, 360).

After death, the soul is judged for its actions. It is drawn up by the sun's rays for judgement at dawn, on the fourth day after death. The soul is confronted by the Chinvat Bridge, which grows wider or narrower depending on the quality of the person's life. The wicked fall into hell as the bridge becomes too thin to cross (dozakh). Kind and generous souls, on the other hand, travel to one of the seven paradises (behesht). There is a place of gloom called hamestegan for those whose actions are neither particularly good nor particularly evil (Taylor 2000, 359).

According to Zoroastrian doctrine, there will also be a great day of reckoning when the 12,000 year struggle between the cosmic forces of good and evil will close. Then, the great God Ahura Mazda will forever overcome the God of the Lie (Angra Mainyu). Besides, at the frashokereti (renovation), all souls will be resurrected (ristakhez) and given a final dispensation. After that, all people may experience eternal life with God, called ameretat (ultimate immortality) (Taylor 2000, 360).

However, it is believed that the souls of ashavan, or people who have lived their lives in accordance with the precepts of asha (goodness), unite with the fravashi (divine spark) to form a united fravashi, which becomes a guardian angel. However, in Zoroastrianism, the ultimate goal of one's life is to achieve ushta (peace and happiness)—both for oneself and for humanity as a whole.

IV
The Tower of Silence

The Towers of Silence, also known as dakhmas in Persian, are squat circular stone structures inside which the bodies of the deceased are placed to be consumed by birds such as vultures and crows (Zykov 2016). Despite the fact that many cultures expose corpses rather than burying or cremating them, Towers of Silence are unique to Iranian Zoroastrianism and later among Parsis in India. Burial and cremation were thought to pollute the holy elements of earth and fire, according to Zoroastrian sacred texts (Taylor 2000, 377).

In the fifth century BCE, Herodotus wrote in *The Histories of Matters* which are secretly and obscurely told–how the dead bodies of Persians are not buried before they have been mangled by birds or dogs. A few hundred years later, Zoroastrians built a *dakhma* in present-day Uzbekistan that still survives today: a squat, forty-nine-foot-tall stone tower near the Amu Darya River, upon which corpses were left for vultures' (Subramanian 2020).

The modern-day towers, which are built in a relatively uniform manner, have an almost flat roof with the perimeter slightly higher than the centre. The top is divided into three concentric rings, with men's bodies arranged around the outer ring, women's bodies in the second ring, and children's bodies in the innermost circle (Taylor 2000, 377).

The remaining bones are dried and bleached by the sun and wind after the scavenging birds have devoured the flesh (Subramanian 2020). The dried bones are later collected by the nasu-salars and thrown into a pit with layers of lime and rock salt to decompose. In dry climates, however, the bones naturally disintegrate into powder. Robert Murphy, a translator for the British colonial government in India, coined the phrase 'Tower of Silence'. Because Zoroastrians value purity and ritual, the Towers of Silence are given special consideration by the community. In Mumbai, the Tower of Silence is known as the Doongerwadi dakhma, and it was initially isolated from the rest of the population.

V
Funeral Practices

1.   Preparatory Arrangements

When death is imminent, relatives and friends are summoned to spend the last moments with the dying individual. Moreover, the family invites two or more priests to recite the 'Patet', prayers for repentance of past sins. It is considered auspicious for the ailing person to join the priest in reciting the last repentance prayers or hear the priest recite them on behalf of the ailing individual. Besides, shortly before death, the ailing person is made to drink a few drops of the consecrated *Haoma* water, a plant symbolic of immortality. However, sometimes the juice of a few pomegranate grains, considered essential in Parsi ceremonies, is dropped into the dying person's mouth (Modi 1928).

Furthermore, the venue where one intends to place the body is washed clean with water. Other preparations include washing the old white cotton clothes for the corpse to be clothed after a ritual bath. In addition, a white sheet four metres in length for an adult to be used as a shroud and two other white bedsheets for lying under and over the body is required (Modi 1928).

2. The Death Ceremony

The practices I elaborate on symbolically represent the Zoroastrian belief system around death, which might differ regionally.

The ceremonies, rituals and prayers conducted immediately following the person's demise are called Geh Sarnu, presided by two priests. Since fire is considered sacred in the religion, the fire is kept alight throughout the ceremonies. In addition, incense is sprinkled on the fire from time to time.

Shortly after death, the deceased's body is washed ceremonially by the family members or individuals well-versed in the process. After drying, the body is clothed in clean white clothing with a prayer cap on the head.

After that, the kusti is girded around the body by a relative while reciting the 'Ahura-Mazda Khodai' prayer. Ideally, the rite is performed by the eldest son or daughter of the deceased.

After that, the deceased is placed on a clean white sheet of cotton cloth spread over the ground. Then two family members keeping themselves in touch with the dead, sit by the deceased's side and recite the prayer, 'Ashem Vohu', close to the ear. At that point, other family members and friends touch and approach the body. However, after this ceremony, the deceased's relatives are forbidden from touching the body (Taylor 2000, 150).

Besides, while participating in the funerary rites, saying goodbyes and paying respects to the deceased, Zoroastrians refrain from excessively displaying grief—they believe that excessive mourning will hinder the soul in its journey to the other world.

After this, the deceased's body is entrusted to the nasu-salars, keeper or controller of nasu. While performing the rituals, the pallbearers wear the dastana (white gloves) and padan (a veil) covering their faces. After the funeral, the pallbearers undergo strict preparatory rites like a ritual bath, performing the kusti prayers and wearing clean clothes (Taylor 2000, 150).

Subsequently, the two family members stationed beside the deceased are replaced by nasu-salars. From this point, the nasu-salars solely handle the dead body since it falls under the influence of the nasu—the evil power of decomposition (Modi 1928).

The pallbearers shift the body from its temporary resting place to a large stone slab in the corner of the room. While doing so, they ritually wrap the body with a shroud while leaving the face uncovered. The top corners of the shroud are tied under the chin, whereas the bottom corners are twisted under the feet with hands arranged upon the chest crosswise.

After covering the body with the shroud, the nasu-salars demarcate the area by outlining the kash/kasha, a protected space around the body only accessible to pallbearers. The line is commonly placed three paces away from the body, a distance designed in the olden times to prevent infections from spreading to surviving family members. After this ritual, the priests preside over the prayer ceremony where the 'Yasna' and 'Gathas' are recited for the deceased (Modi 1928).

Halfway through the recital of 'Yasna', a ritual called sagdid is performed where a unique chatur-chasma (four eyed-dog) is brought to confirm the death. If the dog steadily stares at the body, the person is believed to be alive. However, if the dog does not look at the body, the person's death is confirmed (Taylor 2000, 150). In the olden times, when there were no doctors to confirm the end, the sagdid ritual was significant in ruling out conditions such as a coma. After the sangdid, the praying of the 'Yasna' continues (Modi 1928).

Subsequently, the nasu-salars enter the hall carrying a gehan. After covering the bier with the white cotton bed sheet, they lift the body, placing it on the bier. Afterwards, they tie a string to the bier handle and wrap the cotton strap string seven times around the bier while repeating the prayer, 'Yatha-Ahu-Variyo', each time. It is believed that this ritual aids in providing the body with spiritual protection against demonic forces during its journey to the tower (Taylor 2000, 150).

After this, the nasu-salars carry the body to the tower. Later, the deceased is followed by a procession of family and friends dressed in white, walking in pairs led by two officiating priests. The people following the procession walk by holding hands or two ends of a handkerchief forming a payyand (connect). After reaching the tower, the body is placed on a raised platform close to the tower's outer walls to enable the final sangdid to confirm death by the dog (Modi 1928).

Subsequently, the procession stays back while the nasu-salars take the body to the Tower of Silence. Only the designated pallbearers have access to the tower—the tower's insides remain invisible to the congregation.

The body is placed naked in the tower before sunset to allow the body to be bathed by the sun's light, called khursheed nigerishn (beholding of the sun). Finally, the shroud of the deceased is systematically disposed of in a pit outside the tower.

While the pallbearers perform the rituals inside the tower, the family members, in the meantime, assemble in a nearby sagri and say their farewell prayers for the deceased's soul. After the pallbearers exit the tower, the family and friends return home.

Special prayers are offered for the departed soul for the next three days, culminating at 3.30 a.m. on the fourth day, when the soul journeys across the Chinvat bridge (Modi 1928).

'After death, paydast or funeral services are held at the funeral home. Later in the day, prayers, sarosh nu patru, are done. On the third night, the family organizes uthamnu, a condolence meeting. On the fourth morning, Charam prayers are offered for the departed soul,' said a priest.

Generally, the Tower of Silence is open to all community members. However, Jehangir Patel, the editor of the journal *Parsiana*, told me,

'In the past, suicidal deaths were confined to a different, smaller Tower of Silence.'

VI
Customary Funerary Practices: Challenges

Dokhmenashini, or sky burial in India, was thought to be one of the most environmentally friendly ways of disposing of the dead until the extinction of vultures a few years ago.

According to a 2016 survey conducted by the Bombay Natural History Society (BNHS), India's vulture population has decreased by 99 per cent over the last fifteen years. When vultures fed on carcasses, diclofenac, a drug given to livestock, poisoned them. The Indian government banned the use of diclofenac in 2006. However, another drug called meloxicam was available in the market that was less expensive than diclofenac and was not toxic to vultures, so it was replaced (Subramanian 2020).

'When the vultures died off, they stopped eating the bodies of Zoroastrians, Tibetan Buddhists and farmed cattle. Their extinction and sudden absence from our lives and our deaths marked the severance of yet another human tie with nature' (Subramanian 2020).

The traditional Parsi funerary practise was thus jeopardised. The corpses at dakhmas that vultures quickly scavenged rotted for a long time, spreading a foul stench in the area (Walker 2020).

A Parsi woman shared photographs of bodies rotting inside Mumbai's Tower of Silence with the media in 2006, sparking a heated debate about last rites (Subramanian 2020). The Bombay Parsi Punchayet, on the other hand, denied the accusations and fiercely defended their age-old method.

'Although some orthodox members were opposed to alternatives, the bodies rotted there for months. We couldn't keep our eyes closed.

As a result, some of us felt compelled to look for alternatives. I had to step in. I was not only a priest, but also a coordinator at Doongerwadi. As a result, I assessed the situation more carefully,' Framroze Mirza, a priest, informed me.

Although there is a push to resurrect the vulture population, this will take time. Meanwhile, to deal with the crisis in Mumbai and Hyderabad, the Parsis introduced artificial mechanisms such as solar concentrators at the Towers to dehydrate the body faster. However, because of the clouds, these innovations are ineffective during the monsoon season (Lasania 2015). Furthermore, because of the high heat generation, these concentrators keep other birds, such as crows, away during the day. Besides, these concentrators can work efficiently on a limited number of corpses (Lasania 2015). 'These solar insulators are a complete eye-wash. We have to shut them down during the rainy season,' confirmed Mirza.

Because of the crisis, some Parsis have begun burying or cremating the dead, which most orthodox community members oppose. They believe that such practises call into question the age-old Zoroastrian funeral custom, contaminating the earth. Some believe that those who choose cremation will go to hell (Walker 2020). However, I understand how difficult it must have been for the Parsi community to accept a new method that contradicted their beliefs.

The priests who assisted members in conducting cremations were barred from the community and were served with legal notices. 'The entire community despised me and took me to the Supreme Court. I've even received threats, but I'm unconcerned. If I am born into a priestly family, it is my moral obligation to assist bereaved families in their method of choice—I cannot turn my back on the people,' Mirza told me.

'The Parsi community members opting for cremation use Worli electric crematorium and adjoining Prayer Hall for funerary services,' confirmed Jehangir Patel, who has edited the community's monthly magazine, *Parsiana*, for fifty years. A designated priest who presides over the last rites and rituals assists the members at the crematorium, he said.

Similarly, Framroze Mirza believes that the Parsi community is becoming more accepting of cremations. Initially, there were only two to five people per year. It gradually grew to seven people in a month. Sometimes there are close to forty funerals per month these days. He and his team are among the few priests in the country who provide cremation services, particularly in Mumbai.

The community was prohibited from performing Dokhmenashini/ last rites in dakhmas under the Covid-19 guidelines issued by the Union Ministry of Health and Family Welfare. These restrictions, however, were not well received by the larger Parsi community. Due to dissatisfaction, the Parsi Punchayet filed a petition with the Supreme Court, after losing the case in the Gujarat high court, seeking the right to complete the last rites and rituals of the Parsi faith (Sinha 2022).

According to Mirza, for the past two years, the cremation method has greatly benefited the community. Mirza claims to be the only Parsi priest providing cremation services for Covid victims. 'The irony is that I presided over the cremations of people who had previously opposed this method and criticised me. For example, I assisted in the last rites of the lawyer who fought me in the Supreme Court,' he recalled.

I'm not sure what the future holds for the shrinking Parsi community in India. However, I am hopeful that the community will be able to restore the vulture population in India as well as the age-old practise of laying the dead to rest at dakhmas.

4

Funerary Customs Among Christians

I
Christian Belief About Death

In Christianity, beliefs about death are shaped by various theological concepts found in the Bible. According to the Christian faith, humans are immortal. It is believed that since Adam and Eve sinned, humans were denied access to the Tree of Life and hence dispossessed of physical immortality. As per Christian theology, death is universal. No one is spared. Everyone dies, either through accident, natural calamities, sickness, or old age. In Christianity, death is believed to be the end of life for the body. It puts an end to human existence on Earth (Joo 2020). The religion holds that life continues after death. However, the precise nature of the afterlife may vary depending on the denominational and theological differences, but the common belief is that the soul will go to heaven or hell. Christians also believe in the resurrection of the dead. However, it is important to note that there are variations in beliefs and interpretations among different Christian denominations and individuals. These beliefs are a general overview and may not encompass the entire spectrum of Christian perspectives on death.

II
Last Rites and Rituals

Practices and customs related to last rites and rituals can vary among different Christian communities and regions in India. Some denominations may have specific rituals and traditions that are unique to their faith. Likewise, cultural differences can also shape the funeral customs observed by Indian Christians. As per Richard Taylor, the general structure of funerary rites in the major Christian traditions (Protestant, Roman Catholic and Eastern Orthodox) does not differ much, though local ethnic customs create some variation in minor aspects of the services. In his comprehensive book, he writes: 'What does create bewildering funerary variety is the growing secularization of many Christians, who to varying degrees are moving away from established tradition. For example, it is common for Christians today to engage the services of funeral homes rather than churches, read modern poems for the dead rather than Scripture, and cremate rather than bury the body—when the body is not given over entirely to medical science.' (Taylor 2000, 129).

According to him, such nineteenth-century trends, which have gained tremendous momentum in this century, make it difficult to say anything definitive about how Christians observe funerary customs. (Taylor 2000, 129). Keeping this premise in the backdrop, let's look at the funerary rites among Christians in India.

As per Cyril Joseph, a funeral director from JCJ Funerals in Delhi, outside of India, funeral directors handle the entire funeral. Families may not even choose the date of the funeral. The decision is made by the crematorium or a funeral parlour. Cyril believes that the funerary rites and rituals of Christians in India have changed little. 'Some things are changing now. For instance, many members of the community are now hiring funeral directors. However, my family has been in this business for a long time. Mr Morris Morgan, my grandfather, was a pioneer in funeral work. My grandmother, Mrs Penzy Morgan, became the first woman funeral director in India,' said Cyril. This section will explain some common elements seen in Christian funerals in India.

1.   Notifying the Church

Informing the Church is the first thing to do after the death of a family member. 'We notify the Church priest shortly after the death, and the priest issues a letter mentioning that the deceased was a respected member of the Church. The Church then informs the cemetery, which prepares a burial pit. The Church also maintains death records of the members,' said Cyril.

2.   Body Preparation

Among Christians, close attention is paid to preparing the dead. The dressing of the body after death for Christians can vary depending on cultural traditions, local customs, and personal preferences. As a symbol of purification and preparation for the afterlife, the deceased's body is traditionally washed and cleansed. Bathing rituals are gender specific. All the family's men bathe the man, and if the deceased is woman it is done by the women.

Anointing the body with holy oil or perfumed oils may also be performed as a ritual act in some Christian denominations. After cleaning, the body is then dressed appropriately. This usually entails wearing clothing that is modest, respectful and appropriate for a funeral or burial.

The attire chosen may differ depending on cultural practises and personal preferences, but it is typically formal and conservative. Religious symbols or items may be placed on the deceased by some families. A crucifix, rosary beads, or other meaningful religious objects that were valued by the individual or the faith could be included. Sometimes, families may choose to dress the deceased in their favourite or significant clothing, which may hold a special meaning (see Taylor 2000, 47).

After dressing, the people gather to pay their last tributes. The body is presented for a final viewing, if deemed appropriate, before placing it in the coffin, allowing for last farewells and expressions of condolences.

'The families receive support from their neighbours and friends during this time. For instance, during the mourning period, the grieving family doesn't cook food at home. It is arranged by friends and relatives,' said Cyril.

There are mobile mortuaries available for the families in case there is a waiting. In the meantime, the families continue to pray. Every day until the body is buried, a pastor offers prayers.

3.   Coffin Preparation

In most Christian communities in India, wooden coffins are commonly used for burials. 'The interior of the coffin may be lined with fabric or cushioning material to provide an image of comfort and dignity. This lining can vary in colour and design, depending on personal or cultural preferences. One may include additional elements inside the coffin. These can include belongings, photographs, or items of significance to the deceased,' confirmed Cyril. Sometimes, a cross or other religious symbols may be placed on the coffin as a visible expression of the deceased's faith and a reminder of the Christian beliefs surrounding death and resurrection. Families may consult the funeral directors or local authorities to ensure compliance with applicable guidelines and to honour any specific cultural and religious customs.

'We exquisitely decorate the coffins to ensure that the deceased is resting in peace and comfort. In India, coffins are made of plywood or teak wood. Some people also prefer rosewood cedar. Other options include polished or unpolished coffins, as well as laminated or unlaminated ones. The cost can range from ₹3000 to a lakh. Aside from that, we must personalise coffins for the deceased suffering from communicable diseases,' added Cyril.

'After placing the body in the coffin, the close male family members walk the coffin to the ambulance or the hearse. The act is considered an honourable duty and shows support for the grieving family. A procession may be held, with the coffin being taken to the burial site. During the procession, hymns and prayers are sung or recited,' said Cyril.

4. Burial

The gravesite is prepared before the body is buried. This typically involves digging the grave to the appropriate depth and size. A final prayer service is held after the members gather at the cemetery. The coffin may be kept open for final viewing until this point.

Before the coffin is lowered into a grave, the family members and friends say their last farewells. These can include prayers, words of remembrance, or personal gestures of farewell, such as placing flowers on the coffin. After sealing, the coffin is lowered gently into the grave by family members, friends, or funeral professionals. A lowering mechanism such as straps or ropes is used to lower the coffin into the grave.

Once the coffin has been lowered into the grave, it is carefully positioned in its ultimate resting place with the help of funeral professionals or burial staff. After placing the coffin, the grave is covered with soil. Family members, friends, or cemetery workers may take part in this process by shovelling soil into the grave, symbolizing the last act of laying the deceased to rest. Throughout the placing of the coffin into the grave, religious prayers or readings may be performed.

In exceptional cases, cremation services may be performed instead of burial. In such circumstances, the ashes are later buried in the cemetery.

'The body sometimes starts decomposing or is brought in later for burial. Since the conditions of mortuaries in India not very good, cremation may be preferable if the repatriation process is taking too long. In such cases, there is a risk of bodily fluid leakage. The ashes are then returned to the country. The mortal remains are collected from the airport by funeral directors, and the remains are buried in a cemetery near the loved ones. I am in charge of coordinating repatriation from Middle Eastern countries,' said Cyril.

5. Memorial Service

Sometimes, memorial services may be held after the burial. These services provide an opportunity for friends and family to gather and remember the deceased, offer support to one another, and continue to pray for the soul of the departed. Some members also organize feasts and make donations on this day.

The service may begin with opening remarks, which may include a welcome, words of comfort and an introduction to the purpose of the memorial service. Prayers and hymns play an essential role in Christian memorial service. Prayers may include expressions of thanksgiving, petitions for comfort and peace, and intercession for the soul of the deceased. Passages from the Bible are typically read during the memorial service. These passages may contain themes of hope, comfort and the promise of eternal life.

A eulogy is often delivered to honour the life and accomplishments of the deceased. Family members, friends, or clergy may share personal remembrances, stories, and anecdotes that reflect the character, values, and impact of the departed soul. Other than this, several prayers are offered for the deceased member during the first year.

5

Antim Sanskar in Hindus

I
Introduction

Death is fascinating, as are the last rites and rituals that surround it. This is the final sanskar in a series of life-cycle sanskars for Hindus. It is also known as anvarohanyya, antya-kriya, antima sanskar, or vahni sanskar. Sanskar in Sanskrit broadly refers to any auspicious rite or ritual that affects the body or the soul.

Furthermore, ancient Hindu scriptures such as the Vedas contain a wealth of knowledge about approaching the final sanskar. The aggrieved families pay their last respects to the deceased member and prepare the soul for its journey to the next life by performing antima sanskar. It encompasses all rites and rituals performed just before, during and after death.

Death, according to Hindu belief, separates the immortal atma from the mortal physical body, whereas life is viewed as a continuous unbroken chain of existence. 'We Hindus believe in rebirth. As a result, the antim sanskar is critical for the soul's ascension. It is believed that the soul's ascension into swarg does not begin until these rituals are successfully completed,' Dr Manisha Shete, a practising priestess from Pune, said.

The primary goal of Hindu death and dying rituals is to cut the deceased person's ties with the survivors, allowing the departed soul to sail freely.

With a few exceptions, open pyre cremation, or agni sanskar, has been the most common method used by Hindus since ancient times. Children under the age of two, for example, are buried. Furthermore, burying or immersing sadhus in samadhi is an exception. However, cremation is gaining popularity not only among Buddhists, Hindus and Sikhs, but also among other faiths around the world.

Beliefs and practises concerning the end of life may differ depending on caste, region and culture. Nonetheless, according to Knipe, a scholar on Hindu last rites, with a few exceptions, Hindu rites of death and cremation procedures are relatively uniform throughout India (Knipe 2019, 22). In this section, I try to capture the essence of how Hindus perform the last rites while simplifying it. I also intend to explain the final rites and rituals in the current context of changing times.

II
Hindu Views on Death and Afterlife: a Brief Description

As previously stated, death is viewed as a continuation rather than an end in Hindu philosophy. Furthermore, the physical body is thought to be conditioned by current and previous life events. The body is a tool through which various experiences are gained, influenced by past karam (deeds). When these experiences are realized, the body's purpose is fulfilled, and it is then shed at death. For example, the Bhagavad

Gita (2:22) compares death to changing clothes: after discarding worn-out garments, one puts on new ones. Similarly, the embodied 'Self' encounters new ones after discarding worn-out bodies (Rambachan 2003, 642).

Rambachan explains this verse in detail: 'The analogy is rich with suggestions. First, a suit of clothing is not identical to the wearer. Similarly, the changing physical body, which is likened to clothing, is not the repository of the person's true identity. Second, there is the similarity of continuity of being. When a suit of clothing is changed, the wearer continues to exist, and with the death of the physical body, the dweller does not die. The subtle body links continuity between the old and new bodies' (Rambachan 2003, 642).

The Brihadaranyaka Upanishad elucidates beautifully: just as a goldsmith takes a small amount of gold and refashions it into a newer and better form, the soul discards its current body and takes on a new form each time.

As a result, the Upanishads propose that the nature of a person's consciousness determines the individual's journey and destiny after death. The course of a person's life before death is determined by their thoughts, desires, hopes, and actions. Similarly, these aspects guide an individual's journey after death. Let us look for these connections in the final rites and rituals.

III
The Rites of Dying and Good Death

Among Hindus, the rituals of separation should begin before a person dies. Therefore, Hindus perform a series of rites before death, helping the atma leave the body. Therefore, individuals whose death is imminent, like terminally ill patients, or people with extreme old age, can be offered premortem rituals. Moreover, these rituals allow families and ailing individuals to prepare for the imminent end.

The practices like placing a leaf of the sacred tulsi to ingest and pouring a few drops of Ganga jal (Ganges water) on the tongue are considered beneficial. These potent cleansing substances are meant to destroy one's paap and bring about a quick and easy end—releasing the deceased from the binding ties of this life. Besides, for moral cleansing, forgoing food some days before death and consuming only Ganga jal is also considered crucial for the easy departure of the atma still attached to the body.

I was told that feelings and thoughts at the time of death ultimately determine the soul's subsequent fate. Hence purity of thought is considered crucial at the time of death. Therefore, chanting the name of God and reciting the 'Gayatri Mantra' or the 'Mahamrityunjaya Mantra' is considered desirable. Furthermore, one may invite sadhus or spiritually inclined people to recite 'mantras' and verses from holy scriptures.

In addition, I was told by a karam-kandi brahmin in Varanasi that offering daan to sadhus and brahmins, especially a gau daan (cow daan), is considered auspicious. 'But these days, people don't perform these rituals. They think a pandit is greedy, so he is suggesting this daan.' But, he said, 'We must do some daan before we die.'

Furthermore, at this time, the person's last wish should be sought and fulfilled, if possible. These rituals are considered crucial because, according to the Bhagavad Gita, the feelings and sentiments that a person recalls at the time of the soul's departure are the feelings that the person attains after death. Therefore, family members are advised against loud crying and lamentations that may hinder the soul's ascent into heaven.

The scriptures even mention the appropriate place for dying. For instance, the bank of the Ganga at Varanasi or another pilgrimage site is considered auspicious. Besides, many people come to Varanasi and live there until they die. It is believed that Varanasi is a gateway to moksha. I heard numerous stories of individuals staying in Varanasi for years (Kashi Vaasi), waiting for death to arrive. Some hospices and dharmsalas serve this purpose by providing rooms to mokshaarthis (moksha seekers).

When this is impossible, the desirable location is one's own home, on the ground, on which mustard and sesame seeds have been spread and in the open air facing north (Parry 1994, 172).

It is believed that by lying on the ground, one returns to the earth, the source and keeper of life. Moreover, placing a dying person on the floor, a neutral place, is believed to ease the release of the Atma from the physical body, cutting the material attachments. According to Sarah Lamb, beds were unsuitable places to die because they were considered relatively comfortable household possessions, expressing attachment and obstructing the soul's departure (Lamb 2000, 159).

However, laying the person on the ground may not be possible in urban settings, where the terminally ill die in hospitals. Moreover, many hospitals may not accommodate rituals like administering Ganga jal or Tulsi leaves.

Dying at home makes performing the necessary pre-death rituals more manageable and meaningful because you are surrounded by immediate family members. As a result, when death is imminent, hospitals in India frequently discharge critically ill patients to return home (Rambachan 2003, 644).

Connected to this is the theory of a good and bad death among Hindus. I am discussing it here because this understanding is crucial in determining the future of the soul. For Hindus, the sumaran (good end) occurs at the proper time, place and under appropriate circumstances (Parry 1994, 162). In Hinduism, for example, a good death occurs in old age, after one has lived a full life. 'A good death is when one has seen the face of one's grandchildren or great-grandchildren and is surrounded by loved ones,' a pandit in Varanasi said.

An untimely death (akasmik mrityu), on the other hand, is sudden. It is perceived to be premature, violent and painful. These include fatal accidents, suicides and women dying during childbirth (Parry 1994, 162). This understanding was confirmed by many pandits I spoke with in Varanasi. Furthermore, a pandit told me that if the last rites of these people who died unexpectedly are not performed ritually, the dissatisfied spirits may hover around restlessly due to unfulfilled wishes, causing distress to the family in the form of illness and disputes.

Furthermore, there is a mention of an auspicious time/month for death among Hindus. For example, dying during the six months following the winter solstice (uttarayana) is thought to be desirable. Death, on the other hand, is considered unlucky during the remaining six months (dakshinayana). However, spiritual people believe that a person's bhakti, upasana (understanding of God's form), and karmas determine their fate after death, not the time and place of death.

IV
Pre-Cremation Rituals

Nobody knows when or where they will die. Without a doubt, the loss of a loved one is devastating. But we must say our final goodbyes while performing the last rites ritually.

More specifically, among Hindus, cremation should take place within twenty-four hours of death (Rambachan 2003, 645). As a result, the grieving family members must arrange for end-of-life rituals as soon as possible.

If the death occurs in a hospital, family members must complete the necessary paperwork before the deceased's body can be released. Furthermore, in the event of organ donation, the family must notify hospital authorities immediately.

Following the acquisition of the deceased body, the families carry out the desired pre-cremation rituals in accordance with customs and traditions. The time and date of cremation are also communicated to extended family members at this time. As previously stated, the Hindu funeral is usually performed shortly after death, but it may be delayed in exceptional circumstances. In the case of an accidental death, for example, families may have to wait before the body is released from the hospital or mortuary.

In some cases, one must wait for family members who live abroad to arrive. For example, a friend stated that her father's cremation had to be postponed because her brothers lived on different continents. 'We had to go for Appa's embalming because my brothers had to travel from the United Kingdom and Alaska,' Suchitra explained. In such cases, families usually place the body in the hospital morgue or mobile mortuaries.

In such instances, the deceased person is commemorated through home rituals such as placing the deceased person's picture alongside God's picture over a table. Furthermore, the images are displayed with fresh flowers and a diya (oil lamp). Until the body is cremated, prayers for the departed soul are offered on a regular basis.

The domestic hearth is extinguished for at least a day after death. During this time, relatives and friends bring food to the bereaved family. These traditions are incorporated into end-of-life rituals to ease and comfort the bereaved family.

After obtaining the body, the family members lovingly bathe the corpse for the final shuddhikaran (cleansing). 'It is believed that the person has terrifying visions before death, which cause urination or stool passing. As a result, we must cleanse the deceased body before agni sanskar,' a priest said.

Male relatives clean and dress the male corpse, while female relatives clean and dress the female corpse. Finally, for fragrance and purity, chandan powder is smeared on the person's forehead, and the corpse is adorned with flowers. In Varanasi, for example, the dead are revered as if they were God. 'Among Hindus, a deceased is honoured as would befit a God, and in Kaashi, it is said that the dead take on the very form of God' (Eck 2013, 341).

There are also specific ways in which to dress the deceased. Cremation attire is generally guided by regional customs and traditions. Males are typically dressed in new white dhotis and kurtas. The bodies of women who have predeceased their husbands, on the other hand, are the most ornately adorned, traditionally dressed in a red wedding sari. Unmarried women are dressed in red or white depending on their age. A widow, on the other hand, is dressed in white (Rambachan 2003, 644).

In India, funeral arrangements are made by friends and relatives. For example, a small-town friend mentioned, 'I had an uncle who assisted everyone in the neighbourhood during their last rites.' Professional funeral services, on the other hand, have begun to assist families in organizing funerals in recent years.

Following the preparation of the body, a Tulsi leaf and Ganga jal are placed in the deceased's mouth, followed by loved ones performing the ritual of offering flowers and praying.

The body is then placed on a tikhti (bier made of two bamboo shafts and thirty-two boards), which is adorned with flower garlands and covered with a white shroud with the face exposed. Finally, a sutli is used to secure the body to the bier (string made from bamboo grass, cotton or wool). Before leaving, family members honour the deceased with circumambulations three times in the auspicious clockwise direction around the body and by touching the feet of the departed as the final act of respect.

However, due to the fear of spreading infections and Covid-related protocols issued by international bodies and the State, families were forced to forego these pre-cremation rituals during the pandemic.

V
Antim Yatra: the Funeral Procession

The body is ritually carried on the shoulders of male relatives to the cremation site, known as kandha dena. If the crematorium is a long distance away, a hearse van is rented for the same purpose.

Women are not usually allowed to accompany the procession, but women from Punjabi communities enter the crematorium and even take part in cremation rituals. Furthermore, in some communities, women have begun actively performing the last rites of deceased family members. However, I will go over these changes in a separate section.

Typically, the chief mourner, the eldest son or family priest, leads the funeral procession with a pot containing fire from the domestic hearth. However, with electric or CNG-powered cremations, some customs, such as taking fire from home, may gradually fade.

When leaving the house, the corpse is taken head-first because that is how a baby is born and a person must leave the world (Parry 1994, 175). *Ram Naam Satya Hai* (Ram's name is the only truth) is chanted throughout the procession, with the priest leading the chant and the mourners repeating it in unison. This is said to ward off malevolent spirits (Parry 1994, 175). Carrying the dead on their final journey is considered righteous by Hindus. As a result, family members and acquaintances take turns carrying the bier.

Mourners throw small coins, puffed paddy and mustard seeds over the bier as the funeral procession passes. According to anthropologist Parry, puffed paddy represents prosperity and mustard seeds attract ghosts and ancestors (Parry 1994, 175).

It's interesting how Hindus celebrate the death of an elderly person, and the funeral procession is described as a second wedding, treated like a barat (wedding procession) (Parry 1994, 157). As a result, the bier is festooned with balloons, streamers, and garlands. Furthermore, on some occasions, the procession is accompanied by a band of musicians, as if it were a wedding. I wasn't sure if these customs were still in effect. So I asked a funeral pandit. 'If a person dies in old age, their bier is decorated,' he explained. 'For example, a 103-year-old woman died last month. Her funeral was carried like a marriage procession with bands playing,' he added.

VI
The Cremation: Dah Sanskar

According to anthropologists, after all the preparatory rites, the central separative act is dah sanskar. Cremation attempts to disintegrate the body as completely as possible. The body is disseminated back into the five cosmic elements (panch tattva), from which it originated, through cremation, leaving no traces of the body as it once was (Lamb 2000, 160).

The funeral procession comes to a halt outside the crematorium before entering the funeral home's gates. The body is now placed on the ground before being lifted again. The final stop, however, is the cremation site, where the corpse is laid on the pyre with its head facing south.

The body is bathed in holy Ganga river on the Harishchandra and Manikarnika ghats in Varanasi before being placed on the funeral pyre. Furthermore, some communities prefer to perform cremations near holy rivers. For example, I discovered that people from the Garhwal and Bihar regions perform last rites near a holy river.

As mentioned, crematoriums in big cities also offer CNG and electric-run furnaces in India. However, it is up to the family to choose the system most compatible with their religious beliefs. For example, some believe that open pyre cremations are most suited for the Hindus where the traditions laid in the scriptures can be followed. However, others believe that CNG-run and electric crematoriums are more environmentally friendly.

After arriving at the cremation site, the funeral pandits assist the families in performing the last rites. Furthermore, there are community-specific pandits at larger crematoriums that cater to various communities such as Pahadi, Garhwali, Punjabi, and so on.

If people opt for open-pyre cremations, the type of wood used is determined by availability and the financial situation of the family. For example, the sacred chandan, aam (mango), and bel (wood apple) are very expensive.

'Usually, we use the wood of mango, banyan and eucalyptus because chandan is very expensive. Families, on the other hand, use a small amount of chandan as a ritual. As a result, even the poor can afford a small amount of sandalwood,' said a funeral pandit at Nigambodh Ghat.

Furthermore, there are specifics to erecting the pyre. According to Parry, the wood purchased for the pyre should weigh an odd number of mounds for auspiciousness. To create a bed for the body, five to seven thick, split logs should be laid horizontally. After placing the body on a pyre, the eyes, ears, nose, chest, and feet are anointed with ghee (Parry 1994,176).

After assembling the pyre, the relatives conduct the final viewing of the deceased (antim darshan) while reciting a short prayer. Dashang (an aromatic compound of ten substances) is thrown into the flames after the pyre has been lit. The chief mourner circles the pyre counter-clockwise. The dead are now an offering to Agni, the fire (Eck 2013, 341). Midway through the cremation, the chief mourner performs kapal-kriya, or the skull rite, by breaking up the partially burned corpse and stoking the fire to ensure that it is completely consumed (Parry 1994, 177).

However, the ritual of kapal-kriya is forsaken for mourners who choose electric or CNG cremations. Moreover, the practice of kapal-kriya is becoming less common with changing times. In Varanasi and other parts of India, a pot is symbolically smashed towards the end of the cremation (Parry 1994, 177). However, some communities still believe that the atma will remain trapped if the kapal-kriya ritual is skipped.

Finally, family members register the death at the cremation office and receive a slip to be presented at the government office for death registration and the issuance of a death certificate. However, at

Nigambodh Ghat, I noticed that families must first obtain a rasid (receipt) from the office before proceeding with the cremation service.

Finally, before returning home, mourners take a ceremonial bath to cleanse themselves of the ritual pollution of contact with the dead. This aids in the removal of all pollutants from the cremation site.

VII
Post Cremation Rituals

1.   Collection and Immersion of Ashes/Pravah

After that, the ashes are cooled before the remains are collected. Asthi-sanchayan is the ritual of gathering the remains. It is also known as phul chugna in some areas. After the pyre has been extinguished, ashes are ritually collected in an earthenware pot the next day. Some groups, however, gather the asthi on the third, fifth, or seventh day following the cremation. Asthi-sanchayan must be performed ritualistically, with specific steps. For instance, I witnessed a funeral pandit handing over a printed list of ingredients to be made available by family members for ritually collecting ashes at the crematorium.

The labelled jars containing ashes are occasionally stored in crematorium lockers for later immersion. Furthermore, in some cases, the pot of ashes can be taken home and safely stored for future immersions. In some instances, people travel long distances to immerse the ashes in the holy waters of the Ganga. The remains of the unclaimed bodies, however, are immersed by the crematorium staff. Sometimes, the NGOs carry the ashes and submerge them in Hindu holy places like Kashi, Gaya, Pehva and Haridwar.

Pravah in a sacred river is the preferred method. Ritual specialists such as tirath purohits (pilgrimage priests) assist in the immersion of ashes in holy places such as Haridwar. Boatmen who ferry mourners in Varanasi typically assist in asthi pravah (immersion of ashes).

2. The Memorial Service: Shraddhanjali or Shok Sabha

Another important post-cremation custom observed by many Hindu families is the memorial service, also known as shraddhanjali/kirya. Prayer services are typically held at homes, community centres, or temples. Some people prefer a simple ceremony, while others prefer an elaborate one.

A framed photo of the deceased member is placed on a raised platform adorned with flowers during this ceremony. A flower garland is usually placed around the framed picture. In addition, the family members light an incense stick or a diya near the image.

Friends and family members attend the service to pay their respects to the deceased. Furthermore, those who were unable to attend the cremation pay tribute to the departed soul on this occasion.

The assembly is typically an hour long. During the programme, the holy scriptures are read aloud, or a satsang (devotional singing) is organized. During the assembly, family members also recount the deceased's virtues or good deeds. On this occasion, some families also serve snacks or meals to relatives and friends.

3. Pind Daan

Pind daan, or the offering of pind, is a rite in which homage is paid to a deceased family member. Pinds are round-shaped balls made of cooked rice, barley flour, black sesame and ghee that are served to the pret.

Six pinds, known as khat pinds, are initially offered at various locations such as the place of death, the front door, on the way to the crematorium, the cremation site, the corpse's belly as it lies on the pyre, and finally when the cremated bones are collected. At the Nigambodh Ghat, for example, I observed pandits assisting families in performing the pind daan before cremation. Another school of thought, however, believes in completing all six pinds simultaneously while collecting the ashes for immersion in the Ganga.

Aside from that, the ten-day pind daan is performed after the cremation. On the first day after death, the chief mourner, accompanied by a priest, goes to a riverbank and makes an offering of a pind to the deceased. The rice ball represents the spirit of the departed as a pret. While the priest recites the deceased's lineage, name, and month of death, a small clay cup filled with sesame seeds is emptied onto the ball. This process is repeated ten times. However, some families offer all ten pinds together on the tenth day (Rambachan 2003, 647).

As seen above, we create the disembodied spirit's temporary body, through this ritual (Knipe 2019, 137). The ten rice balls given to the pret represent ten lunar months of pregnancy. Each daily offering is thought to generate a new body part or organ, beginning with the head on the first day and ending with digestive system on the tenth. A son produces a new body for his parent or elder, just like the parent gave the child his own body at birth (Lamb 2000, 171). A ritual pandit explained it like this: 'It takes ten days for the pret swarup (spirit) to transform into a body. Until then, the pret hovers around the house restlessly—some may even see the dead person. So the food offered for ten days is meant to nourish the pret.'

According to Parry, there is a lack of consensus around the purpose of performing the pind daan. However, the most typical view is that these sacrifices buy off the evil ghosts hovering around the corpse, threatening to reanimate it (Parry 1994, 176).

'If the pind daan is not performed correctly. The dissatisfied pret atma may then roam around indefinitely, becoming a pishach (fiend) and causing pitr dosh—illness and misfortune in the family,' confirmed a priest in Varanasi. Eck also mentions this: 'Pishachas are also unsatisfied spirits of the dead, particularly those who died violent or unnatural deaths, or whose rites were improperly performed' (Eck 2013, 339). As a result, pind daan is regarded as an important end-of-life ritual among Hindus for ensuring the well-being of both the living and the dead.

The pind must be ritually disposed of. 'The pind should ideally be immersed in the water. Sometimes, it's fed to cows. These days, we recommend that families bury it in a pot and plant a tree in the name of a deceased person,' explained a priest.

The pind of the tenth day completes the offerings and signals the end of the most intense pollution period. On the tenth day, the chief mourner officiating the last rites is considered highly polluted and must undergo a cleansing ritual such as nail cutting and head shaving.

4.   Eleventh Day: Shraddh

It is marked as a significant day in the soul's journey. The soul's journey into the next world begins on the ekadasha (the eleventh day), after shraddh. The eleventh day rituals are presided over by a mahapatra or mahabrahmin, a special pandit. On this day, the mahapatra is fed food on behalf of the pret.

In addition, families give daan in the form of utensils, clothing, bedding, shoes, grains, toiletries and so on (Knipe 2019, 245). In some cases, cash is given in lieu of these items. It is believed that the deceased will receive these offerings through the brahmin in the next world—considered crucial in the dead's journey to the other world.

After the ritual, the pandit confers salvation and allows the soul to swim across to the other world. As a result, it is believed that the pandit must be satisfied with gifts in order for the last rites to be completed successfully. 'Mahapatra never asks for less money. He sometimes demands ₹10,000 or more,' said a ritual priest in Varanasi. He added, 'The brahmin is ritually bid farewell after performing the eleventh-day ritual—no one wants to see his unlucky face. However, one keeps running into them these days.'

Some new-age pandits, however, have a different perspective on these rituals. Dr Manisha Pandit, for example, compared the shraddh ceremony to giving thanks to the departed soul.

5.   Twelfth Day: Sapindikarna

On the dwadasha (twelfth day) of death, a special ritual known as sapindikarana is performed. Knipe, explaining the significance of sapindikarna, writes: 'Of all the complex stages in the Hindu rites of death and dying, the most arresting moment comes at the *sapindikarna*, the time-filled action of blending the deceased with his/her forefathers, of transforming the vulnerable, disembodied spirit (*preta*) of this world into the secure pitr (ancestor) of that other world' (Knipe 2019, 22).

The pinds of father, grandfather, and great grandfather are merged with the deceased, sapindikarna, during this ritual (see Knipe 2019, 24 & 25). The chief mourner divides a ball of rice representing the deceased into three pieces and combines it with three other rice balls representing the three ancestors.

'Through this ritual, one assists the pret in becoming a pitr. The pret-sarir becomes a pitr after taking this pind and can enter the world of ancestors. If we don't know the names of our ancestors, we remember Brahma, Vishnu, and Mahesh,' said a pandit in Varanasi. Following this ritual, the family bestows daan on a brahmin in the name of the newly formed ancestor.

However, it is believed that with pret-sarir, a deceased person cannot enter the world of ancestors. As a result, if sapindikarna is not performed on the twelfth day, pret-sarir becomes a ghost instead of entering the world of the ancestors.

6.   The Thirteenth: Day

Then, on the thirteenth day, one performs the havan, feeds thirteen brahmins, and gives thirteen daans, concluding the thirteen-day rituals. 'With changing times, the rituals have changed. For example, people used to wear white clothes and abstained from visiting people for a year. Besides, in the olden times, these rituals used to last for twelve years. These days everything is a shortcut—done in three days. For instance, now the monthly shraddh is only performed by a handful of communities like Marwaris and Brahmins,' said a ritual priest in Varanasi (see Knipe 2019, 25). However, he believes that we should annually perform shraddh for our ancestors till we are alive.

But, Shete believes that the soul's salvation doesn't depend on these rituals. 'The idea behind these rituals is to honour our ancestors. I inform the families that the shraddha (the purity of thoughts) matters. But, the means to pay respect might change/vary with time,' she told me. According to her, the idea of performing death rituals together was to bind the family and pay respect to the deceased.

VIII
Immersion of Corpses

Hindus traditionally cremate their dead. However, certain corpses are immersed in water (jal pravah). Ascetics' bodies are among them. Furthermore, stillborn babies and aborted foetuses are sometimes immersed in water.

Cremating the bodies of people who die from infectious diseases is frowned upon because it defiles agni. For example, I've heard that cremating the bodies of cancer victims is frowned upon by Doms in Varanasi. Similarly, the bodies of people with leprosy are not cremated, and smallpox victims were not cremated in the past (Parry 1994, 185).

Furthermore, many poor people who cannot afford cremation end up wrapping the dead bodies of their loved ones in a white muslin cloth and pushing them into water. In addition, the bodies of people who die as a result of snake bites are immersed. Many pandits I spoke with in Varanasi confirmed this ritual.

As a result, corpses can be found floating in the Ganga in Varanasi. The well-known Ganga Action Project (GAP) of the Government of India aimed to clean the Ganga of floating corpses in order to reduce pollution in the river. During my visit to Varanasi, I saw a cleaner Ganga.

IX
Funeral of Sanyasis

The sanyasi (renouncer) who had left the social world, abandoned the material ties and possessed no worldly attachment to his mortal body is not cremated. Instead, his corpse is either immersed or buried. Since the renouncer has burned all bodily desires, a crematory fire is deemed redundant (Parry 1994, 184). Moreover, he has already attained a sense of detachment from physical needs through spiritual training, discipline and being away from family.

After bathing the body of a deceased sanyasi, it is adorned with flowers and garlands. Then, the body is lowered into the deep pit in the padmasan (lotus) pose. However, in Varanasi, the bodies of these sanyasis are immersed in the Ganga. Before immersion, the skull of the renouncer is smashed by one of the renouncers with a coconut. Next, the body is circled around with fire, which is touched to his mouth on each revolution. Finally, the corpse is weighed down and ferried into mid-stream by boat (Parry1994, 184). After that, their shraddh is performed by the sanyasi community on the twelfth day.

X
The Final Rites of Babies

Infants under the age of two are buried rather than cremated. The general consensus is that a child is ineligible for cremation before he or she has teeth. Furthermore, it is believed that the tender bodies of children are unsuitable for the harshness of the cremation fire. Moreover, because the babies are not attached to their bodies, cremation is not required to sever worldly ties. 'Children are like flowers; we shouldn't burn their tender bodies,' a priest explained.

Close relatives carry the body, which has been adorned and laid in the bier. Following a ritual prayer, the body is buried in a new plot of land with liberal amounts of salt for quick decomposition. Other rites, however, are not performed for children. However, the family may commemorate the child's death anniversary by feeding young children.

It's fascinating to discover how Hindu funeral rites and rituals are linked to the basic philosophy of death in the scriptures. Furthermore, it is interesting to see how some end-of-life rituals, such as cremation, shraddh ceremony, or pind daan, are gradually evolving over time. In the end, we must remember that the essence of the last rites and practises is, above all, to say goodbye to the deceased member with shraddha.

6

Ritual Specialists Among Hindus

While performing my father's last rites, I remember asking the funeral pandit about his role in other life-cycle rituals. He told me, '*Hum sirf mrityu se jude kaam karte hain* (we only do death-related work).' I was slightly amused by his response, if not shocked. This anecdote motivated me to dismantle different specialist roles in the death drama.

I learned that a separate category of pandits oversees the final rites among Hindus for eleven days. However, I thought these distinctions were more theoretical/superficial when I started dismantling them. Later I discovered that these divisions existed even in practice. Therefore, I attempt to combine the puzzle pieces, delineating each person's role at different stages of the last rites. Besides funeral pandits, I look at the part tirath purohits play during end-of-life rituals. Finally, I present how nais (barbers) contribute to mortuary rites for Hindus.

I
Funeral Priests

During my interviews with pandits, I discovered a separate category of priests who preside over the eleven-day last rites among Hindus. However, they are addressed by different names across India. For instance, in much of North India, a familiar name is mahapatra (great vessels). They are called mahabrahmin (great brahmin) in Maharashtra. On the other hand, they are addressed as apara brahmins in the South—dealing with rituals required apara (later) (Knipe 2019, 240).

When I was trying to solve the puzzle, the distinction was confirmed by experts and practising priests alike in their unique ways. For instance, when I spoke to Sociologist Dr Ravi Nandan Singh, he said, 'The funeral pandits are different from other pandits across India—called mahabrahmin or acharya. They are involved in the eleven-day last rites.'

Similarly, a ritual priest in Varanasi told me, 'He is the acharya of eleven days' last rites.'

When I spoke to Rajesh, a funeral pandit at Nigambodh Ghat of Delhi, he interestingly explained this distinction: 'Brahma Bhagawan (God) had created sixteen karams in an individual's life. The other brahmins perform fifteen—we perform the last karam. They don't enter our work—we don't enter theirs. My work involves performing the pind daan and asthi visarjan—karam kand for my clients. I recite the mantras and guide the aggrieved families in performing the last rites of the deceased.'

Similarly, Sultan Singh, a crematorium supervisor, said, 'These pandits are called mahabrahmins, *yeh sirf mrityu se jude kaam hi karte hain. Yeh gharon main havan nahin karate* (they only do death-related work, not auspicious work).'

Funeral priests like Rajesh serve their regional communities like Pahadi, Garhwali, Punjabi, etc. in pilgrimage (tirath) places like

Varanasi. I observed them performing rituals for their jajmans (clients) hailing from different areas in Varanasi and Nigambodh Ghat of Delhi.

During my discussions, I understood how other ritual pandits (karam-kandi brahmin) don't like associating with funeral work barring some roles. For instance, when I asked a tirath purohit (pilgrimage priest) about funeral work, demarking his territory and protecting his position in the formal hierarchy, he instantly said, 'Yeh kaam hum nahin karte, (we don't do this task). A separate set of brahmins, mahaacharya, assists in the martak work. We manage shubh karya like naming ceremonies, mundan (head shaving ceremony) and marriage ceremonies, whereas they perform the eleven-day last rites and accept daan in return. However, on the twelfth day, we take a different set of donations made in the name of a pitr.'

While talking to Rajesh, I learned how death work is considered polluting. 'People treat funeral work as ganda,' said Rajesh, a funeral pandit. Since death in the Hindu religion is seen as ritually polluting, work related to death is also seen as polluting. Therefore the death-related work is relegated to these lower-order priests in the hierarchy.

According to Knipe, the highly polluting work related to funerals is left to these particular brahmins. They perform polluted services, like bearing corpses from the place of death to the cremation ground. They are called faceless brahmins in the South because one should never remember seeing their ill-omened faces. Otherwise, they might haunt you like ghosts (Knipe 2019, 241).

When trying to disentangle, I was perplexed by a question—why is funeral work considered ritually inferior/polluting? For example, a ritual pandit said, 'They are pret swarup (ghost-like)—therefore, they are polluted.' Initially, I didn't understand what he meant to say. However, I moved forward in this journey and discovered that according to Hindu scriptures, the soul becomes a disembodied ghost or pret, in a hungry and malevolent state, at death. The mahabrahmins preside over the rituals addressed to the pret during the first eleven days (a highly polluting period after death) and accept gifts in the ghost's name. Therefore, they are treated as ashuddh (ritually impure) because they accumulate paap by presiding over the eleven-day rituals and accepting gifts in the deceased's name. Hence, they are not allowed inside the threshold of the house after eleven days (Parry 1994, 77).

Not just are these brahmins subordinates, they are treated as untouchables. In his book, Parry describes them as lower-degree brahmins: 'Though unequivocally brahmins, mahabrahmins are pret-brahmins—who are treated as untouchables or *achhut* (not to be touched). Therefore, no fastidious person of a clean caste will dine with them. Hence, in theory, they should live outside the village and the South, in the direction of death' (Parry 1994,77).

According to Knipe: 'No one should see their inauspicious face after 11 days' (Knipe 2019, 241).

Like, a ritual priest in Varanasi told me, 'After performing the eleventh-day ritual, the brahmin should leave—people don't want to see his face. But, unfortunately, one keeps bumping into them these days.'

Moreover, since death is polluting among Hindus, the mahabrahmins, who participate in the death pollution by serving multiple jajmans, are considered permanently impure (Parry 1994, 77).

However, some new-age brahmins don't see death as inauspicious or funeral work polluting. Dr Manisha Shete, a progressive pandit, believes death is painful but not inauspicious. According to her, even scriptures like the Bhagavad Gita mention death like changing the soul's clothes. Therefore, it is inevitable and natural. 'Many believe that rituals related to death are inauspicious, but I don't ascribe to this belief,' she asserted.

I agree with Shete that why should funeral work, a crucial life cycle ritual, be relegated to an inferior position. This differentiation is, however, profound in many parts of the country.

Mahabrahmins, although considered ill-omened, are nevertheless critical in the performance of the last rites. Their role in the death drama is indispensable, playing a crucial part in end-of-life rituals. They officiate the deceased's last rites till the eleventh day until the pret is ready to become a pitr. Their work is to accept food on behalf of the dead pret on the eleventh day. Following the presentation of the food, their visual enjoyment shows that the deceased is satisfied with the food and has no ill will toward one's relatives (Knipe 2019, 241).

Moreover, fearing these brahmins' curse—the families dutifully fulfil their demands. Therefore, before their departure, mahabrahmins claim sajja daan in utensils, clothes, bedding, shoes, grains, toiletries, etc. Sometimes, a cash payment is given instead of these items. Therefore they are alternatively called daan brahmins (Knipe 2019, 241). It is believed that the deceased receive these offerings through the brahmin in the next world—considered crucial in the journey to the next world. I remember giving all these items to our funeral priest at my father's eleventh-day mourning ceremony.

'He doesn't ask for less money—sometimes he demands ₹10,000 or more. He doesn't eat food till you fulfil his demands. But he can never flourish—all his earnings just fly like a pret. There were not many mahabrahmins—these days, one sees many,' said a ritual priest in Varanasi. The above statement substantiates how mahabrahmins are treated with disdain by other higher-order priests.

After receiving gifts, these priests bestow salvation and allow the soul to travel to the other world. Therefore, it is believed that they must be satisfied with daan for the successful completion of the last rites. Else, the dissatisfied pret might haunt you forever, bringing misfortune to the family.

When I spoke to a family about the role of mahabrahmins, Ram Maheshwari told me, 'Mahabrahmin *ko khush rakhna zaruri hai. Nahin to humare purvaj ko moksha ki prapti kaise hogi* (it is crucial to keep our mahabrahmin happy. Otherwise, how will our ancestors attain moksha)?'

Some even see this work as their moral duty. 'If I don't do this— who will do this work? God has chosen me to help people in distress.

The other pandits won't do this work. They don't even accept water from the death house—let alone funeral work,' said Rajesh.

Shete believes that the essence of the rituals should remain alive, not the conventions, 'In the past, families sacrificed sixteen kinds of daan, including a cow—things have changed with time. We must question if we need such elaborate rituals in the present context. In my opinion, daan should be given to the needy instead.'

I interviewed a karam-kandi brahmin in Varanasi who presided over the last rites and rituals of their jajmans, barring the eleventh-day daan (considered highly polluting). I found that other higher-order karam-kandi ritual pandits often offer their services at funerals trying to diversify their work. For instance, in many Marwari families, the kul (family) purohits or tirath purohits conduct last rites like pind daan. Besides, they accompany the families to the ghats. In these scenarios, mahabrahmin is merely present on the eleventh day to accept gifts. So, the family priests can do the funeral work, whereas funeral priests are barred from family work.

II
The Work of Pilgrimage Priest or Tirath Purohit

I remember my visit to Haridwar, one of the holiest places for Hindus, to immerse my father's ashes in the sacred Ganga—a part of the family tradition. My grandfather's and great-grandfather's remains were immersed in the same holy waters.

Tirath purohits/pandas, the genealogical experts who assist families in immersing the ashes and conducting the tirath shraddh, are sought-after religious specialists in Haridwar and Varanasi. While performing papa's last rites, I saw several families at the mercy of tirath purohits in completing the post-cremation funerary rites of their loved ones, ensuring a good afterlife. I even observed pilgrims making ritual offerings to their ancestors at the Manikarnika Ghat of Varanasi.

After completing the rituals related to last rites at the ghats, families customarily visit these specialists to update the genealogical records. Tirath purohits theoretically serve a never-ending hereditary relationship with their jajmans, serving many generations.

After finishing the immersion rituals, we headed to the family tirath purohit's office to conclude the custom of updating the family's genealogical records. We were escorted by his assistant through the narrow galis and climbed a dark, narrow staircase leading us to his dimly lit office. I am sure I would have lost my way had I been alone.

I remember the damp smell of the mattresses on the floor in an otherwise empty room. The faded pictures of the Hindu Gods and Goddesses were mounted on the walls looking after the ritual specialist.

After a brief greeting, the tirath purohit, clad in pure white clothes with a vermilion tilak on his forehead, politely enquired the name of our ancestral village and gotra (subcaste) to dig out the correct vahi records—genealogy register. Purohits arrange these documents first by the village name of the ancestors, followed by the gotra from that village.

These records, vahis, have been kept safe with the purohit's family for ten generations. Once we confirmed the family name, clan name, and ancestral village name, he quickly opened a steel vault to retrieve a rolled-up, bound document.

Then the entire family history unfolded, written on archival paper with special ink, recorded with great precision and expertise, carrying each visit's month and date. The sheer joy my family and I felt—reading the notes left by my grandfather and his siblings written in dark sooty ink, is incomparable.

I retrieved one record from 21 December 1941, when my great-grandfather visited Haridwar from Dadwal, Jhelum district—now in Pakistan. In the olden days, the ink was made with the sap of banana trees, burnt apricot peels and other secret ingredients prepared by these ritual specialists.

According to him, pilgrims used to come by foot, sometimes taking six months to reach. Only the wealthy could afford pilgrimage. Sometimes, they even carried their neighbours' phul (remains) to be immersed.

'In pre-partition days, the train Lahori took the pilgrims from Pakistan. We used to visit the station to receive our jajmans. Now, of course, things have changed. People come in Maruti cars and even helicopters. There were no hotels or dharmsalas in Haridwar. There were only tirath purohits catering for everything—dining, staying, and arranging temple visits for their jajmans. We provided chulas (traditional stoves) to cook food,' he recounted, reminiscing those times.

Literature suggests that these specialists have exclusive rights over written records and the communities he caters to. Parry explains the undisputed power of a tirath purohit: 'The tirath purohit's proof of his rights in his record books (vahis), in which the previous visits of the members of the pilgrim's descent line, village or caste are recorded. These books are his patrimony and are heritable property that can also, in theory, be sold or mortgaged—though in practice they are more likely to be transferred by theft than a sale' (Parry 1994, 97).

Since the 1990s, these documents have been granted legal status in India and are even admissible in court in family disputes, giving these specialists more power (Kundalia 2015, 51).

These specialists charge fees for the upkeep of the vahis, which vary according to the family's social status. Mahendra has an extensive repertoire of clients. We paid him his dakshina after we updated our records. However, I can't deny a sense of pride and joy upon seeing the vahi.

Utah's Genealogical society has microfilmed the information in the vahis since 1977. They undertook this project in India as part of their genealogical research project. However, purohits are averse to sharing records—perhaps fearing their misuse and threat to their livelihood (Kundalia 2015, 57).

According to Mahendra, approximately 1700 surviving tirath purohit in Haridwar serve the Hindus of the entire world. 'By the grace of Lord Ram, we are still the keepers of this tradition. The gaddi is hereditary. Originally there were 2500, but the number diminished either because of deaths or the absence of male heirs,' he said.

Some families employ lower-level purohits or agents/assistants—colloquially called gumashtas. These are tirath purohit's agents who are based in the city. 'After keeping their fees of 25 per cent, these gumashta's share the daan with the tirath purohits,' he told me. I also learned that the pandas and gumashtas have their own code language, through which such shares are negotiated in front of the pilgrims.

With digitization, these specialist professions may fade and become history. However, I am glad I witnessed my family vahi in its original avatar, written in sooty ink by my forefathers.

III
The Barbers: Role in Last Rites and Rituals

Like other traditional professions, barbering is practised intergenerationally, called by names like nai, navi and navik across India. Besides cutting hair, barbers have played critical social roles like arranging marriage alliances, ceremonies associated with childbirth, and even last rites and rituals. They also served as surgeons in India because of their expertise in handling razors. Not only this, some of them even served as musicians.

In ancient India, barbers traditionally doubled as messengers and confidants, resolving social matters. Some of them even enjoyed royal patronage. Even today, when arranging a marriage, barbers are the preferred mediators.

In olden times when there were no postal services, the barbers were given the task of carrying the news of death to the relatives of the bereaved family. The barber has a crucial role in lower-caste and high-caste mortuary rituals. Among Hindus, the tonsuring of hair is an essential aspect of last rites, and barbers perform these rituals. At various stages, they tonsure the mourners and may even tonsure the corpse. Moreover, they shave and pare the nails of the mourners on the tenth-day rites. 'Some family barbers accompany the families to the cremation ground, assisting them in various life cycle rituals at the ghats in Varanasi. These days most of them prefer tonsuring the hair at the ghats since that's more lucrative,' said Amrit Sharma, my respondent from Varanasi.

These barbers serve a particular purpose at pilgrimage places like Gaya, Varanasi and Haridwar. For instance, I saw several pilgrims and mourners getting their heads shaved during my visit. The barbers who have exclusive rights on Manikarnika also shave large numbers of bathers and pilgrims who visit the ghat. In addition, some have a profitable side business selling hair to dealers from Calcutta and Bombay who export it to the West to manufacture wigs (Parry 1994, 92).

The barber's influence on Indian culture is undeniable. Although the grooming landscape is changing in India, barbers still play an essential role in mortuary rites in the urban and rural landscape.

I was amused to learn that these distinctions exist even in today's world. Perhaps because the death culture is the slowest to respond to changes however, I believe the strict roles of ritual technicians may become less rigid with time or in different settings.

7

Women Performing the Last Rites: the Hindu and Sikh Faith

'I performed the last rites of my papa because he wished so,' said Anupama Singh. Does it sound offbeat? Among Hindus, the eldest son usually lights the parents' funeral pyre It is believed that one attains moksha if sons light the chita of their parents. Considering the health of their afterlife, the Hindu families wish for a son. Moreover, men traditionally perform end-of-life rituals, and women are kept from morbid places like crematoriums and funeral homes. However, in some Hindu families, women have stepped into these male-dominated zones to perform the last rites of their loved ones, like offering fire and immersion of ashes—sometimes circumstantially, and as an informed choice in other scenarios.

Many famous women, film and political personalities, have been in the news for lighting the pyre of their deceased family members, setting a precedent. For instance, Indian actor and TV presenter Mandira Bedi hit the headlines for performing her husband's last rites in the recent past. In 2014, Pankaja Munde lit the pyre of her father, Gopinath Munde, a senior BJP leader in the western state of Maharashtra. Further, in 2018, foster daughter Namita Kaul performed the end-of-life rituals of former prime minister Atal Behari Vajpayee (Pandey 2021).

Minor changes are underway in the arena of last rites and rituals. While analysing these changes, I spoke to sociologists and ritual specialists. According to sociologist Dr Ravi Nandan Singh, people are ready to accommodate minor alterations until other significant traditions like mukhagni and funeral pyre are kept intact. He told me, 'If one has to let go of some practices, then a daughter performing the final rites will be more conducive than tampering with the structural traditions. However, the essential traditions are retained here, but positions are adjusted.' According to him, perhaps more challenging would be daughters seeking a distinctive funerary practice than the traditionally prescribed one.

But, I feel daughters and wives performing the last rites is a significant change. It questions the stereotypical beliefs around the cruciality of male members offering mukhagni to the deceased. Moreover, it gives women the agency to dismantle age-old traditions by deciding on their involvement in life-cycle rituals.

When I spoke to a funeral priest, he had something interesting to share. 'These days, even women are coming forward. We have seen in many instances where daughters perform the last rites of the parents even though a son is present. With changing times, we need to accept these alterations. We equally support women's participation in the last rites of the deceased,' confirmed a funeral priest from Delhi. However, this might vary in other geographies, where women are barred from entering the crematoriums.

In the Sikh religion, theoretically, any family member can perform the last rites. While talking to Gyani Atma Singh, a senior Granthi, he said, 'When we bring up our sons and daughters equally—why can't daughters light the pyre? Likewise, a wife can light the husband's funeral pyre too.' But, I am not sure how many women in practice participate in the final rites of their loved ones among Sikhs.

My sister and I conducted my father's final rites. '*Yeh mere do ladke hain* (these are my two sons),' papa used to say with pride. We are two sisters, and there was no question of anyone else performing papa's final rituals. Even he wanted it that way, and we honoured his last wish. My Hindu extended family members were seemingly comfortable with this decision. I was the designated chief mourner for papa's antim sanskars. However, I would say it was a mixed bag of feelings—challenging and satisfying simultaneously. First, I lit the funeral pyre and saw his flesh burning, leaving bones and ashes behind. Then, I ritually cracked papa's skull with a long stick in the middle, releasing his soul. At that point, I felt relieved to have fulfilled papa's antim ichchha (final wish).

Inspired by my experience as the chief mourner during papa's last rites, I wanted to capture the involvement of other women during the end-of-life rituals of their loved ones. I tried to understand the motivations and sentiments involved. So, I wrote a lengthy Facebook post asking women friends and acquaintances to share their stories. In a few hours, I received an overwhelming response resulting in heart-warming conversations with women from different walks of life.

Madhumita, an author-journalist, contacted me. She told me, 'I lost my parents very young. My father was a devout brahmin who liked following traditional rituals. So when Ma died, he involved my sister and me in performing her rites. However, my sister was not in the country when he passed away. So I did the cremation ceremony, but we conducted the thirteen-days rituals together. None of my relatives flinched. My dad had an older brother, but no one objected. I had a conversation with the priest, who told me that it's nowhere in Hindu scriptures that women shouldn't be doing this. It's more to do with convention than what's written in scriptures. So even though I am not religious, I performed everything for my father—fulfilling his wishes.' There have undoubtedly been shifts in how people think. However, she told me there would be a substantial regional and urban-rural divide regarding women's participation. 'I conversed with a friend from Karnataka who said that Bengalis tend to be less rigid than other communities,' she told me.

I understand that the changes would not happen at the same pace in a remote village compared to an urban metropolis. Even Dr Ravi corroborated that these modifications would be context-specific. There are regions in India that are more progressive. He said, 'The entire Punjab region has been more reformist than other parts in India—the social reform movements like Arya Samaj could be the reason. Likewise, West Bengal is reformed partly because of social reform movements. Moreover, saw the first crematoria getting built. In contrast, one won't find many women at the crematoriums in Banaras. Furthermore, things would be different if you were to go down to eastern Uttar Pradesh or Bihar. In these regions, gender segregation would be more profound. So specific changes would be allowed in some parts—they may not become routine—not an industrial change.'

Similarly, Madhavi Gupta, who works with the differently-abled, shared her touching story. She participated in the last rites of her father-in-law, whom she dearly loved. 'It was baba's wish that I participate in his final rites. We shared an excellent bond. Therefore, he wanted me to participate in these rituals just like his sons. Although I didn't light his funeral pyre, I was involved in other rituals like phul chugna and immersing ashes,' she told me.

Likewise, I discovered many exciting facets in a detailed conversation with Suchitra, an entrepreneur from Bangalore. While sharing her extraordinary story, she told me, 'I was in Berlin, travelling for work, when Appa took his last breath. So, my journey from Berlin to Bangalore was the most challenging one. After reaching home, I first gave him a hug and kiss and played his favourite song. People must have thought that I have gone crazy—this was how we related—through food and music.'

Her father wasn't a devout Hindu, so they went the Arya Samaj way. Her elder brothers, who lived abroad, were present at her father's funeral. But somehow, she was appointed the chief mourner. 'So, strangely, when the pujari came, he asked me to do everything. He said, 'Aap betho—aap sab karo (You sit and do everything).' Perhaps he sensed that my brothers were not as comfortable. Moreover, my husband and I had looked after my ailing father. So, we shared a special bond with him. Therefore, I felt I had the absolute right to send him off,' she told me.

Moreover, she felt that she was comfortable handling rituals. She practically did everything from kandha dena to saying the last prayers. While talking, she narrated a delightful anecdote, 'I took along the T-shirt that I had gifted appa and covered him in that T-shirt before letting his body in the furnace at the electric crematorium. I even saw his body burning in the furnace. We made sure that our mother accompanied us to the crematorium. That way, it was good closure for everyone,' she recounted. According to her, the extended family members were comfortable with her taking the lead. Suchitra comes from a progressive Tamil family where children were treated equally in every respect. She believes that any child has fundamental right to participate in the last rites of their parents regardless of their gender.

Likewise, women pandits are setting a precedent by performing the last rites of their family members. For instance, Dr Manisha Shete, a practising pandit and scholar, passionately shared her thoughts with me, 'We need to change with the world. For instance, women in the past were not allowed to participate in the last rites due to security threats. Even in today's world, women are barred from attending funerals in many communities based on traditional customs. However, there has been a change in these traditions.' She believes that the antim sanskar can be performed by a daughter or a son. 'I conducted the antim sanskar of my grandmother and father both—change is imminent. During the pandemic, didn't we have to mould the rituals? We had to resort to the online mediums and forgo some rites,' Shete asserted. Shete, who is very progressive in her thoughts, believes these reformist ideas should reach the wider society.

I don't know what the Hindu scriptures say about the women performing the last rites of the family members. But, I know how the parents would smile from their new abode at their heartfelt desire fulfilled by their daughters. In the end, what matters is respectfully saying goodbyes to our loved ones, not the gender of the chief mourner.

Not only this, but during the pandemic, many women who were previously barred from entering the crematorium assisted with the last rites of strangers. I heard countless stories and interviewed the brave hearts who carried the bodies from the ambulances, lit the pyres and collected the remains—recasting the traditional beliefs and customs. I have described these elsewhere in the book. However, I wonder if we should wait for these unprecedented times to determine the future of women's participation in the rituals, especially the last rites.

These narratives are immensely encouraging—making me feel hopeful. But unfortunately, for now, these rights are accessible to a privileged few. But, I am confident it would reach the wider society. In the end, I believe the gender of the mourner shouldn't matter until the rituals are performed with love and respect.

8

Ritual Technicians

Initially, I anticipated interviewing the ritual experts to be the most daunting task of writing this book. But, to my surprise, it was an enriching exercise—humorous, insightful, and thought-provoking. Each interaction was unique—the Parsi priest candid and funny. Manisha Shete a feminist revolutionary Hindu priestess in her own right. Atma Singh, a serious Sikh Granthi who takes pride in his work and Mahendra Kumar Gautam, a tirath purohit with an elephant's memory. The funeral priest is an honest and prudent soul. Let's read their stories to understand the future of priesthood and last rites in India.

I
A Practising Women Priest

Although female priests have recently sparked the digital world's buzz, women leading the front in the priesthood began in the early '80s, with Shankar Seva Samiti in Pune training women to recite the Vedic mantras and perform Vedic rituals. Now Pune city has two schools for female priests—Jnana Prabodhini and Shankar Seva Samiti.

So when a friend shared the contact of Dr Manisha Shete, a female priest, I was thrilled. Keen on understanding how gender operates in this male-dominated profession—I quickly grabbed the opportunity and scheduled an interview with Dr Shete. I was particularly impressed by Shete's courage and passion for studying ancient scriptures. But more so, how she negotiated her space with grace and knowledge.

Dr Manisha Shete has been a practising pandit for the last thirteen years with deep knowledge of Hindu ancient texts. 'Other than me, no one in my family practices priesthood. However, I pursued this work because of my interest in ancient scriptures. I decided to study the scriptures because women had entered every field except priesthood,' Dr Shete told me.

Her passion for the subject led her to complete her doctorate in the same discipline. Dr Shete is currently associated with Jnana Prabodhini, a Hindu reformist organization training men and women across castes to perform rituals since the '90s.

Besides, she has presented papers in various international and national forums reflecting her deep interest and dedication to research. When I enquired, she instantly shared her publications through an email. She is passionate about her work and apprentices the young generation at the Jnana Prabodhini organization. 'There are no restrictions. However, our biggest achievement is to open the gates to everyone irrespective of caste and gender,' she said proudly.

She went to a college in Pune to study Indology. While narrating her journey, Shete enthusiastically said, 'In 2007, I re-joined the organization and pursued a degree in paurohitya (priesthood). As I started practising, I found it exciting and challenging simultaneously.

It became a medium to interact and counsel people on Hindu rites and rituals and communicate their deeper meanings. During my interactions, I introduce/communicate sanskars rooted in Hindu tradition. Perhaps I would have lost interest if my work was only confined to karma kand. However, research and training excite me to stay.'

In India, paurahitya is a male-dominated profession. When I asked Shete about her experience as a woman pandit she paused a little before answering, 'In my thirteen-year long career, I have never been outrightly questioned for practising priesthood. However, sometimes families demand that a male pandit accompanies me during the ceremonies.'

According to Dr Shete, people have started accepting women priests. However, she believes that every reform comes with some obstacles.

She said that the demand for female priests is growing in cities, and she often receives requests from Indian families overseas to conduct rituals. She told me she has travelled to Germany and Dubai to perform marriage ceremonies for Hindus living in that part of the world. She offers a rich repertoire of services, from naam karan (naming ceremony) to antyesthi (last sacrifice). 'I like explaining the relevance of each mantra while performing the rituals, making it understandable to ordinary people. Moreover, there are many doubts surrounding life cycle rituals—especially last rites.' She said, 'People ask, "What will happen if we don't ritually perform the rites?"' Therefore, I clear those misconceptions.'

She has witnessed several changes in the profession with the coming of the internet. 'In the beginning, there was no website. We used to perform rituals for friends and relatives. Now the exposure is wider, and so is our reach. Moreover, the students at Jana Prabodhini come from different parts of the country. As a result, the centre has become more versatile, established, vibrant and well known,' she said.

Manisha is exceptionally dedicated to the field. Besides, she was most forthcoming and helpful whenever I approached her with queries. I believe if women are given adequate opportunities, they can excel in any sphere, whether flying jet planes or reciting mantras for the salvation of the departed souls.

II
A Panda From Haridwar

In 2019 I visited Haridwar to immerse my father's ashes in the holy Ganga. That's when I met Mahendra Kumar Gautam, our family tirath priest. When I started researching, I retrieved the old pictures we had clicked during the visit and scratched my memory to recollect the events, creating a sketch in my head.

Then I contacted Mahendra to gain deeper insights into the professional work of pandagiri. As soon as I told him my gotra, he recounted everything as if creating a family tree in his head—surprising me with his precision and craftiness. '*Haan mujhe yaad hai, aap apni sister aur parivaar ke saath aayen thi* (I remember you came with your sister and family),' he told me confidently.

Pandas are the heredity genealogists who maintain the vahis for their jajmans. 'I am the tenth generation involved in this work, contributing for the last 300 years or so—we are the tirth purohit or kul purohit living in the lap of Ganga ji. Five-six family members are engaged in pandagiri, helped by my son and nephew. Sometimes, my wife helps me maintain the vahis,' he told me, narrating his family's legacy.

Mahendra Kumar primarily serves the Punjabi community of *Khatris, Aroras* and *Brahmins* hailing from the Punjab area—Rawalpindi, Sialkot, and Gujranwala in Pakistan. Mahendra has a steady clientele. 'We are purohit of Sunil Dutt, Dr Manmohan Singh and Virat Kohli,' he told me boisterously, naming a few well-known personalities from film, sports and politics among his clients.

He takes pride in his elite and wealthy jajmans. 'Big gotras have big jajmans. I have jajmans around the globe—England, South Africa, America,' he told me.

Lately, he was in the news for assisting the asthi visarjan of a reputed Nanda business family from Delhi. '*Agar app Google karenge to video mil jaye ga*, you will find the video if you Google,' he informed me. Not only this, he has been featured in a book, he claimed.

'How do you find your jajmans?' I asked him curiously. 'The baby fish in Ganga ji learn how to swim on their own—no one teaches them,' he told me. I was astonished when he said, 'If we see someone on the *Har Ki Pauri* from a distance, we can tell the region the person belongs to.'

Besides pandagiri, he performs other life cycle rituals like mundan ceremonies, naming, and marriage ceremonies and knows astrology. 'We manage shubh karya while a separate set of pandits assists in martak karya (death rites) called maha acharya,' he informed me.

Pandas have absolute authority over their vahis. Mahendra owns 150 vahis traditionally stored in heavy steel/metal cupboards. He regularly takes care of the upkeep of his vahis, 'We are the caretakers of these vahis—we worship the vahis just like a Bhagwan by lighting dhoop-batti (incense) and showing them to the Suraj Bhagwan (to put in the sun).'

He told me that these books are their punji (wealth) and a source of livelihood. Therefore, they don't share the records with anyone except their jajmans. But unfortunately, some innocent ones from the community traded the documents, impacting the reputation and livelihood of the community.

When I enquired about digitizing his records, he said mockingly, 'By the time you straighten the wire of your computer, I will make the recording in my vahi.' However, later, he added that his children might use computers because the current generation is savvier with technology.

He has two sons studying law. I asked him if his children would join this hereditary work? He said, 'They will certainly practice the pushtani (hereditary) work and their newly acquired professions.'

According to Mahendra, the girls are also involved in this work. However, I slightly doubt his claims regarding that. 'My wife is very knowledgeable—she holds a master's degree,' he added proudly.

Before concluding, he invited me to visit his family. The bond between the pandas and jajmans is inseparable because they are the ultimate gatekeepers of the family vahis—their history. He concluded the call by saying, 'if purohits are well-taken care of, then they will contribute to the prosperity of their jajmans.' Thus connecting the fortune of the jajmans to their pandas and vice versa.

III
A Funeral Priest From the Nigambodh Ghat

In February, during my visit to Nigambodh Ghat, I met Rajesh Sharma, a funeral priest. Dressed in white kurta-pyjama, sitting at the bench of the ghat, amidst the hustle-bustle of the aggrieved families carrying the arthis while reciting *Ram Naam Satya Hai*—he spoke to me.

Rajesh, forty-four, a migrant from Uttar Pradesh, the northern state of India, has been among the team of sixty to eighty pandits delivering services at the famous Nigambodh Ghat for eighteen years. He worked with the Aditya-Birla group before joining the funeral work. After that, however, he left his job because it involved excessive travelling.

There are pandits from all over the country like Garhwal, Maharashtra and Bihar presiding over the last rites of the respective communities. These funeral pandits acquire the skill by apprenticing under some senior brahmins. 'I worked under a pandit before starting here. My grandfather was also involved in the funeral work, but my father worked with the MCD,' Rajesh told me.

The pandits take turns in presiding over the last rites. So, one needs to be enterprising to survive in this competitive environment. I saw Rajesh coordinating with the other pandits in the middle of our conversation. His work involves performing the pind daan karam kand for his clients. 'I recite the mantras and guide the aggrieved families in conducting the last rites of the deceased member. God Brahma has created sixteen karams in our life, of which the other brahmins perform fifteen, and we perform the last karam,' he told me.

The funeral pandits also belong to the brahman samaj but are treated differently and are discriminated against. When I enquired about his caste, he underscored that he belongs to the Sharma caste of the Bhardwaj Gotra. But it's not the same as other brahmins.

Rajesh conducts four to five funerals in a day on this busy ghat. However, he is not interested in having his children pursue funeral work, and they are currently studying. 'I don't want them to join this job—there is no scope. Moreover, many people treat this as ganda,' he said.

Nevertheless, he regards funeral work as crucial. 'If I don't do this, who will do this? God has chosen me to help people. The other pandits won't do funerals,' he said. Besides, Rajesh told me that other ritual pandits don't even accept water from the house where someone died.

When I inquired about his fees, he said, ' It depends on the jajman. The family's socioeconomic status is also crucial—I don't put pressure on anyone. However, charges are fixed at ₹750 for cremations and ₹250 for phul chugne (collecting the ashes).' He believes that since antim sanskaar is the last sanskaar—there is no harm if one pays a slightly higher amount to the brahmin priest.

He said people prefer open pyre cremations despite greener cremation systems like Mokshada and CNG units installed at the crematorium. Although, his role doesn't alter much with newer methods.

Rajesh feels that the work is not easy. 'We have to tread the path carefully. Tending to the burning corpses and the remains after family members leave is important,' he said. Not only this, I feel staying amidst the burning pyres and inhaling the sooty smoke must be detrimental to their physical and mental wellbeing.

Their role is crucial to society, especially when other pandits are unwilling to put their hands into this important but stigmatized work.

IV
A Karam-Kandi Priest from Varanasi

Walking through the narrow lanes of Varanasi, I reached the house of Arun Dhital, a Karam Kandi ritual priest in his late sixties. I approached Pandit Dhital with questions about Hindu last rites and rituals, which he answered with utmost patience, demonstrating his deep knowledge and experience. He is a Shastri (expert in scriptures) who graduated from Sampurnanand Sanskrit University Varanasi.

Although originally from Nepal, he has lived in Varanasi all his life. 'My great grandfather came to study shastras here in Varanasi. He was a karam-kandi pandit and a Geeta Paathi (Geeta reciter),' he said. Arun's children returned to Nepal some years ago, but he intends to live in Varanasi until his death. '*Ab yeh hi ghar hai humara—Gangaji ke charno mein rehna hai* (now this is my house, I want to live at the feet of the revered Ganga),' he told me. His son and daughter insist he joins them in Nepal, but he resists.

'No one in my family followed in my father's footsteps. So I am the only practising priest in the clan. My children are not keen on practising Karam kand but only interested in anushthan (yagya and havan) because it pays better,' he said.

He follows a strict morning routine waking up at four and there after taking a snan (bath) in Gangaji. Not only this, like a genuine pandit, he follows an elaborate prayer routine every day before heading out for work. He proudly showed me a small temple he had nurtured for many years next to his living quarters. From the window of his room, I saw the stairs leading to the serene Ganga River.

While discussing his diminishing patronage, he told me that people are not keen on performing elaborate end-of-life rituals. However, he swears by his Marwari patrons, who do follow the traditions. In the past, these rituals used to last for almost a year. 'Everything is done in haste nowadays. These days, the monthly shraddh is only performed by a handful of communities, like Marwaris,' he said.

He also mentioned how mourning rituals have changed with times. 'People used to wear white clothes and abstained from visiting relatives for a year. Besides, in the olden times, death rituals lasted for twelve years,' he said, reminiscing. He firmly believes that one should perform the pind daan shraddh for our ancestors annually. He thinks this is our way of showing gratitude to our loved ones.

He also believes some less knowledgeable pandits have turned life cycle rituals into a business by cheating people. 'My father used to be paid a meagre salary of One rupee. But, he worked with shraddha. But, these days, pandits have become lobhi (greedy). They are busier operating their mobiles than doing puja-path,' he said cynically. Pandit Arun is perhaps old-school but rooted in his knowledge of scriptures and dedication.

V
A Sikh Granthi

Gyani Atma Singh, fifty-three, is a learned Granthi who graduated from Sikh Missionary College in Amritsar. Although there is no ordained priesthood in Sikhism, a Granthi equates to a priest. Gyani Atma Singh is a Head Granthi at a Gurudwara Sahib in Gurugram—learned and thorough.

One appointed as a full-time Granthi should be an Amritdhari practising Sikh following the prescribed code of religious discipline— Sikh Rahit Maryada. Besides, Gyani Atma Singh is a pracharak who travels worldwide, taking discourses on the holy Sikh scriptures. 'The current generation is not well-versed with the holy scriptures. So I think it's our responsibility to educate them,' said Atma Singh.

When I enquired about the Sikh last rites, he described the Antam Sanskar with pride—his eyes bright and demeanour composed. Then, sitting in the calm and pious environment of the Gurudwara Sahib, he explained different aspects to me.

While describing the last rites, he shared numerous interesting anecdotes describing his work and journey. For instance, he was in Thailand when the tsunami hit. 'We recited Ardas for the departed souls during the apda,' he told me. Furthermore, he recalls how the King of Thailand complimented him for his commendable work during the tsunami.

He also shared another exciting anecdote about travelling to America. He narrated how he faced the American embassy when they enquired about his purpose of visiting.

He has three children—none keen on carrying his legacy forward. 'I wanted my son to follow in my footsteps, but he wasn't interested—it's all destiny,' said Atma Singh with a sigh.

During our conversation, he had to leave several times to attend to his ritual duties.

When I told him I was writing a book on last rites, he paused and told me, 'Write a nishpaksh (unbiased) book.' So I left the Gurudwara premises with a thought—something to ponder later. It's incredible how I enriched my understanding with every conversation—gaining deeper insights into the philosophy of life and death.

VI
A Parsi Priest

Framroze Sorabji Mirza took some time to respond to my messages, but there was no stopping once he nodded. At the onset, Mirza told me—'Ask me any questions, *mujhe kisi ka dar nahin* (I am not scared of anyone).' I believe this response best describes Mirza—fearless and prudent.

Mirza, sixty-eight, has been practising priesthood for nearly five decades. Belonging to a priestly family, he was trained in a Madrassa. Mirza was initiated into the order at the Iranshah Atash Behram, the holiest fire temple in Udvada, Gujarat.

Not only Parsi tradition, Mirza claims to be well versed with the funeral methods across religions—dedicated to understanding the system in other religious traditions. 'I can write a book based on my deep conversations with the workers and the staff members,' he told me.

He likes to call himself a freelancer offering his clients a wide array of services like marriage, navjote, and cremation services. When I inquired about his fees, he insisted that it varies depending on the prayer services. 'I manage everything from hiring assistants to acquiring required materials for the funerals. However, I am totally against misleading my clients for monetary gain,' he said.

Mirza is a revolutionary in his own right. When sky burials at Doongerwadi came under the scanner a few years back, he introduced cremation as a funeral method among his community. He and his team were amongst the few who started cremation services for the Parsi community at Worli crematorium in Mumbai. Mirza is very outspoken and candid about his role—humorously comparing himself to a revolutionary historical character Ahilya Bai. 'The community ostracized me, taking me to Supreme Court. I even received threats. However, I am not bothered anymore. I was born into a priestly family, and it's my moral duty to assist bereaved folk with their choice of method. I can't turn my back on people and deny them my services,' he told me with pain in his voice.

According to him, slowly, the community is becoming more open to cremations. Moreover, he believes that Parsis had benefitted tremendously from this method during the pandemic when the gates of Doongerwadi were closed for funerals. Finally, Mirza proudly confirms that he was the only Parsi priest performing the final funerary rites for the Covid victims.

'I have served my community 24/7 during the lockdowns. No one stopped me because the Government and the Municipal Corporation issued me a permit,' he said. He believes people shouldn't dispose of bodies at Towers of Silence, especially for pandemic deaths. Since, at Doongerwadi, there is a scare of spreading infection.

Due to shrinking numbers, there is a shortage of Parsi priests in the community. Moreover, the priesthood is restricted to a few families. When I enquired about priesthood status in the Parsi community, he shared something meaningful. Unfortunately, he believes not many people are interested in joining the profession. In the '60s, when he started, more than 200 priests were associated with a prominent fire temple in Mumbai. 'There would be no room to stand. There were so many priests at the fire temple. Yet, there are only a handful of priests in the temple because no one wants to do this thankless job,' said Mirza. He said that the community is responsible for this—neglecting the priesthood in the country.

According to him, it's not an easy job. A priest is bound by many restrictions. Due to this, many people receive training but eventually lose interest and discontinue practising. He believes that the younger generations are attracted to more well-paid professions. 'I started my career with a meagre payment of four and eight annas. However, the young people are not keen on joining the priesthood because it's not lucrative,' he said. Mirza follows what he preaches, 'I have informed my family that I wish to be cremated instead of Doongerwadi—I can't be a hypocrite.' He is happy that he doesn't have children, 'I wouldn't want my family to suffer the same plight, facing trials with the highest court in the country.'

He humorously told me, 'I have a direct setting with my God. So I have spoken to him, please don't have me reborn into the Parsi community and don't make me a priest in my next life. I want to enjoy life without any jhik-jhik (nagging).'

It was interesting talking to him. Unfortunately, I am yet to come across other people who speak their minds without inhibitions the way he does.

VII
Hafiz Gulam Sarwar

Gulam Sahib is a Hafiz in Ranchi. He teaches children in a Madrassa and is associated with a mosque in Ranchi. Hafiz is a title given to a person who knows the Quran by heart.

He patiently explained the last rites to me in his beautiful Urdu. He was hesitant at the beginning of the interview, thinking I would not be able to comprehend the language he was comfortable with. I am glad that I went ahead and spoke with him.

I have excerpts of his interview quoted throughout my section on Islamic last rites. However, in the end, I had to interpret some parts of his interview, taking the help of friends well-versed in Urdu.

When I asked him about the Imam's job, he said, 'Theoretically, anyone in the village who can read the Quran well can be appointed an Imam. In addition, the person should be a pious and a good human. But, unfortunately, one doesn't pay the Imams well these days; therefore, sometimes less knowledgeable ones are appointed for the same. At least, they would do the Azaan, if nothing else.' It takes years of experience and depth of understanding of scripture that makes a good Imam and Hafiz. His deep knowledge of Hadiths and the Quran was apparent during our conversation.

I don't know about what the future of last rites in India looks like, with fewer people coming forward to join. Among Parsis, the number of priests is diminishing. Although, among Hindus, there are enough practising pandits. But, I can't say with certainty how many of them are ritually competent with proper knowledge of scriptures. Moreover, with other professions luring the current generations, how many of them would be keen on joining this work in the future? Without many ritual specialists, the time is not far when we would have to rely on technology to attain salvation. Besides, some new-age pandits have already adopted newer ways of reaching their tech-savvy clients worldwide. I believe, if nothing else, the pandemic has taught us to look for more unique ways of performing rituals.

9

People Involved in Laying the Dead to Rest: Cremation Workers and Mortuary Staff

Can you imagine the plight of someone working amidst the sooty smoke of the burning pyres—attending to the dead day and night? Some professions are seldom mentioned in non-academic discourses—funeral or death work is one of them. I wonder how we can ignore the work that comes with death.

However, it comes to the centre-stage during disasters or public health emergencies. Didn't we experience innumerable challenges during the Covid-19 pandemic? The situation was alarming. During the second pandemic wave, we heard numerous stories when laying the dead became challenging because of the enormous death toll, lack of space and dwindling workforce.

Although challenging, the army of cemetery and cremation workers worked tirelessly—never giving up. While talking to these workers, one told me, 'We fought the war against Corona—just like the army. The situation was difficult, but we worked day and night. It's our dharam to serve people.' This was the spirit and responsibility these people displayed—risking their own lives and well-being to serve their fellow humans.

I dedicate this section to these everyday superheroes—shedding light on their work, struggles and day-to-day hardships. Without their vital contribution, human bodies would rot in the open, and the surroundings would become a breeding ground for infection.

I wrote this section based on my enriching conversations with these workers. The humility with which they shared their stories, pouring their hearts out, was an overwhelming experience.

I
Funeral Workers: Buriers and Cremation Workers

1. The Caste Work

'This work is considered ganda. But *humare log* have to do this. *Bade log shav ko haath nahin lagayege* (no upper-caste person will ever touch a corpse),' said Manish, a cremation worker from Delhi.

In India, Dealing with dead bodies has been traditionally confined to India's dalit communities based on oppressive belief systems that also draw from notions of purity and pollution. Moreover, people born in these families are forced to continue in hereditary occupations because of strict caste divisions. I saw this division, these ideas, prevalent across religions.

Dignity Disposed, a Report on Crematorium and Burial Groundworkers in Bengaluru during the COVID-19 pandemic also highlighted the caste-based hereditary nature of work limited to the Dalit community, with third to sixth-generation workers engaged in funeral work (Dignity Disposed 2021).

Across India, these workers are addressed by various caste names. In north India, they are known as Doms/Chamars, while in western India, they are known as Mahars. However, in the south, common caste names include Mala, Madiga, Pariah, Pulaya, and Holeya (Laxmaiah 2021).

Not only workers, but in many contexts, even the funeral priests who deal with the dead are treated with disdain and described as achhut—not to be touched (Parry 77, 1994). This discrimination was corroborated by many funeral pandits whom I interviewed while writing the book.

2. The Work of Funeral Staff

'I work here the entire day—I lay the pyre, assist the family members in handling the bodies, and clean up the place after the families leave (*saaf safai ka dhyan rakhta hun*),' said Munnalal, a funeral worker.

Among Hindus and Sikhs, the work involves setting the pyre with wood and tending it until it becomes embers and ashes. On the other hand, in Muslim kabristans, the funeral work entails digging the graves, cleaning up and plastering the grave after the families leave. The elected body at the kabristans appoints two to three workers to do the job on a fixed salary. Digging graves is a learned job. However, not everyone can do this. 'Only a jaankaar person is adept at doing this work,' confirmed Hafiz Gulam.

The people who deal with the dead—the buriers or crematorium workers, play a significant role in society. But unfortunately, this stigmatized labour remains unrecognized as important public health work. I wonder, can we think of saying goodbyes to our loved ones without their crucial assistance?

However, just like today, these workers' roles were ignored even during the British regime. Nevertheless, the British reports and archives fleetingly mention these workers' contributions.

The social stigmatization of mortuary work explains the silence in the colonial archives. What archives choose to tell is equally revealing. Colonial archives contain snippets of payrolls for mortuary workers, enlisted by caste names such as *doms*, *mahars*, and linguistically fluid terms such as *murdafarashis*. Documents on civic administration, such as municipal, administrative and health reports, summarily acknowledge the number of mortuary workers on the respective department's payrolls but do not clearly state how much the city's public health depended upon their work (Chattopadhyay 2020).

However, the documents written during epidemics like the bubonic plague recognize their contribution—albeit briefly. But unfortunately, the trend continues even today, with these workers receiving little recognition and mention in the media reports/newspapers, barring unprecedented times like the Covid-19 pandemic. During emergencies, the inadequacies of the systems and the work involving human disposal that is otherwise neglected gains prominence.

Although critical, the work remains exploitative and underpaid— falling under unorganized and informal labour.

'Most crematoriums in big cities are managed by Non-Government Organizations (NGOs). This is because the Municipal Corporations have outsourced the upkeep of the crematoriums. So NGOs manage everything from employing the contractual staff to paying them salaries,' said Anshul Garg, a volunteer from the NGO Mokshda.

During my visits, I noticed how organizations oversee the upkeep of crematoriums. Besides, my conversations with the staff were equally revealing. I gathered how the crematorium workers are at the mercy of organizations for hiring and paying salaries.

The report Dignity Disposed highlights that, in Bengaluru, most workers work contractually and are not registered on the payrolls. Even the payment cycles are highly erratic. As per the report, sometimes the wages were not paid for months altogether (Dignity Disposed 2021).

The payment of the burial workers is not fixed either. However, in some better run kabristans, the workers earn a decent amount. 'The workers are paid well here. We pay them a fixed salary of ₹4,000. Moreover, they receive tips from deceased family members. We also give them a yearly bonus,' confirmed Jawadul Hasan, a kabristan management committee president.

I also discovered that the payments varied depending on the nature of the work. For example, someone who recites mantras and adds a mixture of herbs to the pyre is considered more skilled and higher in the funeral-work hierarchy and paid more. In contrast, the sevadars who assist in carrying the wood and cleaning the pyre rank lower in the work hierarchy are paid less.

The SDMC (South Delhi Municipal Corporation) has pre-set the charges to control any inconsistency. 'The corporation has fixed the amount we can charge from the families. The pandits are paid ₹300 per cremation while the sevadars get ₹125 per cremation. Besides, sometimes the staff members are tipped by the family. But, that is purely dependent on the family's wishes,' confirmed a funeral pandit (See Times of India 2021).

I spoke to Sanjay, who has worked as a safai karamchari at the famous Nigambodh Ghat of Delhi for twenty years. He manages the section where the corpses are offered a ritual bath before the cremation. He said he gets two monthly leaves and is paid ₹12,000. However, I can't comment on other crematoriums since Nigambodh ghat is one of the better-managed shamshan ghats in Delhi and perhaps remunerates better than others.

Besides, it's not easy working in the crematoriums amidst the hazardous smoke and pollutants rising from the pyres. The report Dignity Disposed also pointed out that the funeral workers worked in hazardous environments with negligible social security and protection. Although, the government is promoting the CNG crematoriums in big cities. But the open pyre crematoriums are still sought after in the Hindu religion over the CNG-operated pyres.

Although beneficial from the environmental perspective, the modernization of the crematorium requires training and expertise, making it more challenging for workers adept at managing the traditional pyre (Selvaraj and Jagannathan 2013). Some of these hurdles were confirmed by workers at electrical and CNG-operated crematoriums. For instance, an operator at the CNG crematorium in Varanasi confirmed that the CNG units are riskier because they involve gas leakage. He showed the burn injury marks on his leg endured while operating the furnace. 'I was more comfortable with the electrical unit. With CNG, one wrong button pressed, you are gone,' he told me.

We are far from fully mechanizing funerals because Hindus and Sikhs across India prefer open-pyre cremations. However, for workers managing the mechanized pyres, rigorous training is necessary to ensure their safety.

Even though stigmatic and exploitative, it's challenging to break away from the traditional caste-based work practised inter-generationally in the same extended family. 'My father and grandfather used to work at crematoriums. So I automatically picked up this work. It's difficult for us to find work elsewhere. So my son also joined me,' said a worker from a crematorium in Delhi.

In some cases, the job is hereditary. '*Apke vaalid ye kaam karte the phir aap bhi karne lage* (first your father did the job, and you later joined the work),' said Jawadul.

'*Main nahin chahta mere bacche yeh kaam karen* (I don't want my children to do this work),' said another funeral worker. Although practised inter-generationally, some try hard to break away from this caste-specific work.

Because of the exploitative stigmatized nature of work and low pay, many are discouraged from joining the occupation. 'My father used to work in the crematorium back in Uttarakhand village. So, my brothers and I slowly picked up the work. We both migrated to Delhi fifteen years ago to earn a better living while my family stayed back in the village. Since then, my brother and I have been doing funeral work. However, we barely make ends meet. The work is challenging, underpaid and not well-respected. Besides, since we are not on the payroll, we are at the mercy of the bereaved families for payments. In addition, there is no job security. We are not even regularized like sarkari karamcharis (government employees). So after getting educated, I want my children to do something more meaningful and respectful (*izzat ka kaam*),' a worker, who works at a crematorium in New Delhi, told me.

Lack of job security because of the contractual nature of work impacts the well-being of the workers and is highlighted as a deterrent in joining this work (Selvaraj and Jagannathan 2013).

Amidst discrimination, I heard some positive stories too. Although the work's lack of job security and hazardous nature makes it challenging, the community feeling and the mutual help among the workers help them survive the challenging environment. For example, a funeral worker told me, '*jab sab milke kaam karte hain to thoda aasan lagta hai* (work is easier when we do it together).' Similarly, I was pleasantly surprised when Sanjay said, 'I come from the Valmiki (Dalit) community. There is no bhedbhav (discrimination) at this crematorium—we all eat and drink together.'

During the Covid pandemic, workers' problems were accentuated due to the increased workload, long working hours, and even the risk of contracting Covid. Moreover, workers were not appropriately compensated for their work. The human rights groups raised concerns about their mental and physical well-being during the pandemic. I elaborated on these struggles later in the book.

3. Nasu-salars: The Pallbearers in Parsi Community

Pallbearers among the Parsi community are nasu-salars (those who control the demon nasu). The Zoroastrian laws strictly prohibit any contact between the dead and living beings, even prohibiting the deceased's family from touching the dead after a certain point, making the role of nasu-salars crucial during the Parsi last rites. Unfortunately, these pallbearers are considered contaminated until they undergo a purifying bath to clean themselves (Zykov 2016).

The translation of Videvdat (texts representing Parsi ritual and civil law) emphasises the qualities of the people for the nasu-salar job. The text, for example, suggests that anyone from the Zoroastrian community who can recite specific prayers while carrying the body and has gone through the purification ceremonies could work as nasu-salars (Zykov 2012, 34). Furthermore, the position is not a professional or hereditary one, but rather a paid or voluntary service. However, the text forbids non-Zoroastrian members from participating in the work (Zykov 2012, 34). Texts such as the Kama Bohara and Kaus Kama Rivayats elaborate on the role and eligibility of nasu-salars.

These texts, however, do not indicate the social standing of people in these roles. They should, in theory, be treated equally. However, newspaper articles and reports indicate that they are subjected to discrimination within the community—even their gaze and touch are regarded as polluting (Baria 1995).

Similarly, Cyrus Mistry's novel *Chronicle of the Corpse Bearer* highlights the discrimination against nasu-salars and related segregation within their community. Zykov writes in his review of the novel that the community still adheres to the purity rules. According to these rules, corpse-bearers are not permitted to dine with the rest of the population during jashns (ceremonies). He mentions that the perception of permanent contamination associated with nasu-salars persists. There is no basis for such discrimination in religious texts. After a nahn purifying ceremony, a corpse-bearer is completely cleansed (Zykov 2012, 39). However, the novel vividly depicts instances of discrimination.

Finally, Zykov writes that the community must decide the future of their afterlife by valuing nasu-salars' work and status within the community (Zykov 2012, 40).

The number of nasu-salars working in dakhmas in India is dwindling (Zykov 2012, 33).

However, unlike other death workers, nasu-salars are fairly compensated by Parsi community members. 'The Parsi panchayat hires and pays the employees. So they are well compensated, and they even receive gifts in cash and kind from family members in addition to their wages,' a Parsi priest confirmed. Unfortunately, I did not have the opportunity to interview a nasu-salar. To capture their role in the community, I had to rely on secondary sources.

4.   The Doms of Varanasi: Custodians of Salvation

Varanasi is the spiritual capital of India. It is one of the oldest and holiest of the seven sacred cities in Hinduism. People come here from around the world to cremate their dead at the Manikarnika and Harishchandra ghats of Varanasi.

Many of the city's residents make a living from death. These include the Doms, a caste that has been discriminated against, and who work at the cremation sites.

In Varanasi, the task of cremating bodies on these ghats is carried forward through inheritance. The Doms, belonging to the lowest rung of the social ladder, have been assigned this task for centuries.

'*Yeh to humara kaam hai* (this is our work). We have been doing cremation work for generations—no one else here can do this,' said Laalu Chaudhary, a Dom working at the CNG crematorium of Harishchandra Ghat.

Similarly, Harish from Varanasi Walking Tour said that work areas are demarked in Varanasi. For instance, Doms exclusively perform all the cremations at Manikarnika and Harishchandra ghats.

According to a popular myth, it is believed that receiving the auspicious fire from the eternal flame through the Doms helps attain moksha, from the cycle of life and death (Kumari 2019).

During my visit, I noticed the chief mourners receiving the eternal fire from the Doms to be put in the deceased's mouth. Not just this, I saw them tending to the burning corpses after the families left. I also spotted the Doms sifting through the ashes for gold and silver left on the corpse, squatting around a heap of ashes. '*Yahan par paari lagta hai* (Dom families take turns in doing business),' my boatman told me when I enquired.

The Doms have a traditional uncontested power over the bodies in Varanasi. For example, they collect kar (tax) for offering agni at the cremation ghats of Varanasi. However, not just the tax but their right to sort and wash the ashes for gold and silver ornaments left on the corpse are more prized (Parry 1994, 91).

Not just this, Doms have received attention from different segments of society—politicians, researchers and filmmakers alike. Besides, they have also been featured in mainstream Hindi cinema films like *Masaan*, highlighting the caste struggle of the community.

The work is gender-specific and confined to male members. 'Only one Dom woman, a matriarchal figure from the Choudhary family, worked at the ghats. After she passed away, I didn't see any women members working at the ghats,' confirmed Jeremy Oltmann, the founder of Varanasi Walks, which organizes walks around the holy city.

Although they are discriminated against, their power in funeral work is undeniable. Dr Ravi Nandan Singh, a sociologist, confirmed this, 'In Varanasi, the Doms have exclusive rights when it comes to handling the corpse. As a result, they have bargaining power that others may not have. That power is derived from their caste position. For example, if you try to bargain with a Dom, he might walk away and tell you to do it yourself.' According to him, it's a two-edged sword—a stigmatised but long-lasting occupation.

Even when talking to the locals, I got the same impression.'You can't ignore them. For example, during Covid-19 first wave, they demanded that open pyre cremations be resumed at the ghats of Varanasi when they were restricted to CNG due to government guidelines. But, after they raised their voices, the government had to reconsider,' said Anil, my boatman.

Some Dom families like Dom Raja are more powerful in Varanasi than other Doms. 'His family owns assets in the prime locations of Varanasi,' said a tour and travel company owner (see Parry 1994, 91).

As per my sources, the Dom workers who work under the maaliks (richer Doms/masters) are at the bottom of the Dom hierarchy—struggling for money and dignity.

Although their role in death-related work is indispensable, the occupational hazards involving this occupation are innumerable. In some instances, workers face specific risks like losing their eyes and even getting burnt by fire. Some of them even fall back on narcotic drugs or alcohol to deal with the stench, stress and abuse the work involves. 'There is a problem of alcoholism among Doms. In addition, there is smoke inhalation from the cremation fires, perhaps reducing their lifespan,' said Jeremy. Their alcohol dependence was confirmed by several people I spoke with. For instance, my boat rider Anil told me, 'Their earnings are not meagre, but their alcoholism problem is enormous, which impacts their health.'

Besides, a newspaper piece eloquently described the plight of Dom workers impacting their health and wellbeing: 'Chaudhary works for close to eighteen hours a day, usually in loose trousers, with a scarf wrapped around his face to protect himself from the heat of the flames. He often removes his flimsy slippers for better traction when running from one pyre to another when handling more than one corpse. When I ask him if he has ever been injured while running barefoot across the cremation ground, with shards of wood and nails lying around, he extends his legs to exhibit his scars. A two-inch-wide wound marks the sole of his right foot' (Iyengar 2017).

Some doms are working hard to break from the caste-specific hereditary work, hoping for a better future for the coming generations. However, time will tell what the future holds for this community. The film *Masaan* depicts how Deepak Kumar, a Varanasi boy from an influential Dom family, works in cremation ghats by burning funeral pyres and transcends the casteist society's restrictions by becoming a civil engineer. However, I wonder how many would be able to break away so easily.

When I asked Dr Ravi about the future of this work in India, he said, 'Unless it's a switch-button job, these occupations will stay, especially when higher-caste groups are unwilling to touch the 'polluting matter'.' But, according to him, it's different in Europe. The work doesn't involve any stigma. 'Moreover, in the West, everything is technologically driven—one doesn't have to touch the body,' he said.

Laalu: a Dom Working at the CNG Crematorium—Breaking From the Traditional Work

Amrit and I were taking a walk around the Harishchandra Ghat when I told him, 'I want to visit the CNG-run crematorium.' Compared to the busy Harishchandra Ghat, it looked deserted with no soul. So we stood there for ten minutes observing and discovering the place before Laalu Chaudhary, dressed in black shorts and a vest with a gamcha around his neck, joined us.

He has been supervising the place for the last twenty years. Lalu's father was also a munshi (account keeper) at a crematorium. 'My entire family has been in government jobs. My baba and dada have been keeping accounts at the crematorium,' said Laalu proudly.

He is happy with his handsome salary of ₹30,000 paid by the municipal corporation. However, Laalu is still not very confident about operating machines even after training. 'Electrically operated machines were better. The CNG ones involve more risk. One wrong button pressed, and you are gone. I burned my leg, and I wasn't even compensated—I bore the entire expenses on my own. It took me a month to get back on my feet,' he said, showing his scars.

Laalu told me mockingly that people try to bargain even though the government has mentioned the rates in bold letters. 'They tell me, *thoda kam karo* (lower the rates). How can they haggle when the 500 rupees are fixed charges? This one is much cheaper than the open pyre cremation,' he laughed, exposing his tobacco-stained teeth.

Since Lalu was getting the machine ready, I asked him if I could stay back and observe the cremation process at the crematorium, and he agreed. Then, while chatting, he talked about his family. Laalu has three children attending school, and his wife looks after the household affairs while he manages the show here. '*Main chahta hun ke mere bacche pad likh ke kuch alag karen* (I want my children to study and do something different),' he said.

While talking, he pointed toward his house in the next galli, surrounded by the homes of other Doms. '*Hum sab ek hi parivaar ki shakhayen hain* (we are the branches of the same family),' Laalu said. However, our conversation got interrupted by the sudden chanting of *ram naam satya hai* as four men entered carrying the arthi of the deceased through the passage leading to the crematorium. The deceased came from south India to die in Kashi. '*Unki ban gayi thi* (he was destined to die in Kashi),' said Laalu when I enquired.

I stood quietly in the corner, observing the entire process with folded hands. Finally, after three accompanying family members paid their last respects to the deceased, Laalu pushed the body inside the furnace. He pressed the buttons while the family members witnessed their member leave. 'It takes two to three hours for the body to turn into ashes. However, this body is weighty—it might take longer,' said Laalu. Managing the machines requires experience and precision.

He told me, unlike the traditional pyres, the families perform the pre-funerary rites like ritual baths and prayers before coming here. 'There are ninety-nine worlds to live in, but only one world to die in—so people come to Kashi,' said Laalu while conversing on death.

Laalu feels secure in his job, but he is uncertain if he can secure a better future for his children.

5. Mallahs: The Boatmen in Varanasi

In Varanasi, another set of workers who play a crucial role in last rites and rituals are boatmen (Mallahs), also belonging to an occupation practised intergenerationally. They ferry the corpses and the ashes into the middle of the river. They also transport vast numbers of pilgrims and make a substantial supplementary income sifting the river mud area in which they have exclusive rights to the coins offered into the Ganges by the pilgrims (Parry 1994, 92).

'We consume high amounts of alcohol and go deep down the Ganga looking for coins—no one else would risk their lives for that money. Not only this, but we also retrieve bodies that go missing in the Ganga. We are Ganga Putra—no one knows the river better than we do. Unfortunately, there are times when the NDRF (National Disaster Response Force) personnel can't retrieve the body, and we are summoned,' said Anil, my boatman, while we took a boat ride early in the morning.

II
The Mortuary Staff

The very sight of a dead body gives many of us a chill up our spines. But some jobs involve opening, dissecting and sewing the bodies back after postmortem. Yes, I am talking about mortuary workers. Can you even imagine the stressful environment under which the mortuary staff works?

In morgues, they are referred to as cleaners, safai karamcharis, Valmiki, and Doms. They take over after the person dies in the hospital, with ward boys and nurses refusing to handle the dead.

These workers tend to be from the Dalit castes, who have traditionally worked in sanitation and the disposal of the deceased (Chattopadhyay 2020).

'Dalits are primarily involved in this work in India,' added Arun Vijai Mathavan, who did a year-long photo documentary project on mortuary workers in Gujarat and Tamil Nadu in 2016—observing over 150 postmortems. His interest in capturing environmentally and socially relevant subjects led him to choose this subject for his graduation project. In addition, the assignment enabled him to visually map the evolution of caste-based discrimination in a technologically advanced society.

'Postmortem is a contemporary practice in India since biomedicine entered the country much later. So, I choose mortuary work to understand the phenomena and how caste penetrated this work,' Arun said.

Arun traced, through his project, how these workers were gradually initiated into mortuary work. 'Initially, they were hired as sanitary staff or helpers but were slowly inducted into mortuary work. For instance, they were asked to clean the mortuary in the beginning. Later they were instructed to bring the body from the freezer room to the table. Eventually, workers were requested to assist the doctors in autopsies. Finally, they were trained in conducting the autopsies independently. Although they are not formally trained, they learn the skill by observing and assisting the doctors,' added Arun.

They do everything like cutting open the body parts for autopsies and stitching the bodies back. And even after the postmortem, they tend the body—washing it and packing the corpse before respectfully handing it to the family. Not only this, but they also assist medical teachers in taking anatomy lessons for medicine students. Their work involves cleaning the bodies and bringing them to the dissection table. Without their crucial contribution, medical studies would be incomplete (Srinivasan 2011).

'These workers independently handle postmortem work under the supervision of doctors in India, barring HIV cases , RTO inquiry, and custodial deaths,' added Arun.

Newspaper reports bring out the struggles that the community faces. 'There are enormous health hazards related to this occupation. Pathogens spreading tuberculosis, blood-borne hepatitis and AIDS can still be transmitted even after the death of a patient. Thus, the possibility of the morticians getting infected is extremely high. General infections and skin disorders are also common for them' (Sengupta 2017).

Moreover, the health settings sometimes lack proper safety equipment. Arun recounted, 'Although the workers are provided with safety gear, sometimes the gear is ill-fitted, because of which workers find it difficult to use the standardized equipment. We perhaps need to take cognizance of these challenges.'

'The Health Ministry lacks any special healthcare scheme for these people and while permanent employees benefit from the government employee health care system, contractual workers have absolutely no health cover' (Sengupta 2017).

However, the physical hazards look insignificant compared to the job's mental stress. According to Sengupta, the pungent stench and the unpleasant sites must haunt them even after leaving the premises (Sengupta 2017). 'My clothes would stink after I left the premises— the smell would just not go away. You can very well understand the condition of these workers,' Arun told me.

'Moreover, handling the bodies of accident victims is more challenging.' These unfavourable working conditions and the absence of fixed working hours make it more difficult.

'Futhermore, the cleaners are paid a meagre amount for this work. The salaries of cleaners vary depending on whether they are on the government payroll or contractual. The average salary of those engaged on a contract is ₹3500 per month. Sometimes, they are voluntarily tipped by the family members of the deceased. Moreover, they perform dual responsibility of sanitation and mortuary work, whereas they are paid just for the sanitary work,' said Arun. This clearly shows how these workers are overburdened and underpaid.

During the Covid-19, the situation became more difficult. In many cases, workers worked long hours without wearing protective gear (Chattopadhyay 2020).

'Because of stigmatization, the mortuary workers hide their work identity from the outside world and even their community. One mortuary worker's daughter revealed that her classmates bullied her, saying she smelled of the dead. That's one reason they conceal their work identity as mortuary workers,' Arun told me.

These workers, like other death workers, are invisible and unrepresented in the healthcare hierarchy. Unlike hospital healthcare staff, their problems are rarely publicized (Chattopadhyay 2020).

10

Last Rites and Rituals: Spending

My grandmother used to say that death is a sad occasion, yet the aggrieved family has to host relatives and friends. Therefore, like other rites of passage, death rituals involve expenditures.

While talking to people, I realized how cultural norms and practices impact death spending. For example, in many communities holding a communal feast is a rule, not a choice. Besides, death is an emotional occasion where families tend to overspend more than their means.

But unfortunately, these societal expectations push poor people to overspend—leading to debt. For instance, while working with rural communities, I have encountered cases where families had to pawn their jewellery to host a mrityu bhoj for the entire village.

Interestingly, for some, it's an event to display wealth by engaging in extravagant rituals. For example, I remember someone telling me how their family hired a leading flower company to decorate the hearse van. Through my conversations with funeral directors, I gathered how some clients demand over-the-top prayer meetings highlighting their social standing.

Through this section, I endeavour to present general death-related expenses and the determining factors based on my conversations with ritual specialists and families. I have broadly classified these expenses into: funerals, service providers' fees, and organizing prayer meetings or feasts.

Calculating the exact cost was difficult because of the unorganized nature of the sector. However, ₹10,000–15,000 is the minimum amount spent just on the cremation/burial. Besides, these are other expenses like organising a funeral feast.

Families incur additional costs like donating to hospitals, schools, or sansthas (institutions) to pay shraddhanjali (tribute) to their deceased relatives. In addition, Daan is considered a crucial part of funeral rites among Hindus. Moreover, sometimes repatriation services also add to the expenses. An obituary in the newspaper can cost between ₹1000-1,00000 depending on the message size and the newspaper's circulation.

In India, the community primarily leads funeral arrangements, unlike in the west. On that side of the world, last rites are left to the funeral directors. But, according to Caitlin Doughty, a famous mortician, the over-dependence on the death industry has a flip side. Due to the corporatization and commercialization of death care, the western world has fallen behind when it comes to proximity, intimacy and rituals around death and deceased loved ones.

However, funeral arrangements are still family and community-run affairs in India. I remember how everyone came together to organize my papa's funeral. While Sharma called the tent vendor, the Guptas contacted the refrigeration service. Furthermore, the neighbours supplied food for mourning members after the cremation.

'In Varanasi, no one would like the body of the loved one to be handled by strangers. So neighbours come together and organize everything,' said Amrit, a tourist guide from Varanasi.

The professional death care industry has mushroomed in India in the last decade. These death care services manage everything—from organizing funerals to arranging prayer meetings and feasts. However, unlike a billion-dollar industry in the West, they are still gaining ground in India.

I
Expenses: Last Rites and Rituals

1. Hindu Rituals

Hindus form the majority of the Indian population. According to Hindu traditions, the body is cremated using wood in an open pyre. However, some families choose incinerators that run on electricity or Compressed Natural Gas (CNG) (see Kaushik 2018).

For an open-pyre cremation, one needs large quantities of wood—close to 400 to 600 kilograms. Although the wood type and quality vary, the minimum cost of timber is ₹8 per kilogram, costing approximately ₹6000-7000 per funeral. Furthermore, a shroud cost can range from ₹600-800. In addition, saamagri, a mixture of dried herbs and ghee offered to the pyre, can cost between ₹2000-3000. However, the prices may vary depending on the quality and quantity of materials. In addition, dakshina to the pallbearer or sevadars ranges between ₹500-1000 (see Kaushik 2018).

There are also some value-added services that crematoriums provide. For example, some families also choose the smokeless pyres with exhaust chimneys for a higher fee at Nigambodh Ghat crematorium in Delhi.

'In Delhi, everything is more expensive. A funeral alone would cost around ₹5000-6000 here. So we suggest the wood of mango, banyan and eucalyptus since chandan is very expensive. Therefore, many people can't afford to buy chandan *ki lakdi*. However, families ritually place a small amount of chandan on the funeral pyre—even the very poor can afford a minimal amount of chandan *ki lakdi*,' said Rajesh, a funeral pandit at Nigambodh ghat—the biggest Ghat in the capital of India.

The pandits charge a dakshina of ₹1000-1500 for presiding over the funeral.

When I inquired about his charges, Rajesh said, 'It depends on the jajmaan. We see the family's paying capacity—we don't put pressure on anyone. However, the charges are fixed at ₹750 for cremations and ₹250 for phul chugne. But, he added, antim sanskaar is the last sanskaar—there is no harm in paying a slightly extra amount to the pandit.' Moreover, when families are grieving, they hardly take account of these expenses.

As mentioned above, the expenses vary depending on the family's economic status and choice. The choice of wood also determines the funeral expenses. For example, some affluent families wish to use sandalwood for cremations—considered more auspicious and purer. 'I chose to use some kilos of sandalwood for my mother's cremation because she was very dear to me,' a family member in Varanasi told me.

Another expense is immersing bones and ashes in the holy river after cremation—the fees of the brahmin for every small or big ritual range from ₹101 to several thousand. But, again, the expenses vary depending on the place of residence/city. For instance, if the rites are performed in religious places like Haridwar or Varanasi, then the costs incurred by the families increase. 'I don't encourage my clients to visit Kashi or Haridwar for immersion because the costs are very high. Moreover, I don't want my clients to get stressed,' said, a funeral director.

However, families often come this far to fulfil the deceased's last wish. 'There was a Russian music artist of Indian origin. He wanted his asthi to be immersed in the Ganges. So his troupe travelled from Russia to fulfil his last wish,' said Amrit.

When he pointed this out, similar scenes flashed in my mind. During our visit to Haridwar to immerse papa's ashes in Ganga, I recalled how ritualists flocked around us, eagerly waiting to offer their services, luring families to perform rituals they barely understand. Similarly, in Varanasi, I saw Doms, tirath purohits and flower sellers keen to assist mourners in death-related and post-cremation practices. *'Poori dukaandari dharam ke naam par chal rahi hai yahan*—everything boils down to economics. This happens everywhere—I have witnessed similar scenes in Rishikesh and Pushkar,' said Harish, owner of a tourist company in Varanasi. Ironically, these sacred rituals have become money-making businesses by a handful of people.

Among Hindus, the post-funeral thirteen-day rituals are elaborate. For instance, pind daan performed by the family members involves expenditure. Besides, the death and other life cycle rituals are demarked among brahmin pandits, determining their rights over the daan. For instance, the Mahapatras, a sect of brahmins who handle the eleventh-day ceremonies, charge a handsome amount of fees on behalf of the dead person. In addition, they demand commodities like television sets, air conditioners, or even a piece of land, costing lakhs of rupees, in the name of ritual offerings. 'He doesn't ask for less money—sometimes a Mahapatra demands ₹10,000 or more. He doesn't eat food till you fulfil his demands,' said a ritual priest in Varanasi.

After the eleventh day, the rituals are presided over by the kul purohit (family pandit) or a karam-kandi brahmin. 'The kul brahmins don't charge any money till the thirteenth day. Instead, they vasool (recover) the entire amount on that day. Then, they make you perform gau daan and charge many other donations like clothes and shoes that sum up to approximately ₹30,000,' a family from Varanasi told me. Besides, the bargaining power of the families is negligible when it comes to last rites and rituals. Therefore, one usually pays the dakshina that the pandit or other ritualists demand.

These days, the pandits in Haridwar and Kashi have added more services to their repertoire. They offer online service packages with live streaming of the pind daan ceremony through Zoom for an additional charge—many Non-Resident Indians (NRI) who travel to India avail of these services.

There are also rituals like holding a grand feast for relatives and friends on the thirteenth day, costing anywhere between a few hundred to lakhs. Again, when I was writing this part, I was reminded of the film *Pagglait*. In the movie, the deceased's distressed father was shown calculating the escalating unbudgeted funeral expenses while making an elaborate list of ingredients they would require for the thirteenth-day ceremony. These expenses could be burdening for many.

While others are willing to walk the extra mile and employ professional funeral services, the costs escalate if one opts for high-end services. A funeral organizer told me, 'My elite clients demand elaborate rituals. The decorations and the flowers are exquisite. Moreover, the food catering is specifically designed depending on the client's needs.'

2.   Islamic Rituals

Muslims constitute 14.2% of the Indian population as per Census 2011 (Census 2011). In some instances, the wealthy Muslims either use their land or buy space for burying their deceased relatives, while the poor bury their dead in public cemeteries (see Kaushik 2018).

The kafan costs up to ₹1,000-2000. Digging the grave costs nearly ₹1,000, and putting wooden planks on the sides of the burial costs ₹3,500–4,000. Bathing and dressing the body costs ₹3000-4000. Besides, scents, flowers and the rates of graveyards approximately cost another ₹2,000-5,000. Among some communities, heavy expenditures are incurred on the fortieth day when a feast is organized for relatives and friends. Among Muslims, the minimum spending incurred in burying a dead body is about ₹6000-10,000 (Kaushik 2018).

3. Christian Rituals

Christians comprise a small part of India's population. The critical expenditure in Christian burial rituals is on the coffin and the cemetery. The cloth in which the body is wrapped costs roughly ₹1,000. Expenses incurred on the coffin cost can range from ₹2,000 to several lakhs depending on the kind of coffin one orders. 'The price varies depending on the decorations. Some coffins are golden-edged, some are brass edged, while others are glass-topped. The cost differs depending on the choice of wood like mango, cedar and plywood. Besides, some are polished, and others are unpolished. The more elaborate ones are made of teakwood, lined with satin cushions, costing more,' said Cyril.

Besides, the cemetery charge varies between ₹8000-16000. The labour charges are upto ₹1,000. The priest also demands fees between ₹2000-3000 depending on the family's economic status. Types of flowers and bouquets offered also add to the cost. Furthermore, families usually have to buy land for the grave, especially in private cemetaries. Additionally, expenses are incurred on prayer meetings held on the twelfth or thirteenth day of burial.

II
Other Expenses

There are other services, such as transporting the body or repatriating it. Repatriation is the process whereby human remains are transferred from a foreign territory to the native land of the deceased. There are two kinds of repatriations—domestic and international, involving import and export.

There are funeral directors/companies engaged in repatriation services. For instance, there are dedicated funeral directors outside India, especially in the western world. The expenses involve transporting, sealing, packing, coffin charges and embalming.

In India, we have a handful of experts involved in these services. However, repatriation could be expensive—especially if the body is taken to Europe or the UK, costing up to ₹1 lakh to embalm and repatriate a body.

According to Cyril, the repatriation involving the body's export is far more manageable than the import. 'I contact the authorities—get the coffin's dimensions, finish the paperwork, and prepare the body for repatriation,' he said.

III
Death Spending: Impacting the families

Studies indicate that disposing of dead bodies demonstrates and perpetuates socioeconomic differences. Besides, while rich people's spending on death rituals reflects their social position, performing last rites is financially draining for the poor. For example, I recollect how in rural Rajasthan families had to borrow large amounts from the local moneylenders to conduct elaborate rituals beyond their economic means.

The literature also suggests that expenditure on death rituals destabilizes family budgets—psychologically and financially draining the low-income households. Although the expenses are variable, ritualists performing death rituals charge their fees for every small and big ceremony (Kaushik 2018). While writing this, I recounted a scene from *Rudali*, a story by Mahasweta Devi, where the pandit scoffed at the protagonist, a Dalit woman, for not appropriately performing the shraddh of her deceased husband. This leads Sanichari into debt of twenty rupees, which she repays by working as a bonded labour on the fields (Devi 1997, 74). 'And after paying for Budhua's father's shraddh, she was so hard-pressed to feed her little son that she never had time to cry for her husband' (Devi 1997, 74). I am sure many in India share a similar plight. However, the rich do not mind spending lavishly on death rites to maintain social status, highlighting the socioeconomic disparity even in the last rites.

Also, bereaved relatives seldom pay attention to additional and unbudgeted spending during such times. Moreover, succumbing to social pressures also influences this sort of spending—the fear of being labelled inconsiderate for neglecting normative death rituals being one. '*Agar acha khana nahin karange to log kya kahange—Gupta ki bete ki hasiyat nahin hai.* (If I don't organize a proper feast, then what would people say—Gupta's son didn't have the capability),' said Gupta.

In the end, I believe the merits of a funeral shouldn't be determined by economics but through the love with which we say our goodbyes to our loved ones in distinct cultural ways. I recounted having a conversation with a priest who said something that stayed with me. The essence of these rituals lies in paying tribute to our deceased family members with pure heart or shraddha.

11

Professional Funeral Services in India

The death-care service industry refers to organizations and communities that provide services associated with death, like funerals, cremations, burials and memorials. Professional services are slowly entering India's urban landscape. Besides, the Covid situation has undoubtedly accelerated the growth of organized funeral services.

The Hindu Business Line article tracked the growth of these services in India: 'While there is no official estimate, the industry is worth about $2.5 billion in India, where about 8.5 million die every year. Still, it is nowhere near its international peers. The US death-care industry is worth nearly $20 billion, and its most prominent player, Service Corp International, had revenues of $2.4 billion in 2012. In addition, the world's largest retailer, Wal-Mart, is a leading seller of caskets in the US and even offers EMI schemes. However, it may be years before a mainstream company in India latches on to the opportunity. Still, already significant changes are underway in the local death-care industry' (Thomas 2015).

Intrigued by this piece, I started my research in this area. In India, death services are primarily unorganized, relying mainly on community and social support. Until I started working on this volume, I was unaware of India's professional funeral service scene, unlike in the west, where funeral directors became indispensable long ago. I always associated funerals with families coming together and organizing them as we did for my father. While surfing the internet, I unearthed start-ups with promising websites. Then I discovered through my conversations with funeral directors and experts how these players are slowly entering India's landscape.

'Outside India, these services are commonly available. However, the death sector is not professionalized in our country. Moreover, in the current times, families are growing smaller. Therefore, one can't rely on their relatives. There are times when people are not even aware of the closest crematorium,' said Jatin Bhargav, a funeral organizer and owner of Noble Sparrows.

As he said, with rapid migration and the increasing number of nuclear families, people find it challenging to manage the logistics without the support of their extended families. Besides, consolidating the legal and digital formalities post-death becomes cumbersome. Moreover, the lack of awareness among the present urban-bred populations regarding last rites may make these services more sought after in the coming years.

These businesses provide professional funeral management services like ambulances, transporting corpses, cremation services and prayer services with personalized packages to fill the gap.

However, while talking to experts, I learned that it had not been smooth sailing for these businesses. During my conversation with Dr Ravi Nandan Singh, a sociologist, he said, 'In big cities like Mumbai and Delhi, private funerary services were trying to gain a foothold for some years. But initially, they were unsuccessful—many of them had a tough time. The death industry is the last to change, and no one wants to meddle with this sensitive territory. Moreover, people think they are doing something fundamentally wrong by monetizing these services. Since the funeral is a communitarian practice—how far can one monetize these services? A decade ago, when I was researching Denmark's funeral industry, they offered funeral service packages. But in India, these professional service providers were too hesitant to enter. So things have been happening more sporadically in India.'

Besides, Thomas aptly stated: 'Ironically, the same social beliefs and taboos that drive its business also ail it in India' (Thomas 2015). Through this section, I unravel these new actors in the drama of Death.

I
Businesses/Organizations

Noble Sparrows, a Gurugram-based business, aims to provide an end-to-end funeral service in the Delhi National Capital Region (NCR). Jatin ventured into this business after working in the corporate sector for twenty years. During the first wave of Covid, when he saw his extended family struggling with arranging funerals, not knowing whom to approach, he got the idea of starting this business. Although initially reluctant, his family eventually supported this venture. Therefore, it was his personal experience that led to Noble Sparrows.

Likewise, JCJ Funerals, based in New Delhi, promises to organize a personalized funeral for their clients. Besides, the company's motto is to deliver a funeral service that reflects the deceased's values, culture, beliefs and relationships. With over thirty-five years of ancestral experience in this work, Cyril Joseph commenced his own business a few years ago. 'My father and grandfather were in this industry, so it came naturally to me. Besides, coming from the hospitality industry is an added advantage,' said Cyril.

Similarly, Kashi Moksha, a registered society in Varanasi, arranges consolidated funeral services for Hindus worldwide. So, on the one hand, we have these start-ups, and on the other, we have registered societies venturing into delivering cremation services professionally.

Breaking away from the traditional cremation services in 2008, a group of like-minded people founded the society. They launched a website to connect with Indian and overseas clients two years later. Since then, the organization has grown with more than 300 regular employees and volunteers.

'We found that there is a lot of confusion around death rituals. People visiting Kashi (Varanasi) often find it hard to locate the right acharya who can assist in performing the rituals aligned with the shastras (scriptures). Also, families get cheated so many times in the name of traditions. Hence, Kashi Moksha was instituted to serve the bereaved families while keeping the Vedic rituals/traditions alive for the coming generations. Besides, we offer services free of cost for the economically challenged,' said Pallavi Gupta, President of Kashi Moksha Foundation.

II
Services/Packages

Many of these businesses have emerged to fulfil the demand for organized funeral services, providing a wide range of services in international and domestic markets. Their motto is to professionalize the industry by delivering top-class funeral services in India, just like in the West. By looking at their websites, I discovered that these businesses offer a rich repertoire of services. For instance, Noble Sparrows provides facilities like transporting bodies, mortuary vans and ambulances. Besides, they offer cremation services and organize online and offline prayer meets. Not just these, they also offer end of life planning services and pet cremations.

Their trained team caters for everything from arranging arthi to kafan to appointing a Pandit. 'As soon as we get a call—our trained team takes over. Once we reach the site—we assist the family with rituals like bathing and dressing the deceased. We carry fragrant flowers and garlands for families to pay their last tributes,' Jatin said.

Not only this, but they also manage the arrangements at the crematorium before the family arrives. After the funeral, Noble Sparrows also assists the families in completing the paperwork like applying for death certificates.

In addition to the above services, JCJ Funerals also provides repatriation services worldwide. Furthermore, they offer road, rail and air ambulance services. Besides this, they provide additional services like transporting ashes, embalming, and manufacturing coffins and urns. Cyril said, 'Embalming is a specialized service wherein the body is preserved against decomposition. Embalming a post-mortem body is tricky since it involves leakages of body fluids, so one must be careful. Besides, the packaging is tricky. We use two boxes—one with zinc lining and another repatriation box. After cleaning and placing the body, we carefully seal the zinc-lined box. Later, a valid embalming certificate needs to be produced to the airport authorities. Besides, the businesses have to pay heavy fines if anything goes wrong.'

Similarly, the Kashi Moksha Foundation provides services like asthi pooja, asthi visarjan (immersing the ashes), shraddh of ancestors, and Brahman bhoj (feeding the brahmins)—aligned with Hindu rituals. Besides, Kashi Moksha provides families value-added services like pictures and video recordings of the ceremonies. Furthermore, Kashi Moksha couriers the prasad if the family desires. 'Devotees from around the world contact us through the website. We were perhaps the first to offer online asthi visarjan and pind daan services. After receiving the ashes by post, our trained priests perform the rituals at the banks of the holy Ganga for the families while live-streaming the same for them,' Pallavi Gupta told me.

III
Empathy With Professionalism

One certainly requires organizational and event-planning skills to run these businesses. But, without formal training in funeral management, these funeral organizers have rich experience in either event management or the hospitality industry. Other skills and traits needed for a funeral service provider are communication skills, compassion and a desire to comfort those coping with death.

These startups aim to cater for clients with empathy and professionalism. For instance, the motto of Noble Sparrows is to deliver a service with kindness. Jatin asserts, 'When a family is grieving—it's torturous for them to bear the burden. But, we assure them they needn't worry about anything—Noble Sparrows will take care of everything. The idea is to provide families with a space to grieve. Mostly, last rites are transactional for people traditionally involved in this work. So I teach the staff to be empathic and sensitive. The first and foremost thing I emphasize with my team is to be respectful towards the deceased. I tell them to be careful about little things like not addressing the deceased as a dead body. I despise this practice—I find it insensitive.'

Similarly, JCJ Funerals is dedicated to a professional approach with tailored services. Their products and the staff are carefully selected—reflecting their commitment. To confirm this, they have four dedicated team members working in India and one public relations staff based out of London—serving all beliefs and faiths. Their motto is to remember and honour the dead with utmost authenticity. Cyril Joseph, the owner of JCJ, said, 'Death is a vulnerable time for families and friends—coming to terms with the imminent or unprecedented loss. Therefore, we try to support and guide the aggrieved amidst the confusion and grief. Besides, we assist them in making informed choices and decisions by creating a personalized funeral experience while honouring and commemorating loved members.' For instance, while managing global clients, they ensure the body reaches on time and the final rites are performed timely and respectfully. 'I don't like sitting behind my desk managing the services while having my team run around—I insist on giving a personal touch to my work,' asserts Cyril.

Similarly, Kashi Moksha believes in earnestly providing services as per Hindu shastras. 'We believe in offering hassle-free services and explaining the relevance of each ritual,' said Pallavi.

IV
Evolving Services

In India, opportunities for the growth of the Death Care Service Industry are emerging. Therefore, these companies are trying to diversify their business models and customize their services to meet complex customer expectations based on religion, culture, subculture, language and location.

According to sociologist Dr Ravi Nandan Singh, a vital cultural aspect is attached to funerals. For example, one wants the coffin to be designed differently. One decides how much daan one intends to make in the dead person's name among Hindus. Moreover, one finds a component of desire in different funeral cultures. In the Caribbean, for instance, it is the kind of coffin one desires—they have Rastafarian pumpkin-shaped caskets. This emotional component surrounding the last rites makes people go overboard at times.

Many businesses diversify by spreading operations across geographies, while others rely on a specialized service package to capture the market. For instance, Noble Sparrows cater to clients with customized packages. In addition, they provide premium vans and high-end prayer services meetings for their elite clientele. Jatin said sometimes families choose their cremation site, like elite families in

Delhi prefer Lodhi Road crematorium. According to him, one needs to fulfil the client's demands. 'Last week, we arranged the funeral for a distinguished corporate lawyer's wife in Delhi. We managed everything from cremation services to advertising an obituary in the newspaper to organizing the high-end prayer service. Since this business involves humans—I put my heart and soul into it,' recounted Jatin.

Besides, companies have been developing creative/innovative ideas, such as pressing human ashes into a vinyl record or compressing them into diamonds. For instance, JCJ Funerals offers value-added services to its clients—creating a niche in the market. A recently added service by JCJ funerals is to provide keepsakes to commemorate the dead. Besides, they transport the remains and ashes to convert them into stone or diamonds. 'It's a six-to-eight-week-long process. There is enormous paperwork involved—I have to deal with customs. Moreover, I have to keep the embassy in the loop. However, it's worth the effort since it's an immensely satisfying experience for the families,' added Cyril.

In addition, JCJ Funerals is planning to expand the services overseas after acquiring the requisite licenses. 'Times have changed. With technology, the reach is farther. I am also looking at extending my operations in other parts of the world since I am one of the few companies dealing with human remains coming from remote areas,' he added.

While in the past Kashi Moksha primarily operated on a traditional model, off-late they have started to offer value-added services like a live telecast of the cremation that relatives can attend from any part of the world. In addition, they offer customized services as per the client's needs. 'We take care of our devotees—realizing their respect and faith in Kashi and Hindu rituals. We even arrange the transport from the airport for them. Moreover, our volunteers promptly assist and attend to their queries. Some of our devotees later join us as overseas volunteers,' she adds.

Besides, they have dedicated teams—IT, marketing, social workers, priests and volunteers assisting them. Moreover, Kashi Moksha has seamlessly digitized the entire process, like customized applications for video calls. Not only this, they are planning to launch a mobile application shortly.

V
Challenges

While there is a market, the startups in the sector have not had it easy since it's an unusual territory to operate in India. Besides, it isn't simple to monetize these services in India. Like a pandit at Nigambodh Ghat said, 'These professional services have expensive packages—which are not affordable for everyone. For example, the ghat authorities provide the hearse vans at subsidized rates, whereas these companies charge a handsome amount from the clients. Why would they want to pay more if families can manage a funeral in ₹ 5000-6000? So why would they want to spend more?'

Although it's a satisfying experience for the organizers, many challenges come along. I spoke to Jatin as he was rushing to the cremation ground. 'It's a relatively new business, and every venture involves hurdles. Initially, I was threatened by the locals who have been in this business for generations. However, slowly I learned to negotiate the rates with the established vendors. Moreover, my experience in event management came in handy in managing adversaries,' recounted Jatin.

Since these services involve humans, there are emotions attached. 'Every profession has its pluses and minuses. Besides, dealing with deaths is not simple—it's not easy seeing families in distress. Even the work timings are not fixed. But I feel some superpower helps me become a pillar for the aggrieved relatives. Moreover, I derive my strength from my family,' said Jatin.

According to Cyril, there is competition in the market, with roughly thirty to forty funeral directors in India undertaking international operations. Therefore, one needs to create goodwill along with personalized packages. Moreover, one needs to diversify services. The company has built a steady network with embassies and multinational companies. But, he adds, 'The work is sometimes challenging and complicated.'

He said, 'One of my counterparts in Chennai went to the airport to collect a corpse. The paperwork and clearances took time. It is a tedious process—sometimes waiting time exceeds eight hours.'

From its inception, Kashi Moksha has focused on developing each process's system. Besides, they try to innovate and put in a new plan whenever issues arise. For instance, they said, 'Initially, private courier companies were reluctant in receiving and delivering parcel packets containing ashes. So, we had to convince these providers to ensure a seamless delivery. Another issue was catering to clients from different time zones like USA and Canada—we had to make our volunteers available 24x7.'

'Oftentimes, we face language barriers. We receive Telegu, Tamil, Malayalam, Kannada, Gujrati, Bengali, Marathi, and English requests. We try to communicate in the receiver's language, it's stressful for our volunteers, but it's a journey and there's so much to learn,' confirmed Pallavi.

VI
What the Clients Say

I visited the websites of these start-ups to gather client reviews. Reading the reviews, I understood how families were particularly grateful to these providers for delivering respectful funerals when practically nobody was available during the pandemic. For instance, in one of the reviews, the person recognized the service provider for the smooth performance of his mother-in-law's last rites, from cremation to the immersion of ashes, in the absence of the family members. Likewise, in another review, the client acknowledged the service provider for ensuring an excellent farewell to her loved ones. Besides, personal service and care were placed on a higher pedestal. Yet, simultaneously, the users valued patience, dignity and empathy above other things.

Time will only tell how these businesses evolve in India's culturally and politically sensitive environment. I don't know how many of us would be comfortable leaving our loved ones in the hands of strangers, unlike in the West. Moreover, I don't know how friendly these services will be with Indian pockets.

'Covid has undoubtedly helped firm up these services, which would be available on call. Anyone who has seen the Delhi Covid situation— seeing pyres in parking areas—would be perhaps more open to these services. Since community services are more scattered, these professional arrangements come in handy during such unprecedented times. However, these businesses have still failed to institutionalize themselves,' said Dr Ravi.

With technology becoming a crucial part of urban lives, these online platforms hold great potential for future funeral solutions with just a click. However, the creativity lies in marketing the businesses through affordable packages.

12

Varanasi: a Site of Death Tourism

Varanasi is India's religious capital. The city was named after the Varuna and Assi rivers that once surrounded it. Its most important gift is the bestowal of moksha. Many people come here to die, choosing Varanasi as their final home before departing from this world.

Many corpses are brought to the ghats for cremation, often from long distances in India and around the world. Others have their ashes brought to the city to be immersed in the sacred Ganga.

Intrigued by death, I delved deeper into the last rites and rituals of the City of Death. It was one thing to read about last rites, but seeing them with my own eyes was quite another. Varanasi celebrates death. It is not feared here like other Indian cities. Death is a source of liberation in Varanasi.

Everyone had something to share about death and the last rites in Varanasi. From my auto driver to boatmen, each enriched my understanding. Moreover, there is something for everyone in the city of light—satiating the deep desire of pilgrims and moksha seekers and the curiosity of researchers and foreign tourists.

I
Death Sites in the City of Light

1.   Manikarnika Ghat of Varanasi: a Gateway to Moksha

My trip to Varanasi took me to the city's Manikarnika and Harishchandra ghats (a section of river frontage). Followers and tourists from all over the world want to touch the soil, bathe in the sacred waters of the Ganga, and take their last breath in the city.

A cremation ground is considered the most inauspicious among Hindus because of ritual 'pollution' by corpses. However, in Kashi, Manikarnika Ghat is the city's focal point—considered the most auspicious of places where Shiva himself bestows salvation (Eck 2015, 33).

Over 200 bodies are cremated daily on wooden pyres at this ghat with the eternal sacred fire, which is said to have burned continuously since time immemorial. Manikarnika, which means 'jewel of the ear' in Sanskrit, is the subject of folklore. However, legend has it that the ghat was formed when Lord Shiva's earring fell, due to violent trembling, into Vishnu's tank while he was dancing (Parry 2004, 14).

Cremation at Manikarnika Ghat ensures liberation from the cycle of birth and death. Here, Lord Shiva, the bestower of salvation, whispers the taraka mantra into the corpse's ear. The mantra allows the dead to sail through the waters of the sansar (universe) (Eck 2015).

Death in Varanasi is liberating. Diana L. Eck explains it in her book: 'Death, which elsewhere is feared, here is welcomed as a long-expected guest. Death, which elsewhere is under the terrifying jurisdiction of Yama, is free from the terror here, for Yama is not allowed within the city limits of Kashi. Death, which elsewhere is polluting, is here holy and auspicious. Death, the most natural and unavoidable, and certain of human realities, is here the sure gate of moksha, the rarest, most precious, most difficult to achieve of spiritual goals' (Eck 2015, 325).

The bodies are carried to the ghat in white shrouds with chants of 'Ram naam satya hai' (God's name is truth) echoing in the air before being ritually immersed in the Ganga. The cremation ceremony is known as the last sacrifice—antyeshti. The corpse is ritually prepared for the sacrifice with ghee, flower garlands and sandalwood oil before it is offered to agni.

In the narrow lane leading to the ghat, one can see a thriving economy centred on death, with shops selling sandalwood, ghee, wooden ladders, and shrouds. Dhabas only serve food to those ritually 'polluted' by death. Large piles of timber can be seen on either side of the galli leading to the ghat entry.

Multiple funeral pyres at Manikarnika Ghat burn nonstop, melting human flesh on woodpiles. Doms, the guardians of salvation, guide the families by lighting an auspicious fire on the corpse.

After receiving the eternal fire from the Doms, the chief mourner lights the funeral pyre with twigs of holy kusha grass. The mourner then walks around the pyre counter-clockwise. About halfway through the cremation, the chief mourner performs kapal-kriya, or the skull rite, by cracking the skull of the partially burned corpse with a long bamboo stick, releasing the soul from its entrapment in the body (Parry 1994, 177).

This ghat is not only used for cremations, but also for other rituals such as pind daan and tirath shraddh. While on a boat ride, one can see the dark smoke rising from the pyres. There is never a dull moment on the ghat. It's common to see Doms and funeral pandits haggling with customers. Witnessing the fire of auspicious Ganga aarti (prayer offered to the Ganga) and corpses burning at the adjoining ghats at the same time is one of the most intriguing sights.

Redevelopment work on the ghat is currently in full swing, with eighteen pyre frames and two greenatoriums proposed. So maybe on my next visit, I'll see the new, modernised Manikarnika Ghat. I'm hoping that this makeover breathes new life into this eternally auspicious place.

2.   Bhasm Holi of Manikarnika Ghat: Celebrating Death

'Have you heard of the Bhasm Holi in Varanasi?' my auto driver inquired. I was unaware of this one-of-a-kind celebration. However, after he piqued my interest, I inquired about this unique Holi. When I asked my boatman, Mohan, he showed me some videos he had taken during the previous Holi. The entire Manikarnika Ghat and the road leading to the burning ghat were flooded with people dancing ecstatically to celebrate the festival. It was a rare sight, enjoyed by both locals and tourists.

The holy city of Varanasi is famous for its ghats, bhang (cannabis), flavuorful paan, Banarasi sarees, chaat and frothy malai (cream). However, it is also famous for its Chita Bhasm Holi, which is celebrated at Manikarnika Ghat in the midst of funeral pyres.

'Chita Bhasm Holi is a Holi celebration played with funeral ashes at Varanasi's Manikarnika Ghat. Because Kashi has a strong connection with Shiva, who has a close relationship with death, we celebrate Holi with ashes at the Manikarnika Ghat,' Amrit Sharma, my guide, informed me.

This kind of Holi can only be imagined in the land of Shiva. Diana L. Eck writes: 'Shiva is the holy one who challenges common distinctions of pure and impure, auspicious and inauspicious. He is the deity who may be beautiful or terrifying, who may anoint his body with the grey ashes of the dead' (Eck 2015, 33).

According to legend, Lord Shiva went to Manikarnika Ghat after his marriage to Parvati to play Holi with ghosts and spirits. As a result, ascetics and saints continue to play Holi at the ghat in order to preserve the tradition. 'The Chita Bhasm Holi has been practised since ancient times, and is also mentioned in ancient texts such as the *Skanda Purana*,' Jeremy Oltmann, a travel company owner explained.

Bhasm Holi has recently gained popularity among tourists due to social media coverage. As a result, in addition to locals, many tourists now participate in the festivities, according to Amrit.

After ritually presenting Shiva with the unique bhog prasad (consecrated leavings of the deity) of ganja (marijuana), madira (alcohol), and bhang (cannabis), the crowd gathers at the ghat to celebrate Holi amidst the music. Interestingly, the famous Hindustani Classical singer Pandit Chhannulal Mishra from Banaras dedicated a geet (song) titled '*Digambar khele Massane Mein Horee*' to this special occasion.

I'd like to see the festival with my own eyes someday. Rejoicing in this unique celebration demonstrates how death is commemorated in Varanasi in a variety of ways.

3. Kashi Labh Mukti Bhawan: Waiting for Death to Arrive

It's fascinating to see how Hindus travel from all over India to die in Kashi. According to popular belief, death in Kashi is death transformed. 'Death in Kashi is liberation—*Kashyam maranam muktih*,' the saying goes (Parry 2004, 21). Many people come to Kashi for Kashivasa or to make Kashi their permanent home (Eck 2015, 329). 'I know of a man who came to Kashi with his wife to die and stayed for 20 years,' Anil, my boatman, said.

Some people make Kashi their permanent home, while others visit at the eleventh hour. For centuries, people have been brought to Varanasi on their deathbeds to reap 'the profit of Kashi' (Kashi labh). They are transported to hospices designed specifically for the dying.

One such hospice is Kashi Labh Mukti Bhawan, which was founded in 1958. (Parry 2004, 52).

Many students, tourists and researchers are drawn to the hospice run by the Dalmia Charitable Trust, a business family, by the unique concept. It offers rooms for two weeks to those who want to spend their final days seeking moksha.

In local parlance, people who come to die in Varanasi to attain moksha are referred to as mokshaarthi (moksha seekers). 'Those who are about to die or are on the death bed, come here. It's not fixed. Sometimes, the administration extends the stay based on the accommodation availability and the condition of the mokshaarthi,' said Mahesh Mishra, a pandit working here for the last many years.

Outsiders are usually not welcomed, if not prohibited, from entering. However, I was delighted to be shown around the hospice, which is unique to Varanasi. When entering the Kashi Labh Mukti Bhavan from the street, one enters a tranquil garden compound with a two-story hospice building that is over 100 years old. When the city outside is smouldering hot, the beautiful architecture with thick high walls makes it pleasant inside.

The atmosphere is pleasant, with tulsi bushes on either side of the path and a well-kept front lawn. After entering the hospice, there is a puja room with many deities and an akhanda jyothi that is kept lit to create a pious environment ideal for dying.

The priests perform a lavish four-hour ritual of undressing the deities and bathing them in milk and water. Finally, the pandits complete the ritual by washing the brass offering plates and glasses and returning them to their proper places.

During the day, hospice pandits are very busy giving holy tulsi leaves and Ganga jal to the inmates—both of which are considered pure and sacred for a dying person. Furthermore, performing kirtan at dawn and dusk with the help of a harmonium, drums and bells is a regular activity intended to benefit moksha seekers. When the staff is occupied, a record player plays the sound of holy mantras throughout the quiet building, creating a soothing environment for the inmates.

Sitting on the benches outside the main entrance, I could hear the birds chirping in the backdrop of music before Mishra called me for a quick tour, narrating the history of the place. 'There are ten bare rooms. During Covid, unfortunately, the Bhawan had to shut its doors due to government regulations. However, we have recently opened it again,' Mishra told me. Each room has two wooden beds where the families look after the ailing/dying members. The stay is free of charge. Besides, the administration provides the gas cylinder. But, the families have to arrange the utensils and cook food independently inside the room.

When I visited, a family from Bihar had occupied one room while all the others were empty. Rahul Jha was accompanying his ailing grandfather and his grandmother, fulfilling the last wish of the 84-year-old to die in the City of Death. Previously Rahul's great-grandfather took his last breath in Kashi. Now, it was his grandfather's turn to die in the holy city.

I saw a cooking stove and some utensils on the floor in an otherwise empty room. On the other side, a frail mokshaarthi lay on a wooden bed murmuring Ram-Ram. I think salvation was the hope that kept the mokshaarthi going in his arduous journey.

According to Amrit Sharma, the place is a mystery, where the members wait for death to arrive. His guests often question, 'How can one wait for death when predestined?' But, he said, 'I tell them that people come here to get liberated from the cycle of life and death. I agree that death is not in one's control—there is still hope.'

He said that there are instances where the unfortunate stayed at the hospice many times but finally took their last breath after reaching homes. Besides, he told me that many who can't get admission to the hospice stay in rented accommodations in Varanasi searching for salvation.

He told me that dying in Varanasi breaks the cycle of death and rebirth. Therefore, those who take their last breath in Kashi are never reborn. 'In the past, 14,689 mokshaarthi's have attained moksha in Mukti Bhawan,' confirmed Mishra. I don't know if Mukti Bhawan is a road to heaven. But the hospice's spiritual environment certainly aids in a peaceful death, if not salvation.

4.   The Aghori Tradition

Among others, some ascetics live in Varanasi to attain moksha. The goal of these renouncers is to become liberated in life. However, Aghoris are the most radical of ascetics.

The Aghori originated from Aghora, which means 'Not Terrible'— an alternative name for Shiva (Barrett 2008). The Aghoris belong to the Saivite tradition of Hinduism, which emphasizes reverence for the God Shiva. The Aghori claim that the sect was started by Kina Ram Baba, an incarnation of Shiva who took samadhi in the second half of the eighteenth century, in 700 AD (Mishra 2016).

As per popular descriptions, the external appearance of an Aghori is sometimes appalling. They are the most feared sadhus in India, known for their esoteric practices. 'Aghoris embrace everything that society discards as uncouth and coarse. They believe in accommodating the most bizarre and shocking rituals' (Mishra 2016). Writings suggest they engage in everything from nudity to smearing their bodies with fresh ashes from the cremation grounds (see Mishra 2016).

The other customary aspects of an Aghori lifestyle include drinking bhang, cooking food on the embers of cremation pyres and shav pujan (Eck 2015, 328). For example, while visiting the famous Manikarnika Ghat, I saw a sadhu bowing to a burning pyre with folded hands. 'These are the usual scenes at the burning ghats,' Amrit, my tour guide, told me. Undoubtedly, these unworldly practices of Aghoris have attracted foreign tourists, philosophers and researchers alike. However, there is another sophisticated/worldly side of Aghor philosophy that one witnesses at the Ashram.

Ashram of Baba Kina Ram: a Seat of Healing

During my visit to Varanasi, I couldn't miss going to the Aghori Ashram, considered an epicentre of Aghor tradition. Baba Kina Ram's Ashram is a spacious compound that reminded me of Japanese architecture. The Baba's samadhi at the Ashram made in red stones is regarded as a seat of power. But the entry to the samadhi is restricted, barring some special occasions when the sight is open for outsiders.

There are skull symbols placed at the main entrance of the Ashram, symbolizing the non-dualistic state of Aghori tradition. In addition, pictures and paintings placed in prominent spaces in the Ashram depict Aghor Baba Kina Ram's life in pictures. My guide Jeremy showed me an image telling me how Baba's power enamoured Aurangzeb, the undefeatable Mughal emperor. The image shows Aurangzeb bowing with a crown in his hands in front of the sage.

When I asked Jeremy why Aghoris engaged in such unworldly practices, he shared something interesting. 'The Aghor theory is to rise above duality. Therefore, one must engage in practices that symbolize non-duality,' said Jeremy.

Baba Kinaram's life was rather intriguing. Literature suggests that Aghoracharya Maharaj Kinaram travelled across India and felt people's suffering. After that, he devoted his whole life to alleviating their misery. Baba's healing practices are well known—connected to his philosophy of alleviating misery. That's why scores of people afflicted with incurable ailments visit the ashram to seek his blessings. It is no coincidence that Baba reached out to women and people from deprived sections to cure stigmatized health conditions such as infertility and leprosy, frowned upon in society otherwise (see Barrett 2008).

Scholars believe that over the last two decades, members of this Aghori sect, the Kina Ram Aghori, have reformed the majority of their unorthodox practises. Furthermore, members of the sect are now politicians and statesmen. Aghoris have become socially and politically legitimate as a result of these changes (Barrett 2008, 4).

Baba's Ashram symbolizes non-duality in every way. On the southeast corner of the pavilion is a bright room with the akhand dhuni (eternal fire). The dhuni is fueled by the leftover wood from burning pyres of Harish Chandra's cremation ghat for three centuries and equated with the cremation pyre. Interestingly, the wood is purchased from the ghat based on customary agreement with the Doms (Barrett 2008, 51).

Everything in the Ashram is unworldly. The ash from the dhuni is the prasad (consecrated leavings of the deity), otherwise considered polluting, crucial for healing and attaining salvation. The visitors seek the grace of the sacred fire through its auspicious darshan (sight) and use vibhuti from the dhuni for healing (see Barrett 2008). I observed devotees consuming and smearing ashes on their bodies during my visit. From my conversations, I gathered how people frequent the ashram to cure conditions like leprosy, skin disease, auto-immune disorders, mental health problems and disabilities.

However, the healing is not completed without devotees bathing in the Krim Kund equated with Ganges water. I was told that Tuesdays and Sundays are considered auspicious for ritual baths at the kund. But, baths on five consecutive Sundays and Tuesdays are crucial to attaining a cure. The naming ceremony anniversary of Baba Kina Ram is when devotees from various castes and creeds, brahmins and Dalits, gather to take a holy dip in the Krim Kund. According to the Aghor philosophy, 'the opposition between the pure and impure and between brahmin and untouchable is illusory' (Barrett 2008, IV). Therefore, all the rituals at the ashram symbolize non-discrimination and non-duality.

From my short trip to the ashram, I learned that the Aghor sect of Baba Kina Ram might have discarded the practices we conventionally associate with Aghoris. However, the ashram still symbolizes the basic Aghor philosophy of non-discrimination. For instance, ashes of the cremation ghats that are frowned upon in ordinary circumstances are consumed and smeared to seek healing at the Aghori Ashram by brahmins and leprosy patients alike—symbolizing the profound Aghor philosophy of equality and non-discrimination (see Barrett 2008).

II
Death Tourism in the City of Death

For ages, Varanasi has fascinated tourists—international and domestic alike. Besides being the most important pilgrimage site for Hindus, the ancient city of Varanasi attracts tourists to cremation ghats and Aghori ritual spaces, among others.

Some call it—'Dark Tourism'. Also known as Grief Tourism, Dark Tourism involves people's keen interest in visiting places linked to death, suffering and tragedy. Sounds bizarre? However, this concept is fast catching up with the trends.

One can't deny that other than spirituality, mystic death rituals and esoteric practices at the burning ghats of the city attracts scores of foreign tourists and visitors drawn to morbid. Newspaper and research articles reveal, among other things, how tourists are attracted to death and associated rituals in Varanasi (Sharma 2016).

For example, a travel blogger for a popular tourist site wrote: 'Being closely connected to travel, I've come across tourism of all kinds— adventure, eco-friendly, cultural and even virtual. But nothing as unusual and macabre as death tourism! The unearthly Manikarnika Ghat in Varanasi thrives solely on that. Not a single day passes when dead bodies are not cremated here, with the number going up to two to three hundred every day. So to know that tourists come here to see the funeral pyres being set to fire in the open is more weird than fascinating' (Jindal 2019).

Another international newspaper article mentioned: 'This morbid site is attracting more than just the dying. Forty thousand foreign tourists travel to Varanasi each year for a holiday of the dark and twisted kind. Travellers can not only watch public cremations but also take canoe rides among the rotting corpses in the river' (Cuskelly 2016).

Intrigued by these clips, I was motivated to unravel varied aspects of tourism in Varanasi. In the process, I interviewed travel and tour company owners operating in Varanasi. However, the conversations revealed that the burning ghats of Varanasi, Aghori ritual practices, and Mukti Bhawan attract foreign tourists.

Travel companies receive queries about these sites around death and cremation in Varanasi. Not only tourists but also international publications show interest in these sites. Based on the demand, these travel companies commenced walking tours to fulfil the tourists' mysterious interest in watching the morbid.

A glance at travel companies' websites reveals a fascination with death in Varanasi. Travel and tour companies like Groovy Tours and Travels, Varanasi Walks and Trip Advisor offer walks to the burning ghats of Varanasi and Aghori Ashram (see Sharma 2016).

For example, Varanasi Walks organizes a walking tour named 'Death and Rebirth in Banaras'. Their website mentions: 'Walk with us through the city and see Banaras as Mahashamshan, the Great Cremation Ground.'

Similarly, Trip Advisor offers a private walking tour called 'Death and Rebirth Lanes in Varanasi'. The owners of these companies told me that foreign tourists dominate a large part of the tourism in Varanasi. Therefore, these walks are organized, keeping their curiosity in mind.

When I tried to understand the motivations for commencing these tours, however, tour companies had different reasons for initiating walks. 'I started walking tours mainly catering to the curious foreign tourists at my homestay. Since not many Indians are interested in visiting the Mukti Bhawan or cremation ghats, I commenced this walk for my foreign tourists,' said Harish Rijhwani, who has been associated with the tourism industry for forty years and the Varanasi Walking Tours for seven years.

Similarly, Jeremey Oltmann from Varanasi Walks had something interesting to share. 'In pre-Covid days, we received 80 per cent of foreign tourists. The walk, "Death and Rebirth in Banaras", was the brainchild of Kuntil Baruwa from Distant Frontiers, a well-known travel company Jeremy told me. 'Kuntil said, "Why don't we give something special to our guests around death in Banaras?"' 'I told him that it sounds so dark. So why would people like it—it sounds spooky. So I suggested, let's cover both death and rebirth instead. Let's talk about a more holistic theme,' said Jeremy.

However, these travel companies are uncomfortable calling it 'Dark Tourism'. Whether Dark Tourism or not, businesses feed the curiosity of tourists attracted to the mystic, albeit more holistically. For instance, Harish said, 'The term 'Dark Tourism' is coined and promoted by media. However, locals won't ascribe to this concept because physical death is not a taboo among Hindus—it's not dark.'

1.   The Burning Ghats

'No other city on earth is as famous for death as is Banaras. More than for her temples and magnificent ghats, more than for her silk and brocade, Banaras, the Great Cremation Ground, is known for death' (Eck 2015, 324). Hence, the city is alternatively called Mahashamshan, the Great Cremation Ground.

Tourists are keen to visit the prominent burning ghats of Manikarnika and Harishchandra, witnessing cremations like nowhere else. 'When we start the walk, the tourists keep nudging me about when they will see the cremation ghats,' Amrit from Varanasi Walks, who left his commerce degree to tell stories to tourists, told me.

In my quest to understand why foreigners are attracted to seeing funerals in Banaras compared to Indians, I gathered varied responses. Some said open-pyre cremations are rare for foreign tourists and culturally different. 'They don't see death [rituals like this] in the West, so they are intrigued by a corpse on fire. They have perhaps seen it on television or in films but not in reality. Moreover, the funeral process is very different in the West ... In India, the ritualistic aspect is much more vital—one must follow several rituals. Otherwise, it is believed that the soul will remain trapped in the cycle of life and death,' Jeremy told me.

The excerpt from George Mitton's book also captures it succinctly. 'The proximity to death is so alien to western visitors that it exerts a hypnotic pull, and many people find themselves lingering a long while, talking in hushed voices as they peer at the flames. Something is compelling about seeing death at such close quarters. The viewer is not sheltered from death's physical realities on the burning ghats. Death in Varanasi is not a mysterious thing. It is a public event by the river banks where cows and water buffaloes wander amid the funeral pyres' (Mitton 2012). These excerpts undoubtedly reveal a keen interest of foreign tourists in seeing Hindu last rites up close.

Seeing Death Closely: Tourist Reactions and Responses

I was curious about the reactions that these sights generated among the tourists. But, when I inquired about the responses of the bereaved family members and the foreign tourists, I learned that the presence of foreign tourists did not perturb families. Either because the aggrieved are too absorbed in their grief, or maybe the company of foreign tourists is familiar in Banaras. When I went to Manikarnika Ghat and witnessed cremations taking place, I noticed that the families performing the last rites least impacted by the presence of an outsider. This is because these ghats are usually flooded with people, and with much activity going around, they hardly notice.

Similarly, Jeremy said, 'People cremating the deceased members don't care about us. In that sense, we are unobtrusive in that space. The families feel least affected. During these rituals, the pyres are mostly surrounded by men displaying sullen faces.' According to Jeremy, women seldom enter these spaces. 'If women come, they are weeping and wailing—that's the role they are expected to play—binary paternalistic response patterns. Once in a while, if women participate in these rituals—it is a big deal here,' said Jeremy.

Harish had an interesting observation to share. According to him, foreign tourists are more respectful towards the end-life rituals—they are more conscious of intruding or interrupting the practices than Indian tourists. However, sometimes, even travel guides help tourists communicate with bereaved families.

Nevertheless, these open pyre cremation sites elicit mixed feelings among foreign tourists—exotic and mysterious to some, whereas intense and frightening for others. Through my interviews, I collected the narratives of tourist operators in Varanasi. Literature suggests that these sites generate multiple meanings among the visitors, shaped by many things like personal death anxieties, death-related rituals, how the cremation ground is symbolically constructed and the religious background of the tourists (Sharma 2016).

Harish confirmed that the experiences of foreign tourists vary depending on their background, ethnicity and religion. Some tourists, in rare cases, react violently upon seeing the cremations on the ghats. But, according to Harish, most foreign tourists are scared of witnessing death. However, some show a keen interest in understanding the philosophy of death in Hinduism. Some even take pictures of the burning ghats, capturing death rituals on their huge camera lenses during the boat ride.

Jeremy had mixed experiences with tourists, 'Some are afraid of death, so they want to experience cremations—facing their fears. Whereas others are not afraid of death, they are simply fascinated by it.' But, according to him, unlike westerners, Indian tourists don't want to accumulate sin by visiting the cremation ghats.

When I spoke to Dr Ravi Nandan, a sociologist, he gave me a fascinating viewpoint. He said that seeing death up close intrigues foreigners and Indians alike. 'Most people don't expect/anticipate seeing the burning pyre so closely—it's a jolt for many. But, it ironically makes it more poignant and deeply spiritual for people,' he said. According to him, these scenes would undoubtedly be more shocking for a person who has backpacked to India and witnessed these sights compared to an Indian. After returning, this individual would share the experience back home in Poland or Germany.

He added, 'One never gets to see the body up close in these countries. I spoke to the funeral workers in Denmark and Italy, who told me that they hadn't seen the face of the dead in last so many years. So, these visuals of the deceased human beings cremated in open pyres are shocking to these people. In Europe, the bodies are closeted inside coffins and buried or put inside the industrial crematorium. Whereas in Banaras, one witnesses the body undergoing open pyre cremation. That treatment through the fire can be challenging for people to see with various emotions attached to funerals.'

However, according to him, we can't disregard the fact that the experience is shocking and educative at the same time. He believes this experience is similar to the exposure one gets while dissecting the first corpse as a medical student. As per anthropologists, one becomes a mini doctor after getting this exposure. One undergoes an elementary transformation after experiencing the dissection of a human body. So, watching cremation up close might be transformative for some.

2. Tourists' Fascination with Aghoris

Kina Ram Ashram, an essential seat of the Aghori sect, is very much on the itinerary of the travel groups. 'One finds pictures of skulls and *trishuls* from British times. Aghoris were on the map to the British—who found them intriguing. But, for hundreds of years, they were found fascinating to outsiders,' said Jeremy, elaborating on tourists' fascination with Aghori tradition.

Harish believes that tourist guides reveal a cliched and incomplete picture of the tradition. 'Westerners generally perceive them as human flesh-eaters—propagated by tourist guides and industry alike. As a result, some even profitably run their businesses with misinformation and glamorizing the tradition,' he told me. On the contrary, Harish believes that Aghori philosophy is much more profound. For instance, according to him, the healing aspect of Aghori tradition often gets overshadowed. The Aghori Baba, Bhagavan Kina Ram, has established Varanasi's most active centre for treating people with leprosy.

There is so much fascination with Aghori tradition that sometimes, these travel companies receive bizarre requests. Jeremy told me that they receive calls from international publications. 'One publication wanted to do a story on Aghoris showcasing them eating flesh from the burning ghats. I told them no way. It was too weird and intrusive. I don't want to show anything without portraying the complete picture—I don't intend to blow things out of proportion,' he said. There are many unknown facts about the tradition. Like, Aghoris can also cremate bodies—people invite Aghoris to preside over the cremations near a river in places with no cremation grounds. Similarly, the healing rituals of Aghoris are unknown.

'There are certain esoteric practices that Aghori sadhus follow—I won't deny. But, since every tradition has a flip side, few Aghori sadhus also engage in harmful practices. But, should we paint the entire tradition based on these clichés?' Harish asked.

Even Barrett, a scholar who has done extensive work around the sect, believes that many popular misconceptions about Aghor have been reinforced by exaggeration in popular media (Barrett 2008, 5).

Besides, based on my conversations with the locals, I gathered that none had seen Aghoris eating the flesh of the corpses. No one here had heard of such an Aghori—this narrative is perhaps just an urban legend.

According to Amrit, any extreme is Aghor—even Shiva was an Aghor. But there is more to Aghori philosophy that one needs to unravel. Aghori philosophy is more profound. Based on my meagre understanding, I believe that Aghors try to transcend the classifications through which we usually comprehend the world—rising above the compartments of worldly distinctions.

3.   Running the Show: Founders of the Travel Companies

My conversations with the tourist guides while walking through the enchanting lanes of Varanasi were illuminating—interspersed with history, philosophy and mythology. The beautiful narratives they weaved through the conversations reflected their skill and experience.

It is fascinating how Varanasi mystically attracts outsiders who make the city their permanent abode. Harish has been associated with tourism in Varanasi for forty years through his textile business, much before the internet era. He runs a homestay with his wife. As a result, he receives foreign tourists from Australia, America and Europe.

'I came to this city when I was eighteen to start my business—it was Baba Vishvanath's (Lord Shiva) calling. However, my journey in tourism began in 1981 with my textiles business. After that, I started the walking tour to cater to my foreign tourists eight years ago. So, I have everything with the Almighty's blessings—a loving family and a flourishing business,' he said.

Similarly, Jeremy has been associated with this business for the last twenty years. I took the Death and Rebirth walk with Jeremy, which was exciting and educative at the same time. Through the walk, he took me through the lanes of Varanasi. While visiting the cremation ghats and the mystic Lolark Kund, he skillfully interwove stories while delivering every tiny detail during the walks, reflecting his passion for the field.

Jeremy, a skilled storyteller, hails from Minneapolis, USA, and has been living in India since 1997. He initially worked as a social worker with a rehabilitation centre in Delhi. 'I was planning to return when someone suggested that a foreign university is looking for a mentor to start a study-abroad program. So, along with mentoring students, I pursued my bachelor's degree and master's in social work and sociology,' he narrated.

While exploring different places in Varanasi with his students, he developed a keen interest and understanding of the place. He met like-minded people across the country when someone suggested registering his business. What started as a mentoring project turned into a career opportunity for him. 'Subsequently, I formally registered my company in 2007 and developed a website with a friend's help. It was on Lonely Planet, and my phone was ringing. I couldn't manage everything alone. Eventually, I trained some local friends to join the team,' he recounted. His friends were skeptical initially. They said, 'Tourists are much more knowledgeable than us. How would we answer their queries?' He told them, 'They may be more well-read, but they don't know the city. You have participated in these rites and rituals—perhaps you are more experienced than them.'

Jeremy's team member, Amrit Sharma, a commerce graduate, left his accounting career fifteen years ago to tell stories. Amrit, who facilitated my walk, knew the city well. Besides, his knowledge of Hindu last rites, rituals, and mythology surrounding death in Varanasi makes it more interesting. 'I love my work—every walk is unique. The most exciting part of this work is meeting new people every time,' said Amrit Sharma.

Amrit narrated an intriguing instance. He once assisted a German photographer on a project around death rituals of sanyasis, which he rates as his most exciting and challenging experience. He said, when the photographer was wrapping up his project documenting the last rites of a Buddhist Lama, he saw a chair in a vision. In his search to find meaning to this vision/dream, the photographer landed in the City of Death, Varanasi. After arriving, he began his quest to explore the relationship between a chair and death. Later, he discovered that during the final journey, a sadhu was carried on a wooden chair. Fortunately, they could film the last rites of a sadhu in Varanasi at Assi Ghat. I heard many such stories walking through the lanes of Varanasi, which must undoubtedly be exciting for tourists, feeding their curiosity.

Both tour companies have interesting yet different approaches and styles of working. Harish has a spiritual disposition. During the conversation, he said, 'I am interested in spirituality. So whatever I pick from the Bhagavad Gita, I practice and share it with my guests. We have extended discussions with our regular guests at the dinner table. If someone comes from the Manikarnika Ghat with negative feedback, I try clarifying their doubts.'

He likes to explain the philosophy of death in Varanasi to his foreign tourists. 'It's difficult for tourists to grasp everything in one visit. However, some international tourists with long-term associations appreciate the Indian philosophy of death and take a keen interest in uncovering it. But, I find it easier communicating with English-speaking tourists,' said Harish.

On the other hand, Jeremy, with a background in sociology, is well versed in history and mythology and good at explaining things. Besides, he believes regular tourism keeps the tourists away from locals to avoid getting caught in long conversations. He wants his guests to interact with locals. 'My approach is more organic and free-flowing rather than relying on Wikipedia. So I mostly provide snapshots of everything during the tours—here are some stories of Kabir and some of baba Keena Ram. I go like this—this is his place, and that is his place. I try to keep it loose and organic for my tourists,' Jeremy told me.

III
Money Matters and Death in the Holy City of Banaras

In one way or another, death in Banaras is a huge business (Parry 2004, 70). I witnessed how death becomes a commodity traded by flower-sellers, pandits, doms and wood traders in the holy city. These individuals flock around the families chasing their prospective customers as soon as they arrive. Doms, tirath purohits and flower sellers eagerly assist you in death-related and post-cremation rituals like tirath shraddh. Besides, from Doms to tirath purohit, everyone has a share in Varanasi.

'The pandas inside the Kashi Viswanath temple are very money-minded. So there are unethical practices that happen under the garb of religion and pilgrimage,' said, my guide.

I learned about certain money-related practices in this sacred city through my interviews in Varanasi. *Poori dukaandari dharam ke naam par chal rahi hai yahan*—everything boils down to economics. This happens everywhere—I have witnessed similar scenes in Rishikesh and Pushkar. It is true that being in this business, even we are a part of this dukaandari,' said Harish.

Harish explained how the boatmen at the Sangam sometimes squeeze money from tourists in the name of the nirvana of their ancestors' atma. 'Tourists get cheated without understanding the meanings behind these rituals. There is so much fear around death rituals that locals take advantage of. However, we helplessly witness the entire drama unfolding every day.'

Locals and sometimes even tourists make undue demands, ignoring the decorum and sanctity of the sacred place. 'For example, taking pictures at cremation grounds is socially frowned upon. Although there is no law or rule—locals find it intrusive. I receive photography groups who tell me to set sadhus for images. They are willing to pay, but I tell them I am not doing this. This sounds cheap and capitalistic. So instead, I communicate to my guests that they can take pictures if any of these things appear organically. That makes it more interesting,' said Jeremy.

Sometimes, tour providers entertain the clients' demands wherever possible without being involved in monetary transactions. 'There are different rules. For example, Doms are different from sadhus. They are much more economically minded, so you provide money and take pictures all day. Therefore, if someone approaches me to take photos of the cremation ground, I tell them to approach the Doms and seek their permission—and you give them whatever they want in return,' Jeremy told me.

13

Funeral Methods: Challenges and the Way Forward

In India, different communities follow varied practices in laying the dead to rest. For example, religious communities like Muslims and Christians bury the dead, while India's Parsis lay their dead on Towers of Silence. Likewise, Buddhists, Hindus, Sikhs and Jains cremate bodies. In contrast, among Hindus, smaller children and sadhus are buried (Davis 2003, 767).

I
Environmental Costs of Burying or Cremating the Dead

We also need to analyse funerary practices from an ecological standpoint. Evidence reveals that the two most common funerary

149

practices worldwide—burial and cremation—have an environmental impact.

For instance, burial, one of the most common funerary practices globally, poses severe environmental problems. It entails using hardwood or metal caskets and toxic chemicals seeping into the soil involved in embalming the body. Hardwood and metal caskets do not decompose quickly, preventing the body's natural decomposition (Kalia 2019). Because coffins are not used in Islamic burials, they are safer. However, the decomposition of the human body itself is polluting, rendering groundwater unfit for human consumption (Knight 2010, 8).

Globally, with over 55 million people dying yearly, the land burden is also very high. Besides, burial spaces are also becoming increasingly scarce and expensive. For instance, India's expanding population and lack of space have made graves a premium proposition, especially in cities.

I spoke to funeral directors in the country to understand the situation. Through my conversations, I found that big cities like Delhi and Mumbai are left with fewer places for burying the dead. 'There are very few government-owned cemeteries in Delhi. However, most cemeteries in the capital are either occupied or expensive. Mainly, there are privately owned ones—my family has been undertakers of seven graveyards with no space left. So if the family members wish to be buried together, we break open the grave and bury them together—called doubling. In some scenarios, tripling is also permitted. However, with land becoming scarce, I feel the government will have to provide land for burial,' said Cyril, a funeral director in Delhi.

The space crunch for burials is a severe problem even among the Muslim community. With many dead people resting in graveyards over the years, coupled with encroachments, finding space to bury the dead is becoming worrisome.

'The kabristan spaces are shrinking—we face this problem regularly. These spaces also suffer from encroachments by land grabbers,' said

Mehfooz Mohammad, section officer, Delhi Wakf Board. Besides, Delhi Wakf Board data showed nearly 500 Muslim graveyards in Delhi in 1970. However, currently, there are less than 100 (Thomas 2018).

Given this backdrop, cremation is becoming a popular option among other religious groups. As a result, small changes are underway. For instance, Madras Cemeteries Board now sells small plots to bury ashes after cremation (Thomas 2018). 'All our five cemeteries are full. Therefore, we have advised people to go for cremations. So people are slowly becoming open to the idea,' said Father Januario Rebello, the Delhi Cemetery Committee chairperson in a newspaper interview managing five of the city's eight Christian cemeteries (Sharma 2014).

In contemporary times, with scarce land resources, cremation is viewed as a crucial alternative worldwide. 'Cremation is gaining ground in the modern world as the most cost-effective means of disposing of the dead; it is also touted for other advantages such as conserving public land and having less of an environmental impact compared to the pollution of the ground that might be caused by decaying bodies resting in synthetic fabrics and cushions encased in chemically treated coffins or the seepage of embalming and other fluids into the water table'(Taylor 2000, 74).

Besides, cremation has surpassed burials as the most popular end-of-life option in the United States over the past four years. Not only this, but with its growing popularity, the Cremation Association of North America has projected a cremation rate of 50% by 2021. The concern for the environment, land use, and economic considerations are the driving factors for this change (Little 2019).

My conversations with experts, funeral workers and pandits reveal that Hindus prefer open pyre cremations in India. According to Dronamraju Ravi Kumar, the president of the All India Brahmin Federation, it is only when one hears the sound of the skull breaking that the journey of a human is considered complete. People don't go home until they hear it. The electric or gas-based burials instantly turn the body into ashes and hand it over to you. So the traditional method is correct, as per shastras (Minhaz 2019).

However, cremation also has an environmental cost, especially the open-air pyre method. It requires a lot of fuel—cutting down millions of trees. In addition, the practice leads to gaseous emissions such as carbon dioxide, carbon monoxide, nitrogen oxide, and mercury vapours that pollute the environment. Moreover, roughly 500 kg of wood is required to burn an adult human body. Therefore, the demand for timber used in cremation also burdens the forests. According to estimates, funeral pyres consume around 50–60 million trees annually, producing 500,000 tonnes of ash and emitting 8 million tonnes of carbon dioxide in India (Kaushik 2018).

Furthermore, these pyres release 2,129 kg of carbon monoxide every day. Besides, the felling of trees results in loss of oxygen and groundwater recharge capacity (Kaushik 2018). Another problem with cremation is mercury emission, which is highly toxic and linked to neurological problems and death (Knight 2010, 8). Moreover, other poisonous emissions from burnt prosthetics and melted bone cement used during surgeries, such as hip replacements, are polluting (Kalia 2019).

Besides, cremation also generates enormous quantities of ash, which are later immersed in rivers, adding to the toxicity of their waters. As a result, environmentalists see an urgent need to look for alternative cremation methods. Environmental concerns like reducing air and river pollution have been the driving force around which the State has promoted electric cremation in India. However, although alternative cremation methods such as CNG crematoriums or electric incinerators are eco-friendly and economical with a fixed rate of ₹1500, their availability is limited. For example, Delhi has only six CNG furnaces and four electric crematoriums (Kaushik 2018).

Accessibility is one issue, but cultural perceptions and notions also come in the way of communities adopting these newer methods. For example, the shift from the open pyre to electric cremation overrides many rituals like parikrama (circumambulating), mukhagni (lighting fire into the mouth) and kapal-kriya, which are opposed to Hindu religious beliefs (Prajapati and Bhaduri 2019). In addition, there are many myths surrounding funeral technology. For instance, while talking to the families, some said, 'Without kapal-kriya, the soul gets trapped in the electric incinerators.'

While talking to a friend, she told me, 'My mother has categorically told me to cremate her on an open pyre whenever the time comes. She doesn't believe in these newer methods.' These are times when sentiments and last wishes take precedence over logic.

Moreover, the quality and quantity of wood used in cremation are sometimes considered a yardstick of social status. Therefore, using precious wood like sandalwood and more wood quantity are signs of prosperity and power (Prajapati and Bhaduri 2019).

Besides, the Brahmin Associations and Dom's Associations opposed the electric cremation in Varanasi on similar grounds. In the past, these religious and cultural beliefs have hindered the adoption of newer technologies. For instance, when the British introduced an incinerator in Bengal in the late nineteenth century, brahmins opposed intermixing the ashes of the dead from other castes. Their opposition led to developing a pentagon-shaped incinerator with a designated space allotted to the brahmin dead bodies (Prajapati and Bhaduri 2019).

Although the conventional system is two to three times costlier than modern cremation methods, there are fewer takers. The gas-fired burners are used only in one out of fourteen cases.

'It's not about money. For instance, in Varanasi, the electrical crematorium has been there for the last ten years, highlighting the flat fee of 500 rupees in bold letters. Moreover, any open pyre cremation would be 3-4 times more expensive, but no one would be keen on using the electrical one unless the ghat is flooded,' said Dr Ravi.

During my visits to crematoriums in Delhi, I found the open pyres releasing dark sooty smoke from the pyres occupied, while the CNG-operated ones looked deserted. Also, the CNG crematoriums' industrial look is divorced from the traditional Hindu system of open pyres, making it less attractive.

Among Hindus, death is seen as the antim sanskaar, a kind of sacrifice for which fire is considered crucial. Moreover, for Hindus, cremation is not just about the destruction of the deceased's body but an act of regeneration through which one is reborn (Parry 1994, 31).

For instance, a pandit at Nigambodh Ghat explained it: '*Lakdi ka sanskaar* (open-air cremation) is the most common one—*logon ka isme vishwas hai* (people believe in this). Mokshada (green cremation system) and CNG are very good from an environmental point of view. However, people are not comfortable with CNG. So I think we need to create awareness about alternate methods. But, eventually, people will have to resort to these methods since one is not sure about the availability of wood in future. *Pata nahin aane vaali pidiyon ke liye kuch bachega ya nahin* (I don't know if anything would be left for the future generations).'

However, during the Covid-19 pandemic, alternative cremation methods gained prominence in Delhi. Non-availability of traditional pyres and faster disposal are the reasons for their wider acceptability during an emergency. But, as soon as things normalized—people returned to conventional funerals. 'Almost everyone now prefers wood-based traditional cremation instead of CNG cremations. When there was urgency due to Covid—the CNG furnaces were in very high demand since people wanted a faster medium. If there are around fifty wood-based cremations in a day—we scarcely get 5-6 requests for CNG units these days,' said Avdhesh Kumar, a supervisor at the Nigambodh Ghat.

Even in Varanasi, the spiritual capital of India, the open pyre cremations were closed during the first wave of Covid. Therefore, the CNG furnaces were in great demand. However, as soon as things normalized, people reverted to the open pyre cremations, confirmed Laalu Chaudhary, a supervisor at the Harishchandra Ghat CNG crematorium in Varanasi.

Social scientists believe the State has not internalized social values in promoting electric cremation technologies in India. Perhaps, the State needs to take cognizance of these cultural barriers and sentiments before advancing any new technology (Prajapati and Bhaduri 2019).

While talking to several experts, I learned that in Europe, the transition from burial to cremation was a part of a broader social movement involving politicians, film personalities and physicians.

During my visits, I also gathered that people were unaware of the alternate cremation technologies. So, like the pandit in Nigambodh said, we need to create awareness around these methods.

Similarly, Dr Ravi told me that newer technologies must be systematically popularised. 'But, because funerals are politically sensitive in India—the State is reluctant to popularise these newer methods. So, one assumes that open pyre cremations are people's choices. But, desire has to be created systematically to bring about a certain kind of normalization around a method. In the Indian context—it's left to people. Then whatever comes their way—they adopt it,' he said.

I also spoke to the environmental crusaders in India, trying to bring about a change. They talked about the challenges and roadblocks in promoting these methods.

II
Greener Funeral Options: Indian Scenario

1.   Mokshda Green Cremation System

In India, social actors are bridging the gap through innovation. For example, the non-profit Mokshda Paryavaran Evam Van Suraksha Samiti has been trying to curb pollution by giving people access to more fuel-efficient structures for last rites. Their semi-open pyre system aims to reconcile social values and technology-efficient systems. The Mokshda Green Cremation System has been developed through enormous research, taking cognizance of the communities' and religious leaders' cultural and religious sentiments. Moreover, the system is less costly than the CNG, which requires enormous investment and maintenance.

Mokshda is a green cremation method, a better and safer alternative than the conventional cremation method, providing proper air combustion and efficiency to the cremation processes and saving trees from deforestation. A metal tray heated with firewood works as a pyre in these structures. This arrangement takes less time and needs less wood than the traditional pyre. Moreover, the transition from one cremation to another is easier by removing the ash-filled metal tray and replacing it with a new tray.

Currently, about 56 such units are spread around seven Indian states. According to Anshul Garg, the Mokshda Green Cremation System volunteer, one metal pyre can handle around six cremations a day, considering the Hindu rituals are performed during the daylight. The system also lowers the wood needed from 400 to 450 kilograms for a conventional cremation to 140-170 kilograms.

Mokshda is also looking for alternatives to wood like cow dung cakes and agro-waste logs to make it more sustainable. 'We are trying to partner with local communities in rural parts to use the locally available materials and create livelihood opportunities for them,' said Garg.

Though there has been some opposition to this method, Garg said, people are more open to the Mokshda system now than in the 1990s. However, some mindsets and sentiments still come in the way of popularising the method.

'More environmentally conscious people are now open to the Mokshda system. However, we must constantly raise awareness among the crematorium staff and users about the effectiveness of the Mokshda system. Moreover, the lobby of the wood mafia is enormous. So the promotion of these methods goes against these timber businesses,' Garg added.

Despite these challenges, more than 150,000 cremations have occurred on Mokshda pyres in India, saving more than 7,50,000 trees, averting about 60,000 metric tons of ash from rivers, and releasing 60,000 fewer metric tons of greenhouse gas emissions.

'We were not aware of Mokshda technology but were informed by the hospital staff where my mother took her last breath. Mokshda is an excellent system—environmentally friendly and reasonable,' said a family member who opted for the Mokshda Green Cremation System to conduct the funeral of their deceased mother in Delhi. I witnessed how the family seamlessly performed the last rites without any hindrances, assisted by the cremation staff. Moreover, the chimney emissions were cleaner than the open-air pyre cremations, where the dark sooty smoke is unbearable for the eyes and lungs.

Moreover, I heard numerous stories during the second pandemic wave where wood was scarce and traditional open-air pyre was less accessible, making the Mokshda system a preferred funeral method—less time-consuming and more fuel-efficient.

Garg said the non-profit has received inquiries from other countries in Africa and Asia about making cremations greener. In addition, CSR and international development organizations are supporting Mokshda projects. So let's see how far one can upscale these energy-efficient and environmentally sustainable methods in India, where big cities are threatened by air pollution—impacting citizens' well-being yearly.

2. Mokshakashtha: Wood for Salvation

Like Mokshda, others strive to save the environment through energy-efficient and environmentally viable alternatives. For instance, Vijay

Limaye, a crusader of environment-friendly cremations, promotes an environment-friendly solution.

Limaye started his research based on his personal experience. 'During my father's cremation. I realized we cut so many trees during the Hindu last rites that I felt like a sinner. So I thought, if we kept cutting trees at this pace, then nothing will be left for future generations,' he said. Therefore, Limaye felt an urgent need to look for alternatives and started his search in 2010. While looking for options, he even studied the scriptures to understand the relevance of wood in Hindu cremations. 'Based on my research, I discovered that as per shastras, the human body is made of panchtatva—the five elements. So, according to the scriptures, the mortal remains need to be returned to the elements by consigning them to the flames. But, the source of fire doesn't necessarily have to be wood, I discovered,' he told me.

Soon after, he started exploring other alternatives. During his work travels in various states, he began visiting crematoriums looking for alternatives to wood. First, he studied cow dung as a substitute, but that failed.

Then one day, while Limaye was passing by an agriculture field, he noticed a burning fire, a common sight in the country as the farmers burn crop residue before the next sowing. That was the end of his search. 'My logic was simple—crop residue is burnt anyway. Therefore, we can save many trees using agricultural waste to replace wood.'

Limaye didn't stop there, and he began his research on briquettes. Initially, he tried various crop residues to get an appropriate result. Finally, after substantial trial and error, he discovered briquettes made of soybean, arhar dal (split pigeon peas) and cotton crop residue feasible (Khandekar 2020).

'After thirteen to fourteen cremations—I got the desired result,' Limaye gave a unique name to his discovery, mokshakashtha (wood for salvation), as they resemble wood.

Initially, he piloted one of the Nagpur Municipal Corporation (NMC) crematoriums. After successfully running the project for three years, Limaye's non-profit was given five more crematoriums for two years. 'Currently, we are cremating 400-450 bodies in a month using briquette,' he said proudly.

Besides this, along with his team at Eco-Friendly Living Foundation, Limaye delivers lectures at several public places and institutions, popularizing alternate fuels among ordinary people. 'It wasn't easy convincing the community. In the beginning, people wouldn't entertain me. Initially, they were sceptical because death is considered inauspicious in our society. Moreover, people thought that these alternatives were against Hindu philosophy. However, once I received support from the local and the national print media—everyone started taking me more seriously,' he told me.

Slowly, as families saw the effectiveness of the fuel, it became easier to convince people. Moreover, the media coverage also helped popularise and promote the method. As a result, during the last three years, approximately 18,000 bodies were cremated using mokshakashtha. 'One funeral pyre needs approximately 300-400 kgs wood, requiring two aged trees. But, on the contrary, we only need 200 kgs of briquettes for a funeral. So we can claim to have saved more than 36,000 adult trees with this calculation,' claimed Limaye.

He has set up a manufacturing unit on the outskirts of Nagpur city that supplies briquettes to the NMC. He feels that using agro-waste for briquettes has led to multiple benefits. For instance, disposal of crop residue is efficient, and the soil remains healthy as burning stubble destroys soil quality and fertility. Finally, briquette making has generated employment opportunities for the locals. 'If everything goes well, the mokshakashtha system will be extended in the city's six other NMC-run crematoriums,' said Limaye, hopeful.

His enthusiasm and spirit about the cause are contagious. Limaye is attempting to popularise briquettes in other parts of the country, especially the northern states that face massive pollution problems due to crop burning. However, it told me about the roadblocks he faces in convincing the people in power.

III
Way Forward

The text reveals that funerals are becoming a significant concern with the rising population and dwindling land resources, leading some environmental crusaders to experiment with sustainable solutions. But, the religious and cultural sentiments attached to last rites come in the way of alterations/innovations leading to more sporadic, fragmented, and unplanned changes in India's death industry.

While talking to sociologist Dr Ravi, he said, 'Most of the changes in the Indian funeral industry are minor. This is because so much of it is improvisation—be it a response to the environment or grieving families responding to different urgency and demands. For instance, some may want to keep the body longer, while others wish to cremate it quickly. Therefore, these changes are not systematic or institutionalized and certainly not industrialized through big technologies. Instead, the funerals have been industrialized through minor changes or makeshift technologies—a response tied to situations that emerge from people's lives.'

Around the globe, people are looking for greener/eco-friendly ways of conducting funerals, leading people to experiment with greener methods. Some examples are Recompose method and Sharpham Trust's natural burial ground at Sharpham Meadow in the UK. For instance, Recompose involves placing a corpse in an above-ground receptacle filled with soil and organic materials. As a result, the body is transformed into usable soil (Kalia 2019).

I don't know how many people will be receptive to newer technologies in India. But, according to Dr Ravi, people's lifestyles are changing.

Besides, mobility and occupation have altered a lot. However, funeral practices haven't changed much worldwide. So, death-related methods traditionally seem to be changing the last globally.

One will have to wait and see how these newer methods gain acceptance in the future. At the same time, one must keep looking for culturally and ecologically viable options until one finds a sustainable solution.

14

State of Cremation and Burial Spaces in India

No one wants to talk about the funeral spaces. These unfortunate sites are the least priority of anyone, the government or the citizens alike. Ideally, cremation and burial places should be well-maintained and clean for the smooth conduct of funerals of the departed souls. Yet, they only gather human attention during unfortunate events. Didn't the kabristans and shamshan bhoomis come to centrestage during the deadly waves of Covid, highlighting the inadequacies? Besides, we heard scary stories of serious under-capacity and malfunctioning of these neglected spaces during the second wave of the Covid-19 pandemic.

I
The Current State of Affairs

Unfortunately, the state of these spaces is dismal in India. Some are managed by the civic bodies, while Non-Governmental Organizations and panchayats run others. For instance, the maintenance of the kabristan is the responsibility of an elected body. 'The body employs two to three workers for the upkeep of the kabristan and digging the grave on a fixed salary,' said Hafez Gulam. There are eleven to twelve elected members of the kabristan management committee. 'We do every small-little activity any organization will undertake. First, we raise funds through donations and the fees we charge from the burials. Then we use the money for various developmental activities and provide different amenities to the bereaved families like water coolers, electricity, ambulances and resting areas at the kabristan. The idea is to ensure hassle-free funerals for the aggrieved family. After that, we use the rest of the funds to pay salaries to the workers. So we make sure we pay our workers well—they also have families to look after,' said Jawadul Hasan, a kabristan committee president. He said their committee actively undertook varied developmental activities in the kabristan in Jamshedpur. As a result, the prominent kabristans are managed well, and others suffer neglect and encroachment.

Similarly, NGOs and charitable organizations look after the cremation grounds in India's capital, with little or no support from government agencies. A few maintained by the civic bodies are smaller and not as well-looked-after as those by the NGOs and other organizations (Mathur 2016). In my recent visit to a crematorium, even a better-maintained shamshan in South Delhi had filthy toilets, missing fixtures and no water access.

'The shamshans in our country are not maintained. A significant worry for a person whose family member dies is whether the burial or cremation will be easy to pull off. When the families are grieving, it's torturous to deal with this. Even the basic amenities are lacking. One dreads using the washrooms in these places. Besides, the hearse vans provided by the crematoriums are shabby,' said, a professional funeral organizer in Delhi.

Reports claim that the country's burial grounds are in no better state. Besides, many look rundown while others suffer encroachments. 'The kabristan spaces are shrinking. This is because these places suffer from encroachments by land grabbers,' said Mehfooz Mohammad, section officer, Delhi Wakf board.

So I went through newspaper clips to better understand the problem. For instance, a report in *The Indian Express* highlighted how one finds shards of broken beer bottles and cigarette packs in Worli Shamshan Bhoomi in Mumbai. Furthermore, the report mentions that slums like Anand Nagar and Jijamata Nagar have encroached into the eighteen-acre Hindu crematorium where young boys play cricket even when dead bodies are brought for final rites. Whereas in some crematoriums, grills and boundary walls are missing. The toilets are dirty with no water facilities and missing taps. Furthermore, some crematoriums have missing streetlights, while others have become the dumping ground for city dwellers. Even the community cemeteries in the city are not well-maintained. Finally, the report highlighted that, unfortunately, the maintenance and upkeep of crematoriums and cemeteries are not on the priority list of the respective departments or civic bodies (*The Indian Express*, February 26, 2014)

Even in Hyderabad, the crematoriums are ill-managed. For example, there is no water at many crematoriums. As a result, people carry buckets and mugs for a ritual bath on the cremation ground before returning home. There is not enough space for performing pre-death rituals either (Minhaz 2015).

This is the picture in the country's metros. In many rural areas, there are only sheds in the name of shamshan bhoomi. On the whole, most of the crematoriums are not in a good state. However, few trust-managed-crematoriums are adequately maintained—Nigambodh Ghat in Delhi is one of them. I visited the crematorium to understand the functioning of the ghat and what makes it one of the better-managed ghats in India's capital.

II
Nigambodh Ghat: a Historical Ghat

Nigambodh Ghat, located behind the Red Fort in the Kashmiri Gate area on the banks of the holy Yamuna river, is the oldest and most historical cremation ghat in Delhi. According to popular legend, the ghat has been used for last rites from the era of the Mahabharata. I also learnt that by bathing in the holy waters of the ghat, lord Brahma regained his divine memory and precious knowledge of religious texts and thus the name Nigambodh, meaning realization of knowledge.

This crematorium has been in the capital for decades now. However, nobody was willing to preside over the inauguration after its construction. Perhaps things associated with death haunt the living, and similar feelings may have deterred the VIPs from entering the site. But Jawaharlal Nehru was infuriated when he learnt that the crematorium was lying unused. Dr Sushila Nayar was eventually persuaded to do the inauguration (*The Hindu*, March 18 2002).

These days, the ghat is famed for hosting cremations of political personalities like Sheela Dixit and Arun Jaitley. Moreover, it is one of the few ghats in India that functions at all hours, making it accessible for the bereaved.

The ghat area is also architecturally prominent, with structures dating back to the medieval era and the British colonial regime in India. One can't miss the well-maintained gardens giving it a serene and pious ambience. As soon as I entered the site, I heard the speakers making announcements interspersed with religious songs blaring in the backdrop. In addition, I couldn't miss the life-sized sculptures of Hindu gods and goddesses planted in different areas watching after the bereaved families. The main gate, inspired by the Kurukshetra battleground, is another attraction.

It is undoubtedly infrastructurally one of the better-equipped crematoriums. It offers well-maintained hearse vans at concessional rates. Besides the traditional pyres, it has six CNG and six Mokshda (green cremation) furnaces. In addition, it has stepped piers for bathing and ritualistic functions leading to the river waters. 'Many Garhwali and Bihari communities like to cremate their deceased near the river bed,' said Avdhesh Sharma, supervisor of the ghat. Hence, the Yamuna riverbed is the centre of ritual activities like pindaan and shraddh, with several burning pyres next to it.

I was told that, on average, forty to fifty bodies are cremated here daily. The ghat is undoubtedly the busiest in the capital city. I noticed the steady arrival of corpses with families carrying the arthi while chanting 'Ram Naam Satya Hai' before resting the deceased under the tomb-shaped structures for pind daan and pre-cremation rituals.

However, one must accomplish the administrative formalities before proceeding with the ritual exigencies. But, the ghat's functional office with well-equipped staff makes the process seamless for the mourners.

Unlike other crematoriums, I was pleasantly surprised to see the functional air-conditioned waiting areas for the bereaved family members and toilet facilities with running water.

In addition, one can't ignore the instructions and the history of the crematorium painted on the walls for the benefit of the visitors in different areas. Besides, the general secretary of the crematorium's managing committee, Suman Gupta's air-conditioned office at the ghat, displaying his trophies and framed certificates, is the centre of activity. The room has screens and speakers for seamless coordination and monitoring work.

When I interviewed him, he proudly mentioned his achievements after taking over the administrative work of this historical ghat. But unfortunately, Suman was distracted several times during our conversation by visitors. Managing this large crematorium while attending to user grievances is not simple.

'This is the oldest and biggest ghat in India—guaranteeing moksha. In 2011, the Aggarwal Trust Badi Panchayat took over the management of the ghat. Unfortunately, when we took over, all the pyres/platforms were broken, and the office was barely a shed. Therefore, we first undertook the repair work of the pyre platforms. We also installed the drinking water coolers and benches for the visitors. In addition, we made sure twenty-four hours of electricity is available here,' he told me.

Besides, the ghat supports low-income families with free wood for cremations, said Suman. Moreover, according to Suman, the ghat offers ten kilos of cow dung cakes and packed Ganga jal for free. 'Madam *ko packet dikhao* (show the packets to the madam),' he instructed his staff members to make the cow dung packets accessible. Other than this, Suman Gupta is associated with many other philanthropic organizations. He also has many people applauding his efforts. 'The face of the ghat changed after the NGO took over. It is a cleaner and a greener place with appropriate facilities and seventy staff members to assist visitors,' confirmed Avdhesh Sharma.

Similarly, a funeral pandit told me, 'We have seen changes in the running of the crematorium after the NGO took over. The staff is trained—even the ghat is cleaner.'

I noticed how the open-pyre platforms were buzzing with people while the CNG-operated ones looked deserted with no takers. Although, according to the staff, the CNG was widely used during the Covid. However, undoubtedly not a preferred cremation method during usual times.

The ghat was in the news during Covid for conducting cremations by constructing make-shift pyres for the Covid victims. 'We arranged food for all staff members during the three months of Covid peak. It was a tough time,' said Suman Gupta.

Visiting a ghat can't be a pleasant experience. However, seeing the happy faces of the staff and the cleaner ambience made it less unpleasant.

The Nigambodh Ghat is undoubtedly one of India's cleaner and better-managed ghats.

III
Vaikunta Mahaprasthanam: a World-Class Crematorium

While most of the crematoriums in the country are in a bad state, some offer world-class facilities. For example, Vaikunta Mahaprasthanam is an eco-friendly crematorium site managed by Phoenix Foundation under the corporate social responsibility (CSR) wing of the Phoenix Group. One of the twin cities, (Hyderabad-Secunderabad) most sophisticated and world-class crematoriums deliver hassle-free last rites and rituals maintained under the Fund Your City program.

Phoenix Foundation looks after the upkeep of Vaikunta Mahaprasthanam with world-class amenities. The Foundation keeps it clean and efficient for the smooth conduct of cremations of the deceased. The clean and green ambience of the crematorium makes it unique and unmatched.

The crematorium has all the facilities and amenities under one roof with traditional and electronic pyres, pandits, flowers, clean restrooms and washrooms, water, storage facility, car park, bookstore and canteen. Moreover, the park-like ambience is a welcome change.

IV
Managing a Crematorium: a Woman's Cup of Tea

Management of the crematoriums is not an easy task. NGOs face umpteen challenges in the upkeep of these places. Praveena Solomon, nevertheless, ventured into the area usually reserved for men. It all started when the India Community Welfare Organisation NGO was assigned to run the 120-year-old Valankadu crematorium in Chennai. Solomon took the challenging task of managing the crematorium.

'The secretary of the NGO thought that if women members contributed to the crematorium's upkeep, then it would be different, and he approached me. I consulted my family and started working,' recounted Praveena, who contributed almost six years to the project.

It wasn't smooth sailing. Praveena, as caretaker of the crematorium, faced umpteen challenges as she was threatened with an acid attack. Initially, she wasn't supported by the local people, who were perturbed by a woman handling the affairs of the dead.

'Men came drunk to the crematorium. They even ridiculed me and talked about my caste. I ignored everything. Since I intended to help others—my confidence didn't waver,' she told me. Even her daughter's teacher ridiculed her. 'Your mother couldn't find a better job,' she said. 'That was very painful for me,' recounted Praveena.

Eventually, her courage and hard work bore fruit. Solomon worked untiringly to change the face of the crematorium that looked filthy and mismanaged before she took over.

Solomon's contribution is unique. It's perhaps the first time a woman ran a cremation ground in Tamil Nadu, where the upkeep of the crematorium is traditionally a male domain like in most parts of the country. In the beginning, Solomon was timid in discussing her role. But, she eventually came along. I salute her courage. I can't think of doing this challenging task alone amidst much criticism and risk.

'This is life. Forget and forgive while helping others,' is Praveena's spirit, who is currently working on another project with India Community Welfare Organisation.

I am happy to learn that historic ghats of the country like the Manikarnika Ghat of Varanasi and Nigambodh Ghat are receiving adequate attention. However, we need functional funeral and burial spaces to say dignified goodbyes and serve the emotional and spiritual needs of the mourners in the rest of the country. But is a well-managed funeral space with basic toilet facilities and proper infrastructures like streetlights, fans, and benches too much to expect? I hope someday we make this country a better place for both the living and the dead. But do we have to be shaken by emergencies to invest in our funeral/burial places?

15

Caste Discrimination in Last Rites

'They don't let us bury our dead on their funeral grounds,' said a member of the Kalbelia community from Rajasthan.

Are the funeral/burial spaces in our country equal for everyone? Or are these spaces fraught with inequalities too? The newspaper reports, films and my conversations with activists across India highlight that caste remains pervasive even in the end-life rituals—following people to their graves.

We might be oblivious to the caste discrimination in India. Yet, it persists across religions in various forms—even in death. Based on this, Dalits are denied access to common burial and cremation grounds and even prevented from using land restricted explicitly for them. Besides, I learned that many Dalit communities are forbidden from reciting Vedic mantras, vedokta during their last rites.

While talking to a member of the Dalit community, he said something hard-hitting, *Aap to sirf sun rahe hain, hum to pidiyon se yeh sehte aa rahe hain* (you are just listening—we have been experiencing this for generations).' These heart-breaking conversations with the victims and the activists across India inform the persistent discrimination these communities faced during the last rites.

Although Article 17 of the Indian Constitution abolishes all forms of untouchability—practising it is considered an offence punishable by law—the reality is different even when it comes to burying/cremating the dead.

I
Discrimination in Last Rites: Echoing Voices

According to the book *Untouchability in Rural India*, denying access to cremation or burial grounds is a widely prevalent form of untouchability in India. Since this is a sensitive issue—it often leads to tensions and violence among communities (Shah et al. 2006, 89).

I spoke to activists who shared the community's struggles and the extent of discrimination. For example, Lalit Babar, general secretary of the National Federation of Dalit Land Rights, shared various instances of discrimination with me. Lalit told me, 'During our work with the communities across India, we found that Dalits were forbidden from cremating/burying their dead in the crematoriums/ cemeteries used by upper-caste groups. Due to this, we found that some buried or cremated their deceased next to the river or road. However, others who owned land also buried or cremated their dead on their farmlands.'

In some cases, just like temples, the funeral spaces are also demarked. 'There are separate shamshans for different caste groups. The upper-caste groups mark their cremation grounds by installing boards specifying the caste names outside the shamshan bhoomi,' said Gopal Ram Verma, secretary of Samajik Nyay Evam Vikas Samiti, a Rajasthan based advocacy group.

The scene is familiar across India. Even in Punjab, the scenario is not any different. The high caste groups disallow the cremation on the main cremation grounds to the Dalit groups like Mazhbis and Ramdasias, comprising 30 per cent of Punjab's population (Pawar 2015). This is contrary to the teachings of the Sikh gurus based on the religious institutions of sangat and langar (communal dining). As a result, there is a gap between doctrinal principles and social practice. 'Sikh religion preaches equality, but some people deviate from the teachings of the gurus,' a Sikh Granthi told me.

Similarly, in hundreds of villages and hamlets across Maharashtra, Dalit communities are denied access to the common burial/cremation grounds and barred from using even the burial grounds demarcated explicitly for them (Pawar 2015).

However, I am pleased that newspapers, films and documentaries focus on these aspects. For instance, in *India Untouched* (K 2007), the documentary underscored perpetual caste-based discrimination faced by Dalits from different religious backgrounds across Indian states during funerals.

'We have no land of our own. So when caste groups (*unchi jati ke log*) don't let us bury our dead on their lands—we bury them around our houses. If we resist—they resort to violence,' said Buddha Nath Kalbeliya, from Kalbeliya Vikas Samiti, Jodhpur, Rajasthan.

Kalbeliya, a scheduled caste group in Rajasthan known for their Kalbeliya folk dance, is shunned by the mainstream and other Dalit communities. He told me, 'We have no place to live or die. We have neither BPL cards (identity proof for Below the Poverty Line communities) nor ration cards.' When I spoke to him, the pain in Buddha Nath's voice was deep, and the sense of betrayal was profound—not knowing where to seek justice was even more heartbreaking.

II
Not Letting the Communities Access the Roads Leading to Funeral Grounds

Listening to these stories, I feel these castes groups don't want Dalits to live in peace. Not only funeral spaces, but I learned that sometimes Dalits are even denied access to the road to the funeral or burial grounds. 'The caste groups don't allow the Dalits to enter their fields or use the road leading to the burial ground. Sometimes, these groups even block the regular paths to the funeral spaces. These upper-caste groups even resort to violence to stop the Dalits from taking the funeral processions. Sometimes, police intervention is required to create the way. Therefore, the Dalits are sometimes forced to bury/cremate their dead on agricultural fields or in their homes. But groups like Kalbeliyas don't own any land. It, therefore, becomes challenging to bury their dead—especially if there is more than one death in the family,' Verma told me.

I heard numerous stories of discrimination and violence. However, this one was exceptionally hard-hitting—Aani Devi of Bairva caste (a Dalit caste) from Beenjarvara village of Ajmer district died on 4 July 2020. While the family was taking the funeral procession through a predetermined route, the path aligned to the agricultural fields of the upper caste community was obstructed by barbed wires. When the community tried to pass through the barbed wires, they were forcefully stopped by the dominant caste members of the village. However, when the family tried to argue, the high caste groups reacted violently. They hurled stones and abused them, leading to severe injuries and fractures of the Dalit members, shared by Gopal Ram Verma.

The injustice that communities face in these situations is enormous. But unfortunately, even their complaints go unattended because of the political and administrative influence of the higher caste groups.

I read a similar account in a newspaper clip where Dalits of Veedhi village in Coimbatore, Tamil Nadu, were forced to carry out a funeral procession through a garbage yard after being denied access to the road used by upper castes Hindus (Murali 2019).

III
Forced to Bury Their Dead on Their Fields or Courtyard

I heard horrifying tales of Dalit members forced to cremate or bury their loved ones next to their living quarters. These communities sometimes delay the burial for several days until they find a place to bury or cremate the deceased due to a lack of access to land (Chandran 2020). The documentary film *Six Feet Under* (Kummil, 2019) showcases stories of Dalit families from several districts of Kerala who have been forced to bury their loved ones in their kitchens, rooms, and even under public pathways. The film links each incident through the conversations with the Dalit families and interviews with activists across six districts of Kerala—Thiruvananthapuram, Kollam, Alappuzha, Palakkad, Kozhikode and Malappuram.

The director, Sanu Kummil, told me, 'Dalit households lead a very deprived life. They don't have enough property or infrastructure to meet their bare necessities. Hence, there is no way to give their loved ones a decent funeral. Due to lack of access to funeral spaces in rural Kerala—Dalits are forced to bury the body of their loved ones by demolishing their house or kitchen.'

Similar issues are highlighted by activists in other states as well. 'In Rajasthan, Dalits are forbidden from cremating/burying their dead on common cremation/burial grounds. Besides, groups like Kalbeliyas are forced to bury under make-shift living tents or in the backyard,' said Navin Narayan, a Dalit activist and researcher from Rajasthan.

Not having access to a funeral space is the height of injustice that any community faces.

IV
The Land Issue

Studies point out that discrimination in funeral spaces involves land, which is always a contentious and relatively scarce resource. 'In India, at least 60 per cent Dalits and 90 percent nomadic groups still do not own land, according to the Socio-economic and Caste Census 2011 and the National Commission for Nomadic Tribes report in 2008, respectively' (Gokhale 2020).

'Dalits do not have land for housing or livelihoods. In India, many poor people live in slums or unauthorized colonies without rights on the land they live on. Not only this, Dalits are also denied land for cremations or burials. These issues have always existed, but private lands have become more contentious since globalization,' said Babar.

In many states, cremation burial grounds suffer encroachment by the dominant castes. These encroachments are often regularized because higher castes groups have access to the state bureaucracy. 'There is an allotment committee in the revenue department that allocates land. But, in many instances, the allocated land is encroached by the upper-caste groups,' said Gopal Verma.

Buddha Nath, with great pain, told me, 'We got some funeral land allotted for our community with immense struggle. But, unfortunately, the upper caste groups even encroached on that land. According to the Maharashtra ministry for social justice, Dalit burial grounds have been grabbed by upper castes in 72.13% of the State's 43,722 villages (Pawar 2015).

The film *Six Feet Under* shows that the available wasteland with panchayats can easily be turned into public graveyards, but the residents protest and get the proposal turned down. So these Dalit families have no choice but to dig their own homes to bury their family members.

Even where Dalit burial/cremation grounds exist, strict regulations about their location happen. For example, the book *Untouchability in Rural India* reveals that Dalit cremation grounds are located on the eastern side of villages in Maharashtra. The prevailing winds are west to east. Therefore the upper castes believe the whole village will be polluted by winds blowing from the Dalit cremation ground (Shah et al. 2006). Can you imagine the extent of discrimination that these groups face?

V
Campaigning for Funeral Spaces/Rights

These issues are not undisclosed—human rights groups, media, and filmmakers have highlighted these issues. Kummil tried bringing focus to the problem by documenting it through the film. 'I had first-hand knowledge of such incidents because I worked as a local correspondent. When I first reported this news in the media, it became a sensation on social media. However, it did not receive the attention of the government and the local bodies. So, looking for a sustainable solution—I decided to document this story,' Kummil told me.

In Maharashtra, activists have been campaigning for equal rights. 'This issue centres around land rights. We have been fighting for Dalit land rights since Independence. After recognizing the problem, we campaigned for rights for common funeral spaces or the allotment of separate funeral spaces. Although Dalits should have the right on the common lands, we demanded separate cremation/burial grounds for the community since it was an urgent issue. Then, we highlighted the issue with the media's help and documented the practice. We even collected information in the respective constituencies of the political leaders to campaign for the cause,' recounted Babar (See Chandran 2020).

There are no easy solutions to the problem. 'When this situation came into the limelight in the news media, the government introduced schemes and plans to handle it. But the implementation of such projects needs land allocation. Moreover, funds were not apportioned properly. In my opinion, the State can do much to improve the situation. Kerala conservation acts have the potential to formulate a sustainable solution for the dignified last rites for Dalits. But the real problem is the lack of government lands for this purpose,' said Kummil.

VI
Concrete Steps: Bearing Fruits

I know the picture is grim, but I see some light. Human rights groups' persistent struggles have borne fruit in some states of India. For example, according to Lalit Babar, there is a provision in Maharashtra where Members of Parliament and the Legislative Assembly can allot funds for funeral spaces from the public representative development fund. In the State, at least 60-70 per cent of villages now have a designated shed. Besides, there is also a provision for lights and roads leading to the shamshan.

Moreover, Lalit Babar said, 'Some progressive 10 per cent villages areas in Maharashtra even allow funerals in shared spaces. We aspire to extend this to every village—but that will take time. Other states are following suit. For instance, in Karnataka, funds are allocated for SC (Scheduled Caste) and ST (Scheduled Caste) groups under the Scheduled Caste Sub-Plan (SCSP). In addition, such funds have been allotted in Telangana state for the development of Dalits.'

Similarly, the former Patiala Member of Parliament (MP) promoted the idea of common cremation grounds. As a result, some villages under his constituency had five cremation grounds—each for a separate caste group. Under his guidance, 144 villages in Patiala passed resolutions to end the practice of different cremation spaces. As a result, special development funds were allocated for the panchayats, ending the system of numerous cremation grounds (Goyal 2020).

I can't fathom what it would feel like to be denied access to a burial or cremation place. These heart-breaking stories of denial are shocking—mirroring the state of our society. It is a pity that, regardless of technological advancement, we live in the shackles of caste-based prejudice. The harsh reality is that the Dalits of our country are discriminated against even in death, and it exists despite progressive legislation. Caste-based discrimination is not a fast-fading remnant of our society but a persistent and flexible part of contemporary reality that must be recognized and addressed. In the end, I believe people like Buddha Nath find justice in life and death.

16

Last Rites Among the Kinnar: a Neglected Group

I have childhood memories of Kinnar, or hijras as they are sometimes called, at the birth of sons and during marriages, merrily singing and entertaining the local audience. Their performance amused the crowds, and their unique style of dancing and clapping intrigued the masses. Their blessings were considered auspicious by many families. There were negotiations, but eventually the families, fearing their curse, paid them whatever they demanded. However, their presence has become occasional during these ceremonies, especially in bigger towns. Instead, I see them begging and asking for money at traffic lights.

In India, the Kinnar community is both revered and despised; some regard them as demigods, while others avoid them. They are even mentioned in old Indian texts such as the *Kama Sutra*. Vatsayana, the author of the *Kama Sutra*, had dedicated an entire chapter to Kinnar courtesans (Zaffrey 1997, 35).

Kinnar stories can also be found in history and mythology. The most famous example is the Ramayana. Lord Ram's subjects attempt to follow him into the forest after being exiled from the kingdom for fourteen years. He summons his men and women followers. His Kinnar followers, who do not fully belong to either gender, feel unbound by this order and remain. Impressed by their devotion, the deity bestows upon them the power to bestow blessings on auspicious occasions such as weddings and births (Goel 2019). That's one reason the Kinnar ritually bless newlywed couples and newborns.

Similarly, many Hindu deities manifested as both male and female—ardhanari. For example, Lord Shiva and Goddess Parvati form ardhanari by merging. Therefore, ardhanari has special significance for the Kinnar community.

Likewise, the Mahabharata includes an episode where the hero Arjuna is sent into exile. During his sojourn, assuming an identity of a Kinnar, he performed rituals during weddings and childbirths, just like the Kinnar of today (Zaffrey 1997, 34).

Also, during the Mughal period, the Kinnar played a prominent role in the court systems of various empires serving as political advisors, influential administrators, chamberlains, trusted generals and guardians of the harem.

However, the British viewed this group as threatening morality and political authority. As a result, the British criminalized being a Hijra under the Criminal Tribes Act of 1871, stripping them of their inheritance rights, leading to further marginalization of the community (Goel 2019).

Despite their illustrious past, the Kinnar face social marginalization today, finding it difficult to survive without work, housing and social support. Such disregard has a direct impact on their social standing, leading to further stigmatization. They, too, live on the outskirts, earning a living by requesting voluntary donations, dancing at birth ceremonies and weddings, and occasionally begging and engaging in sex work (Goel 2019).

Laxmi Narayan Tripathi, a Kinnar, said in an interview: 'Our main occupation is to perform badhai at weddings or when a child is born. At such times we sing and dance to bless the newlyweds or newborns. But can badhai alone fill our stomachs? Obviously not, and so we supplement our earnings by begging on city streets, performing sex work and dancing in bars and night clubs. Dancing comes naturally to us hijras' (Roade 2013).

The Kinnar and their performances make the life cycle rituals merrier. However, we are oblivious to their day-to-day life, including funeral practices, which are unknown to the outside world. Moreover, entry to their community is highly guarded.

For instance, I tried contacting many people of this community for interviews around the last rites, but they either disconnected the phone or outrightly declined the interview request. After a point, I gave up. Therefore, I am writing this section retrieving all the relevant literature I can, trying to weave the threads together.

According to Vidya Rajput, a prominent transgender activist, there are many misbeliefs around the last rites of the Kinnar community. 'Hijras guard their rituals, especially related to last rites. They are bound by strict rules governed by their gurus. I have never attended the community's end-life rituals—I have only heard stories from their members,' Vidya told me.

A Kinnar is initiated into the community through a lengthy adoption process based on customs which differentiate them from other transgender people. On their adoption, they must follow their clans' customs and traditions and maintain secrecy around these aspects.

Other studies pointed out their reluctance to openly talk about their last rites. 'Given the inauspiciousness of even speaking about death, hijras were extremely reluctant to talk to me about their rituals surrounding this event, even if only in the abstract....' (Reddy 2005,

107). Even Zia Zaffrey pointed out the community's hesitancy to disclose their life-cycle rituals—especially those related to death (Zaffrey 1997, 81). Although some authors point out that the Kinnars believe their death signifies the end of a sorrowful life, that the deceased's new life will be full of happiness.

In Zia Zaffery's book, a respondent said: 'There is no Hindu and Muslim hijra ... They're all buried! There is no religion amongst the hijras. No Muslim goes to a mosque, and no Hindu to a temple.' (Zaffrey 1997, 80).

Although, in some clans, all the Kinnar are either Muslim or Hindu. Many gharanas (clans) include Hindus and Muslims and even Christians in their fold. Most of the studies pointed out that whatever the natal religion of the Kinnar, their identity largely stems from being a Kinnar (see Zaffrey 1997).

Gayatri Reddy notes that whatever the natal/religious status of the Kinnar—all the funeral traditions replicate those performed at the death of a Muslim man in Hyderabad. These include: washing the corpse, viewing, praying from the Quran, burial in the Muslim cemetery and conducting a roti (feast) on the fortieth day. Moreover, she mentions that roti was one of the only occasions when Kinnar from across the country came together, apart from Muharram (Reddy 2005, 107).

Reddy describes the funeral rites like this—'The day a hijra dies, her body is thoroughly washed, along with the area around it, by a man referred to as ghasl—a hereditary caste/occupational position in the Muslim community. All ornaments are removed from the body, and the ghasl is given one-half of these, that is, all the ornaments from one side of the body, including one earring, the bangles, nose-ring, toe-ring and anklet, as well as a tablet of silver with which he has to apply surma (kohl) ... The body is now ready for the mayyat or viewing. People who wish to pay their last respects—in this case, primarily other hijras—can come and view the body at this time...' (Reddy 2005,

107). Afterwards, specific prayers are read from the Quran over the body before moving it onto a stretcher. Finally, the body is carried to the cemetery by non-Kinnar Muslim men (Reddy 2005, 107).

However, Reddy also notes that while most end-life rituals match Muslim practices, some resemble Hindu traditions. For example, she mentions that the celas behave as Hindu widows after the death of their gurus, blurring the religious boundaries. They break all their bangles and remove all their jewellery for the period of mourning, much like some Hindu widows (Reddy 2005, 107).

Similarly, Zia Jeffrey notes that the Kinnar are laid to rest in graves, not cremated. Furthermore, she writes that burial rituals were carried out at night, including the burial itself (Jeffrey 1997, 78-79).

Similarly, Vidya Rajput said that most Kinnar bury the dead. However, exceptions may exist among groups like Shiv-Shakti and Jogappa, who follow Hindu funerary rites.

Furthermore, in an interview for a publication, Laxmi, a member of the Kinnar community, said: 'Hijras belong to different religions, and our last rites depend on our religion. A hijra who is a Hindu is cremated, while a Muslim hijra is buried. When carrying the corpse of a dead hijra to the graveyard, we shed our women's clothing and dress instead in shirts and pants or in a kurta and pyjama pants. We do this to hide that the deceased is a hijra' (Roade 2013).

Community members often disguise their identity because they are denied access to cremation and burial grounds. According to activists, discrimination continues despite their efforts to create awareness (KV 2019). Likewise, ritual specialists in different religions reject/refuse to perform their last rites, especially for ones who have undergone castration or breast enlargement. For this reason, many hijras try to conceal their identity (Williams 2017, 131).

Another article confirms the discrimination they continue to face during funeral rites. 'For hundreds of years now, transgenders, irrespective of their religion, have been buried and not cremated.

Most transgenders bury the dead in secluded areas, not in graveyards. Hindu priests refuse to perform post-death rituals for transgenders, and it is due to this the annual shraddh ceremony is not performed for transgenders' (Malhotra 2016).

In the last few years, Kinnar Akhara, a transgender organization, has been campaigning for equality in the funerary rites, questioning the age-old Hindu discriminatory practices. As a result, in 2016, a collective pind daan ceremony was held for the Kinnar community (Indian Express 2016).

There is a lack of consensus around the last rites of this neglected and oppressed community. Moreover, there might be regional variations in the last rites. Therefore, in the end, whether they conduct their funeral rites as per Hindu or Muslim tradition or both doesn't matter. However, one must respect the community's choice to follow the funerary rituals of their choice according to their unique tradition without discrimination. Besides, in 2014, India's Supreme Court officially recognized the third gender. The ruling confers equal opportunities and legal and constitutional protection to trans people. I hope these rights extend to the choice of funerals and the right to funeral spaces without facing any discrimination. Ultimately, dying with dignity is as important as living with it.

17

Gender Discrimination in Last Rites

One morning I got a message on my Facebook messenger, 'I want to share my story.'

Gunjan was responding to my request on Facebook—asking women to share their stories of performing the last rites of their family members. However, Gunjan had something different to tell. I was shocked to hear what she had to say.

Unfortunately, not many people are aware of the persistent gender discrimination in India, let alone that suffered during the last rites. Therefore, I thought it would be crucial to discuss the prejudice women and girls face surrounding end-of-life rituals here.

Not just girls, widows are treated with disdain in many Indian families—aggravating their trauma and agony. As I said, this section took shape when women approached me to share their stories of discrimination, venting their pent-up emotions and anger. Therefore, I dedicate this part to girls and women who face discrimination in life and death.

I
Not Mourning the Death of a Girl Infant

India ranked 135th among 146 countries in the Global Gender Gap Index 2022 because of persistent gender discrimination against girls and women in India (Global Gender Gap Report 2022). We don't have to guess the reasons. Countless girls die an unfortunate death facing neglect due to lack of medical care and food, and many die as foetuses. Thus ensuring fewer daughters for some Indian families to feed, educate and marry—a process usually demanding substantial investment. Moreover, in some population segments, these girls face discrimination in life and death, not celebrating their birth or grieving their deaths.

'The birth of girl children is tolerated, not often welcomed in many families and communities. This is because they are not seen as permanent family members, and it is widely assumed that their links with natal families will get severed once they marry. Moreover, their skills or employment do not presumably add value to their natal families. Therefore, they are seen as a liability. Hence it is likely that a girl's death, especially in infancy, is not seen as a tragedy in most households...' said Parul Sharma, Education Specialist, UNICEF, Jharkhand.

There are many instances where girls are treated unequally. I came across one when a mother shared her pain of losing her newborn girl. 'I thought my heart would feel lighter if I spoke with someone. *Mujhe aaj bhi gussa aata hai vo din yaad kar ke* (I still feel angry, remembering that day),' Gunjan Singh, a mother, told me.

Whether society mourns or not—perinatal deaths can be traumatic for mothers who grieve and mourn their infants' loss in silence. In addition, research suggests that perinatal grief is a phenomenon of varying severity and duration, leading to significant mental health illness and pain.

Listening to Gunjan angered me immensely and compelled me to write about the discrimination girls faced during the last rites. Gunjan told me with a heavy heart that when her one-day-old infant girl passed away, her patriarchal Rajput family from a village in Aligarh hardly grieved. Instead, her mother-in-law commented, '*Ladkiyan nark se aati hain aur narak main hi jati hain tum bhul jao* (girls come from hell and go to hell in the end, you forget about it).' How must have Gunjan felt hearing this? It's been a year, and Gunjan's heart still aches for her daughter.

In villages, the birth of the girls is not seen as a good omen. Even the dai (traditional birth attendant) demands more shagan (ceremonial money) at the birth of a boy.

Her husband's family was upset with her daughter's birth from the onset. Therefore there was hardly any remorse when she passed away. Hindus have different last rites for babies under two, who are not cremated. Their tender bodies are not suited to the harshness of a cremation fire and are therefore buried. However, the deceased child's body is adorned and laid on the bier before performing the funerary rites. Gunjan is angry that the family didn't intend to complete the daughter's death rituals with the same seriousness as a boy.

However, Gunjan ensured a proper send-off to her firstborn. 'I dressed her and insisted they bury her on our farmland. Through this, I intended to prove the girl's right to the landed property. But, more so, I wanted her to remain close to me forever—even after death,' she said.

Usually, there are less elaborate post-death rituals for children under two. However, one may customarily feed small children to remember the deceased child. But, these post-death rituals are absent for girls. Gunjan told me that the death of a boy in the family is remembered for generations. At every critical event, members grieve. In contrast, a girl is forgotten instantly and becomes history very soon.

Gunjan didn't succumb to this discrimination, and there were many instances when she revolted. 'I remember I was given a ritual bath on the seventh day after a nayan's (barber's wife) massage. They placed a rolling pin wrapped in a cloth ritually next to me—wishing the birth of a son in the subsequent pregnancy. However, when I learned the intention behind the ritual, I angrily threw the rolling pin away,' she told me.

Now Gunjan has a baby boy, but she still grieves her daughter's death. 'There is a tradition of drawing a swastik (auspicious sign) at the house entrance welcoming the son. However, I haven't yet performed this ritual since my son's birth—I thought, should it be done for him if they couldn't do it for my daughter?' said Gunjan.

Few women like Gunjan can question the status quo, challenging the age-old patriarchal norms. As a result, most mothers quietly suffer the loss of their girl infants, sobbing in silence. However, I hope these narratives change with women's empowerment and emancipation, where the birth of a daughter is celebrated, and death is mourned, where girls are given an equal chance to live and die respectfully.

II
Becoming a Hindu Widow

The transition to widowhood is one of the most dramatic events in Indian society—seen as a shrap (a curse). In India, the most gruesome ritual was Sati, in which women were expected to die at the same funeral pyre as their husbands since ancient times.

The last recorded case of Sati was of Roop Kanwar in a Rajasthan village in 1987. At eighteen, Roop was forced to commit Sati when her husband died after eight months of marriage. Post this incident, the government enacted the Prevention of Sati Act, making it illegal to force or encourage a woman to commit Sati.

Although widows are no longer expected to die in ritual Sati, they are socially expected to mourn for eternity. Moreover, they must give up wearing symbols of a suhagin (married woman)—sindoor, sakha, bichiya and bangles—signs of fertility and sexuality.

In many cultures, merciless window-making rituals, including breaking the bangles, smudging the sindoor, removing the mangalsutra, and taking off the bichiya, are designed to strip the widow of these marital decorations.

In West Bengal, the woman is also given a widow bath (bidhobar snan) while wearing the bright saree for the last time. From that point, she gives up wearing colourful clothes representing sexuality and reproduction. Instead, she is prescribed white, seen as thanda (cool)—symbolising infertility, asexuality and widowhood. Besides, some higher caste women are even expected to shave off their hair (Lamb 2000, 214).

It's not much different in Banaras. 'A widow has the vermillion rubbed out of her parting before her husband's corpse leaves for the ghat, one of the fingers of his lifeless hand being used to erase it. The bangles on her wrist are removed by being smashed against the side of his bier. She is in some sense responsible for his death, and a high caste widow must expiate the misfortune she has brought him for the rest of her days. While the wife is her husband's 'half-body' (adhangani), one can almost say that she becomes a half-corpse after his death. Henceforth, she must dress in a white shroud-like sari and is excluded from any significant ritual role on auspicious occasions like marriage' (Parry 1994, 174).

Mahasweta Devi described this scene tragically in the story *Rudali*. 'Still crying, she washed off the sindoor from her head in the shallow Kuruda river, broke her bangles, and returned to the village. She had just bought them at the fair' (Devi 1997, 74).

These practices indicate that from now on, the woman lacks the ritual powers of wearing bangles, toe rings and red vermillion she had acquired after marriage.

However, with the husband's death, these women are not only stripped of these signs but are deprived of happiness or pleasure—the most challenging transition for any married woman.

Not only this, these windows are treated as a bad omen and considered inauspicious. Even their parchai (shadow) is deemed ill-fated, bringing bad luck to other married women. Therefore, widows are forbidden from attending auspicious rituals like marriages or naming ceremonies. I remember how my naani (maternal grandmother) deliberately kept herself away from auspicious ceremonies because of her widowed status.

Not only this, many times, women are accused of their husband's death, adding to their trauma and suffering. In many communities, they are called 'husband eaters'. When Neeraj Singh's husband went away, she was barely twenty-four. There were five children to look after. The extended family accused her of the husband's untimely death. 'They called me names like raand (prostitute). No one cared about my mental health,' recounted Neeraj from a Rajput family in Aligarh.

'After the husband's death, his side of the family thinks that you have no business staying here. My husband was a teacher, and my brother-in-law wanted his wife to join his position,' said Neeraj. She was therefore told to leave the house with her children.

While writing a story on witch-hunting in Jharkhand, I learned how tribal women are branded as dayan (witches) at the untimely death of their husbands. The entire community physically and emotionally harasses and ostracises them, denying them any right to the property.

With widowhood, anybody can restrict them and tell them what not to do. Neeraj remembers how she was barred from wearing toe rings. A lady once taunted me, '*Teri himmat kaise hui bichiye pehne ki. Tujhe sharam nahin aati?* (how dare you wear these toe rings. Aren't you ashamed?)' Not only this, Neeraj was even disallowed from wearing bright clothes. 'They treat you as if there is nothing left. They even instructed her to chop off her hair after my father's death,' Gunjan, her daughter, told me.

'I was told to stay inside the house and not interact with the outside world. Not only this, because of my widowed status, my sister-in-law told me to stay away from the ceremonies when my children were getting married,' Neeraj said. Then, however, her children revolted and said, 'Why can't mummy participate in the shubh karya,' Neeraj told me.

However, things changed for the better after Neeraj picked up a job, leaving her husband's house. She pursued higher education and was promoted in her teaching career. 'My children are educated and well-settled. I have nothing else to ask from Paramatma (God),' she said. But, millions of live at the mercy of their husband's families. According to Neeraj, the scenario hasn't changed in the rural hinterland.

Punjab, a more progressive state that gave birth to social reform movements, is not very different. In Punjab, women are remarried to their husbands' younger brothers, even if they dislike it. 'The status of women changes drastically after their husband's death, especially for women of younger age. They are not only accused of their husband's death but are expected to wear plain/dull colours. Moreover, with widowhood, they lose their freedom to interact with the outside world. Seen as a threat to the family's reputation, they are often married to their husband's younger brother. However, women are not encouraged to remarry outside the family. I categorically remember one instance where an acquaintance was forcefully remarried to her husband's younger brother after her husband passed away in Dubai. However, the woman wasn't happy in that marriage,' said Dr Gurjeet Singh Sandhu, an Assistant professor at Punjab University, Rural Centre.

It is different for men. There is no change in their status after their wives' death. 'The death of a male member is perceived differently than a woman. After a woman member's death, the family instantly starts looking for prospective alliances,' added Gunjan.

If a man is widowed, he can marry again and have the entire wedding rites. A woman cannot, suggesting she comes into a permanent state of inauspiciousness after her husband dies.

Unlike males, these women often live in acute poverty and deprivation. Lack of education and any source of income forces them to beg on the streets and many turn to prostitution for survival. As a result, many abandoned widows find themselves in the ashrams of Vrindavan, the Northern Indian state of Uttar Pradesh. Vrindavan is home to over 20,000 widows. Over the years, many shelters for widows run by the government, private enterprises and NGOs have mushroomed—giving it the status of the City of Widows.

Moreover, there is growing anxiety about the future of these women in the absence of social security and state healthcare. Finally, we must consider class, caste and regional variations. Here the urban-rural divide may be significant. For instance, urban educated women are perhaps more economically independent and empowered to make decisions than their rural counterparts.

But unfortunately, a large segment of society is still entrenched in these age-old customs and traditions that treat women differently after their husband's death based on patriarchal norms. I hope these norms change for the better someday, where women have the freedom to embrace colour and live lives of dignity and respect, and women like Neeraj are not treated differently.

18

The Funeral Performances: Parai and Gaana from Tamil Nadu

Can you imagine death being celebrated with music? Yes! Music has been an integral part of human existence in life and death. In Ghana, for instance, carrying the casket is accompanied by dancing pallbearers to joyous music that celebrates the deceased's life.

Similarly, the native Maori people in New Zealand perform Manawa Wera Haka at the funeral after death. A jazz funeral is a procession accompanied by a brass band in New Orleans, Louisiana. We can find similar parallels in the Zapotec funeral traditions of Mexico, where a band plays a piece of happy music to accompany the procession, celebrating the deceased's life (Srinivasan 2018). We have parai and gaana performances in India during funerals, famous in Tamil Nadu.

I
Drumming and Singing at Funerals: the Parai

'Parai chose me. I didn't choose parai,' said Manimaran, a renowned parai performer in a passionate voice. While researching parai, I found Manimaran's contact on the internet.

He instantly responded to my message when I tried speaking with him. But since he didn't speak English, he requested his son to interpret for us. Nevertheless, I could hear his excited voice on the other side of the telephone, waiting to share his story.

Parai is a percussion instrument—a hollow drum made of a wooden ring, with cow skin stretched on one side, played with two unequal sticks. In Tamil, the word means to speak or tell. I genuinely believe that parai has many stories that the world needs to hear.

Although, in olden times, parai was used to mobilize war soldiers, celebrate success and catch thieves. Not only this, it was a vital part of street plays, festivals and nature worship. However, with time, parai became synonymous with funerals, played by Dalit Paraiyars in Tamil Nadu.

Manimaran said, 'I started playing parai when I was six. My drum is my life—parai ensured a steady livelihood and alleviated me from poverty. Then, along came great opportunities like awards and travelling abroad. Besides, my drum taught me crucial life lessons, both humiliations and losses.' He calls parai his dearest friend.

During funerals, the parai performers play the drums, sing praises for the dead, and entertain the community with their humourous acts and witty performances, demonstrating how to live until death. 'Since parai performance involves music, rhythm and coordination, it's natural for the artists to smile while performing as a crew. Playing with a sad face contradicts the very nature of the art. Only when an artist enjoys, the audience delights in the art,' said Manimaran, explaining the art of playing parai.

Besides, detailed ethnographic descriptions of the parai art and its performers help us peer deeper into these folk traditions. For example, Deces describes it eloquently: 'It was the duty of the local Paraiyars to lead the all-male funeral procession through the main streets to the cremation grounds. Dressed simply with towels wrapped around their heads and in long waistcloths tucked to fall like short skirts, these men would dance and sing along the village's main street to the accompaniments of their drums. It was impossible to ignore or simply not hear their pounding....' (Deces 2005, 2-3).

Can you imagine someone getting up from the bier to the beating parai drums? Parai served a unique function at funerals. According to one version, the exceptionally high sound of parai confirmed deaths when medical science was not significantly evolved. If the deceased remained still to the loud and rhythmic music, the end was ascertained—such was the power of the parai.

However, Manimaran contradicts the association of parai solely with funerals. According to him, parai has been an integral part of Tamil life. 'Our parai signifies life and death. Therefore, it was played at all life stages—marriage, birthdays, baby showers, temple festivals, and nature worship. One amongst these is the performance at funeral processions,' said Manimaran, explaining the diversity of parai. According to him, parai and its players are stigmatized because of the drum's association with deaths. However, in ancient times, this was not the case. Instead, death was celebrated, and people danced and played parai on different occasions.

These traditional funeral rituals associated with caste are viewed as oppressive. Therefore, Dalit communities are slowly abandoning these traditions, including parai. These changes would perhaps modify the funeral rituals from the past centred around rigid caste rules.

However, according to Paul Jacob, a music expert, 'Parai is liberating because it is a medium for the oppressed to express pain and agony through music.'

But, according to Manimaran, it is repressive—The artists are obliged to perform even if they need to attend family events or travel. Moreover, there are no fixed hours while performing parai at death rituals. Instead, the artist must perform until the body is taken for the funeral procession, even if it takes two days for the aggrieved relatives to arrive. While discussing the artist's struggles, Manimaran added, 'It's not easy performing non-stop without resting during funeral performances. Moreover, it takes a toll on the bodies, making drummers take respite in alcohol, leading to addiction—a pervasive problem among drum players.' In her book, even Isabelle Clark Deces points out how the drummers drank alcohol to forget the pain in their bodies and feel less inhibited while performing (Deces 2005, 126).

Through my interviews, I learned how individuals are taking concrete steps to transform this age-old tradition from the shackles of caste discrimination by mainstreaming it. For instance, in 2007, Manimaran founded Buddhar Kalai Kazhu, which trains hundreds of people keen on learning the parai. Besides, Buddhar Kalai Kazhu aspires to popularize this traditional art form—free from caste shackles. Manimaran added, 'My motto is to liberate parai and other art forms imprisoned within caste-based rituals and customs—using them as tools for social liberation.'

According to Paul Jacob, the transformation is visible as parai has entered the mainstream, performed at social and political events. Not only this, it has even found space in popular cinema. Besides, parai has travelled to music festivals to celebrate and preserve this traditional folk music. For example, in 2020, the Margazhi music season hosted a five-day event centred around replenishing the dying folk arts by showcasing parai and oppari. 'I have tried upgrading the skills of the folk artists, taking the folk music to the international festivals, making it accessible to a much wider audience,' said Paul. Moreover, he has been actively working towards mainstreaming folk traditions. These efforts will go a long way in preserving these age-old traditions, albeit in their new avatar.

II
The Gaana

Gaana is a form of singing performed at funerals homegrown in Chennai's slums and poor neighbourhoods. It was exciting tracing its musical journey from the funeral grounds to the international stage.

When I spoke to Paul Jacob, he said, 'Gaana was the collective name for the music of the oppressed, expressing life's hardships.' According to him, gaana was initially the music of the slaves that evolved into funeral music over the years.

When I asked Paul about gaana's connection with the funerals, he said something exciting—'Gaana is the music of liberation. Perhaps with death, the person is relieved/liberated from the drudgery of life— that's why they celebrated death with music.'

However, there is no consensus about how the music derived its name, although some believe it may have originated from the Hindi language, meaning song. According to Tenma, a Tamil-indie musician and composer, co-founder and music producer of popular gaana band, 'Since there is no recorded history—everyone has a different version of its origin. However, the most common dominator is gaana, originally performed at funerals. It originated in a fishermen's village in North Madras—called the black town by the British, based on the skin colour of the working class.'

However, born in Chennai's city slums and burial grounds, the present corpus of gaana songs indicates numerous influences. Some pieces are influenced by Sufi saints, while others flourished in the urban landscape absorbing the distinct urban language attributes (Kumar 2018, 32-49). In addition, it has folk roots that reached Chennai through migrants from rural Tamil Nadu. Some also believe that gaana has Burmese language impact along with Sufi influence. All the settlers brought their flavour to the music, making it richer.

Another aspect that highlights the humble gaana origins is its instruments. 'Initially, all the drums were improvisation of hand-made instruments made with available material. But, these drums have become regularized instruments with time,' said Paul. However, experts noted that instruments like satti-mollom are essential in gaana's music performances, made from a large cooking vessel with animal skin pulled over it.

Gaana is a social performance where the singer invokes emotions, telling us about the dead person by singing praises and narrating the life history of the deceased. According to Tenma, the gaana performers depict the life history, achievements, and nature of the person's death through their performance. The pieces are primarily composed and performed by men at the funeral, the sixteenth-day ceremony, and the first death anniversary. However, according to Tenma, the expanse of the concerts may vary depending on the families' paying capacity.

'There are many gaana forms, but Irangal is the adigaana, a complex form of the original gaana sung at funerals. However, these days there are also comedy funeral singers who change the entire vibe of the occasion,' said Tenma.

I have never had a chance to see a gaana performance, but I can imagine how these concerts may transform the entire vibe of the funerals. In gaana singing, birth and death are conceived as the start of life, highlighted through the vibrant performances, helping the aggrieved relieve the negative emotions surrounding death. According to Paul, the gaana concerts serve various functions at funerals—uplifting the mood, diverting the aggrieved family's attention and aiding in accepting death as the way of life. Furthermore, these performances help keep the family awake while waiting for the arrival of the extended family members—similar to the wakes in other parts of the world.

According to Tenma, gaana singers also sing Ambedkar songs, a social reformer who inspired the Dalit Buddhist movement and campaigned against social discrimination towards the Dalits. Besides, Ambedkar Jayanti (Ambedkar's birthday) is celebrated by all the gaana singers as a prominent event. Moreover, in 2020, the first track of the popular gaana band, The Casteless Collective, 'Jai Bheem Anthem', inspired by Ambedkar, was released on Spotify.

According to Paul, the gaana music scene started changing in the late '70s. Since then, the genre has evolved, with variations in old and new ones. Over the years, gaana has become popular with a rich repertoire of love, devotional, and ceremonial songs now performed at weddings, concerts, funerals, and political rallies. Moreover, some funeral songs also feature in popular Tamil film songs. Contemporary gaana bands are also experimenting with new audiences while protesting caste discrimination. In 2018, gaana artists came together to form The Casteless Collective music band.

Tenma, recounting the music band's formation, said, 'In 2017, while I was curating and designing Madras Medai, the Tamil indie festival—the filmmaker and Dalit activist Pa Ranjith approached me. He asked me to mentor gaana singers to form a music band. When we began auditions for the band, I saw these kids' determination, talent and passion. So we came together—worked tirelessly, and performed for an audience of 7000 people. At that time, I read an inspiring book and listened to song lyrics that helped me carve the band. It was the need of the hour to change the vibe of the music scene—music is a massive communication tool.' The band is trying to transform the country's music scene, inspiring many others to come forward. According to one of the prominent band members, art is the most effective way of getting into people's minds.

The songs composed by the band reflect caste discrimination and working-class struggles in a spunky rap-like genre called 'conscious rap', curated by mixing the folk music form with contemporary genres.

The Casteless Collective is one of the bands that has risen to fame, finding mainstream success. 'They have performed in India and the Middle East. Besides, gaana has received empathy and support from Malaysian and South African Tamils,' said Paul, elaborating on the band's popularity. Not only this, these artists have used gaana songs to spread awareness of COVID-19 health guidelines in an exciting format.

While major gaana artists are men with songs usually written from a male viewpoint—women gaana artists are slowly gaining recognition. 'In the beginning, girls were not allowed to be part of the funeral performances because it involved overnight singing. Families didn't want to compromise their safety,' said Tenma.

Recently, Isaivani, a woman member of The Casteless Collective, was recognized for her involvement in the genre. Because of her crucial contribution, she bagged the BBC Hundred Women Awards.

The above narrative reveals that music has been an integral part of funerals in Tamil Nadu, associated with Dalits. They performed other functions like burials and cremations at funerals, along with singing and dancing. However, I believe the spirit of these performances is indisputable—celebrating both life and death zealously. Also, since these music folk forms are constantly evolving and touching new heights, we will have to wait and see what the future holds.

19

Grieving Widows in Hindi Cinema

D o words like Abhagan and Kulachini ring a bell? Unfortunately, there is a stereotypical way women are portrayed as widows in Hindi films. Hindi mainstream films depict grief-stricken women mourning their husbands' deaths as abla naaris, wearing white sarees, violently breaking bangles and wailing at their husbands' loss. These scenes accompany women consoling and sometimes condemning the widow for her ill fate and bringing ill fortune to their husbands.

Apart from being divorced from reality, these portrayals don't change the gendered ways we view women. The scenes of the complete transformation of a woman into a white saree devoid of accessories/symbols of married women have dominated the Hindi silver screen for a long time. The yesteryear films like *Prem Rog* and *Sholay* (1975) painted women as dull and depressed figures with no desires, depicting widowhood as her fate after the husband's death. '80s films like *Prem Rog* had a strong caste angle attached—portraying women within the patriarchal set up,' said MK Raghavendra, an Indian film critic and literary scholar. Similarly, the 2000 film *Mohabbatein* showed Preeti Jhangiani's character, Kiran, as a young widow, wearing a white saree.

However, the stereotypical portrayal of death scenes is changing in Hindi cinema over time, albeit slowly. For example, I looked at films like *Pagglait* (Bist 2021) and *Ramprasad Ki Tehrvi* (Pahwa 2020) to understand the change. These films revolve around death—depicting the mourning period drama of thirteen days. However, the two films are a fresh take on women's representation after their husbands' deaths—shattering numerous gender stereotypes.

I was curious how these new-age films are conceived. How has the portrayal of widows changed over time? So I decided to review these from a gender lens.

In a conversation with Umesh Bist, the director-writer of the film *Pagglait*, he passionately discussed the idea behind writing and directing this powerful women-centric picture. 'This film has come out of intensely lived experiences. I was in my first year of college when I lost my uncle—my father's younger brother. That was my first encounter with rituals around death. I saw how my father treated everyone, especially the widowed wife of my uncle. She was not very educated. But instead of providing for her just through his resources, my father encouraged her to earn independently. After getting a job, I saw my aunt transforming into an independent person. I also saw the family's plight changing after she started working. Incidents like these and being surrounded by strong women impacted me deeply—propelling me to write this film,' Bist told me.

Likewise, Seema Pahwa, the director-writer of *Ramprasad ki Tehrvi*, revealed that the script was inspired by the events around the time of her father's death. 'When my father passed away, I closely observed these aspects—I analyzed grief. Then in real-life scenarios, I saw how people behaved during the mourning period—I watched people discussing work assignments at prayer meets. I also realized how the entire event impacted my mother the most. How did it change her life? These questions stayed with me, which later translated into a script. Initially, I visualized myself doing the role of Amma, the protagonist. Later, I directed the film because of how things unfolded,' Pahwa told me.

The film *Ramprasad ki Tehrvi* depicts the family drama around the thirteen-day mourning period of the protagonist's husband, the patriarch of the Bhargava family. During these thirteen days, Amma faced questions like what to do with her life? However, on the fourteenth day, she takes charge of her life. Instead of behaving like an unfortunate woman, she decides to take her husband's legacy of music forward. The film defies patriarchy—where a widow is expected to depend on her children, especially sons, after the husband's demise under normal circumstances. Pahwa candidly told me, 'The idea was not to portray Amma as a pitiful widow. I didn't want to romanticize Amma's vulnerability. On the contrary, it was vital to depict her search for self. Through the film, I wanted Amma to discover herself.'

Umesh Bisht's *Pagglait* is also centred around a widow who paves her path of liberation during the thirteen days of mourning. In *Pagglait*, Sandhya, a young woman whose husband dies five months after their wedding, is not a weeping widow. Instead, one sees her surfing through Facebook and scrolling the condolence messages while trying to make sense of her grief. Sandhya's depiction breaks from the conventional portrayal of widowhood in Bollywood and society, where a window is expected to behave stereotypically (Srivastava 2021).

After her husband's death, Sandhya doesn't succumb to the newly ascribed status of widowhood, where one is expected to give up one's desires. Instead, she is seen thirsting for Pepsi and craving masala chips the day after her husband's death—not repressing her desires (Srivastava 2021).

According to Bist, grieving is such an intimate, personal experience. And yet it has been stereotyped, and one is expected to do certain things while grieving. 'I had some grief-related questions that I addressed through the film *Pagglait*,' Bist told me. *Pagglait* conveys a powerful message that suffering cannot be the same for everyone—each of us deals with it in our unique ways. So Sandhya's approach toward grief is different. She is trying to make sense of her life while understanding her grief.

Furthermore, both films portray women with agency, able to dismantle the existing stereotypes and negotiate their position within the patriarchal structure. In *Pagglait*, Sandhya sets onto a path to discover her identity while living amidst the quirky members of her joint family. Similarly, *Ramprasad ki Tehrvi* portrays Amma as a progressive woman who intends to move on—figuring out her own identity. 'Amma takes charge and decides to take her husband's music legacy forward by converting her haveli into a music school. That becomes a purpose of her life and source of livelihood—making Amma an independent woman,' Pahwa said.

Bist questioned the age-old beliefs surrounding last rites through his protagonist. He explained this candidly, 'In the film, after the members immerse the ashes, the younger son announces, "*humne bhaiya ki asthiyan Gangaji main visarjit kar di ab vo sidha swarg main jainge* (we have immersed the brother's ashes in the Ganga river now he will attain moksha)." When Sandhya finds out that her husband was cheating on her, she asks, "*Ganga maiya kaise maaf kar sakti hai usko—kya Ganga maiya se uski shaadi hui thi?* (How can mother Ganga forgive him when it is me he wronged)." This thought itself is empowering.' He believes his audience will ask these questions once he triggers them through his film.

These films are gaining popularity among the audience who are perhaps tired of watching stereotypical characterization.

Pahwa was hesitant in the beginning. She wasn't sure if she could do justice to the script. But finally, she found producers and received support from her friends, making the film possible. 'Things are changing in the Hindi film industry slowly. Even the audience is becoming more receptive to these ideas. Films inspired by real-life are becoming popular,' she said. 'Isn't it an achievement that people like you are reaching out to me?' she said when I inquired about the film's success.

Even the film *Pagglait* received an overwhelming response. Bist told me, 'Initially, I was hesitant because it was an offbeat idea. I was reluctant to write the screenplay because writing a script requires two dedicated years. I discussed and bounced the idea with the producer. She sounded excited and started sharing her own experiences. There was complete relatability to the story. People loved the movie so much—not only in India but globally. The audience wrote to me from the world over and shared their experiences. I received an overwhelming response. I feel the audience loved the film so much because it was relatable. So many people said, "this is our life playing on the screen."'

The new-age films more realistically represent the family drama in Indian families, not just women. Movies like *Pagglait* and *Ramprasad ki Tehrvi* show what goes on behind the mourning rituals inside the families. Seema said, 'I didn't want to depict characters in black and white. Amma has her flaws, and so do her children.' Seema told me that children confess their parents' inadequacies and realize their flaws.

These films represent how family conflicts come to the fore during unfortunate events like death. During the mourning period, women taunt each other. Men of the family brag and complain. Boys are looking for places to light up a cigarette. These scenes represent the family drama where the scores are settled amidst the performance of last rites and rituals. These films understand the confusing paradoxes of Indian families—where death can be more revealing than life.

The Way Ahead

Cinema is a popular media of mass consumption, which plays a crucial role in moulding opinions, constructing images and reinforcing dominant cultural values (Sibal 2018). We, therefore, need to break away from the stereotypes and portray women as individuals with desires and ambitions. 'I wanted to break away from that stereotypical depiction of women as 'abla naari'. I had some questions that I wanted to address through the film. Amma is real—she has flaws and desires,' said Seema. She feels happy that she could address these questions through her film and thinks that media plays a crucial role in breaking these stereotypes and addressing questions our society cannot answer. Otherwise, we will end up perpetuating these age-old disparities and notions.

Of course, movies can't and shouldn't shy away from depicting social evils, but scriptwriters should avoid depicting cardboard characters. Umesh Bist aptly said, 'I believe it's a circle. For example, in cinema and popular culture, one picks up things one sees happening in society. So writers start writing something they see around them, and the directors recreate that on the screen. So, the same elements are reinforced repeatedly in society when people watch films—a constant cycle repeating. However, cinema needs to break from that cycle.'

Moreover, women in India are not a homogenous group—they belong to different religions, castes, classes and socio-economic statuses with varied aspirations and desires. Therefore, the portrayal must be sensitive to the category they belong to. Ultimately, the women characters should become an agency to dismantle the existing societal stereotypes and negotiate their position within this structure instead of reinforcing them.

20

Gendered Mourning: Rudaalis, Mirasans and Oppari

In the Indian sub-continent, gender and caste determine who performs end-life rituals. As a result, women are traditionally restricted from actively participating in many observances. However, mourning is one domain socially acceptable and ritually confined for women. In his rich ethnographic work, Jonathan Parry writes: 'The legitimate expression of grief is structured by gender' (Parry 1994, 155). Therefore, based on gendered expectations, women are expected to display grief violently, and men are supposed to suppress it in normal circumstances (Parry 1994, 156).

Also, among rural Tamil communities, women must wail—Deces highlights in her book on mourning rituals in rural Tamil Nadu. 'If we don't cry, people will speak badly of us. They'll say, "Look at her, her father-in-law just died and she stands as still as a tree!"' (Deces 2005, 23).

Besides, among the communities in Rajasthan, I had seen how the women came wailing in groups on the way to the deceased's house— their faces covered in long veils. Then, they started to cry in a rhythmic tone as they came closer to the home. On the contrary, I saw men seldom shedding a tear—barring during exceptional situations. I also noticed how men and women sat separately, sometimes in different areas of the living quarters, during the last rites and rituals—a common practice in rural hinterlands.

Of course, these gender differences always exist. However, during these exceptional times, like funerals, the gender differentiation observed in day-to-day life becomes starker (Deces 2005).

Have you heard of the professional mourners singing laments and eulogies at funerals? I was aware of rudaalis in Rajasthan. However, I was oblivious to the mourning professions in other parts of the country. For example, mirasans in Punjab and oppari in Tamil Nadu.

Hiring lower caste communities to perform mourning rituals/ lamentations in India is common. Usually, the women are hired since men are deemed unfit to display raw emotions publicly. However, there is also a class dimension to mourning—the ability to hire wailers or mourners from lower castes depicts the status and material wealth of the deceased in society.

Performing laments for the dead is not exclusive to India—some women served similar functions in Romania, Ireland and Greece. Professional mourning, on the other hand, is an occupation that has its roots in Egyptian, Chinese, Mediterranean and Near Eastern cultures. Professional mourners were known as moirologists and mutes in the past, and they were paid to lament for the bereaved family. However, they were revered in some cultures while reviled in others. Professional mourning, however, is still practised in some Asian countries. In India, these professions are entwined with class, caste, and gender inequality. This section will explain how rudaalis and mirasans performed lamentations in the Indian subcontinent.

I
Rudaalis of Rajasthan

When I was growing up, I watched the film *Rudaali*. I still remember the solid performances and the melodic soundtrack of the film. In rudaali practice, women from the lower castes are hired to mourn the death of upper-caste men—thus expressing the grief of the family members (Das and Nath 2014). The class division in these societies prevented upper-caste members, even women, from displaying grief openly, thus relegating the task of mourning to the low-caste women called rudaalis (see Kundalia 2015).

The tradition came to light with the story *Rudali,* written by the famous Bengali litterateur Mahasweta Devi (Devi 1997). The story highlighted the plight of these women in the system of exploitation and hunger. The life of the rudaali that Devi describes in her account is poverty-ridden—the occupation of mourning filled by the lowest caste women of the poor communities in the backdrop of caste patriarchy.

In the book, there is a heartbreaking scene where the protagonist doesn't have enough wood to cremate her dead husband or money to perform his last rites. Besides, it portrays how the village priest exploits and criticizes Sanichari, the protagonist, for not ritually performing the pind daan of her dead husband. She eventually borrows money of ₹20 from a moneylender leading Sanichari into debt, which she repays by working as a bonded labour in the fields of the caste communities (Devi 1997, 74).

Later, the story was adapted into a famous play in 1992 by Bengali playwright Usha Ganguli (Ganguli 1997). Finally, this powerful story inspired the film, *Rudaali* in 1993, featuring Dimple Kapadia and Rakhi Gulzar as *rudaalis* (Lajmi 1993). The audience and the critics applauded the powerful performances of the characters.

These women captivated the crowds through their skilful acts of lamentation. As per the popular descriptions, the rudaalis dress in black attires and cover their faces with a veil—symbolizing the colour of mourning. Besides, there is a performative aspect to their work with expressions of weeping, wailing and singing praises of the dead. For example, Mahasweta describes it like this—'The randi rudalis surrounded his swollen corpse and started wailing, hitting their heads on the ground' (Devi 1997, 117).

However, the film further builds on this description with added rocking, hair tossing and dance movements matching the region's folk dances, such as Ghoomar performed on festive occasions. Author Nidhi Dugar Kundalia describes similar scenes in her book—'They gasp and cry loudly, tossing their heads back, and wail to the heavens, beating their chests and slapping the ground in front of them. Their veils drop every now and then, exposing their faces and long necks tattooed with traditional symbols. Soon, thick tears start flowing, straining their cheeks, with black kohl, in the process, falling on their odhnis. They don't wipe the tears away, most dry under the hot sun before fresh ones flow down' (Kundalia 2015, 31).

However, the reasons behind women entering this work remain unexplored. The interplay of caste, class and gender dynamics shoves women into this mourning job. For example, in Mahasweta Devi's story, Sanichari, the protagonist, was initially reluctant to join this work. Rooted in convention, she worries about her fellow villagers' reactions (Devi 1997, 92). However, finally, she becomes a rudaali, succumbing to the material constraints and circumstances.

According to author Nidhi Dugar Kundalia, these women came as dowry to serve the upper caste men in the Rajasthani patriarchal setting and live at their mercy for the rest of their lives. 'Apart from serving as concubines for these thakurs, the daoris also doubled as rudaalis, or mourners, for the family in times of death and sickness' (Kundalia 2015, 23).

Frequent changes in urban and rural hinterlands and corresponding changes in meanings attached to funeral ceremonies and mourning have slowly rendered this mourning tradition less popular. At one point, hiring rudaalis for mourning was symbolic of Thakur's (higher caste men) prestige and status. 'Five rupees each extra for the two of you? Money's no problem, Sanichari. My father's cremation and kriya will be the stuff legends are made of. Everyone will talk about it' (Devi 1997, 102). The above excerpt from the story aptly points out how funerals were an occasion to display wealth and power.

Rudaalis perhaps even enjoyed better patronage during those times. 'The way we'll weep and wail. Huzoor, we'll drown out even the chant of Ram's name! For five rupees and rice. At the kriya ceremony, we'll take cloth and food—nothing more, nothing less. And if you need more Rudalis, we'll arrange it. The gomastha would agree to everything. What option did we have? Everyone wanted them after seeing their performance at Bhairab Singh's funeral' (Devi 1997, 96).

With changing times, rudaalis earn a meagre amount of money, some leftover food and other valuables, depending on the family's status and their performance of grief. However, author Kundalia notes that acculturation and automation are gradually eliminating these mourning practices. As a result, these women, caught in the web of patriarchy and caste hierarchy, are slowly pushed to the margins—making it harder to make ends meet (Kundalia 2015, 37).

II
Mirasans: The Women Singers in Punjab

I am a Punjabi, but I was unaware of the culture of mirasans in the region. Not only me but my friends who hail from Punjab are equally ignorant of these mourning traditions. However, while talking to some locals in Punjab, I discovered this culture of singing laments.

I wished my grandparents were alive to share the tales of these women performers—their inputs would have certainly made this section more nuanced, elaborating on how these women became the raunak (gorgeousness) of life cycle rituals. Later, I stumbled upon some literature and a documentary film based on mirasans, which illuminated the likes of me.

In Punjab, the members of the Mirasi community served as skilled musicians and genealogists belonging to the Muslim religion. They performed a function analogous to the *griot* in West Africa or the piper and harpist in Scottish clans in medieval and colonial times. For generations, some served as musicians in the royal palaces, like the Maharajas of Patiala. The group claims their lineage to Baba Mardana—a close associate of Guru Nanak. In addition, the Mirasi caste groups acted as traditional intermediaries for their patrons—exchanging news and arranging alliances (Schreffler 2011, 14-15).

The women from Mirasi communities, called Mirasans, performed as singers at various life cycle rituals—distinguished as professionals in their own right. However, one of the most critical functions of mirasans was to lead the women's songs called alahuṇia—a group mourning that followed a person's death. Alahuṇia/dirge is a style of mourning—a traditional folk lamentation expressing the bereaved's loss and grief. These communities were also called lagi after the customary dues, lag they collected in return for their services (Schreffler 2011, 18).

Being a Muslim community, most Mirasis left East Punjab at Partition. However, some stayed behind and remained attached to their substantial patrons. Their populations are most densely concentrated in Ludhiana, Sangrur and Patiala districts. These areas are closest to the princely states that remained autonomous after 1947. More significantly, they are close to the town of Malerkotla, which is best known as one of the only towns in Punjab with a majority Muslim population (Schreffler 2011, 18).

A documentary film named *Mirasans of Punjab: Born to Sing* is dedicated to the lives of these Mirasi women singers in Punjab (Jhingan 2001). The documentary points out how Mirasans were once essential to the region's cultural and social fabric—deriving power and prestige from their royal patrons.

The film nostalgically explores this unique tradition of Punjab, in which the Mirasans merrily sang ghodis at weddings and performed alahunia at their patron's deaths. Their trained voices are evidence of their skill and heritage—and their bright faces mirror the passion of these artists (Kohli 2016).

Mirasans proudly reminisce their role during their patrons' happy and sad moments in the film: 'This is a hereditary occupation—our ancestors have been doing this for many generations. *Yeh to humare khoon mein hai* (it's in our blood). Our mother, sisters and grandmothers would keep goading us to learn,' said Sugran smilingly, a Mirasan who was connected to the royal family of Patiala. Sugran discusses her role in marriage and birth ceremonies in the film, whereas Mira and Seedo elaborate on their role during funerals.

Mirasans were traditionally called to perform the siyapas—songs accompanying death rituals. 'When we learn about a certain death in our patron's house—we rush to their place. Then, we ask the older women to start singing the mourning songs—following our notes. Initially, we make the women of the household cry and weep. Then, we tell them to calm down. In the end, we ask them to submit to God's will. We start the lament and bring it to an end,' explained Seedo, a Mirasan (Jhingan 2001).

Their work involved invoking emotions by singing dirges and eventually calming the bereaved at the end of the mourning period—aiding in the catharsis of emotions. 'Our job is to tell women to stop crying and help them lighten their hearts. We plead with them to calm down and talk to each other. Otherwise, they would keep crying—not leading to anything,' said Seedo in the film.

Similarly, Surjeet Singh, in his book, describes the performance of Mirasans. 'Among mourners, there are a large number of women wearing white dupattas, wailing and crying and beating their chests and thighs, chanting songs of lamentations. Mourning the dead is a superb ritual performance with the Mirasan leading the mourning, chanting lamentation songs, and other women following her, ranting the sky with their cries and wails. There are all kinds of lamentation songs, full of pain and anguish, lamenting the sad departure of men and women, old and young, composed from one's relationship with the dead. The continuous wailing and crying of women, with chanting lamentation songs, fully involves the members of the families of the dead to the core of their beings, thus resulting in a catharsis of emotions.....' (Surjeet 2016).

However, in recent times, just like rudaalis, these women singers have been pushed to the margins due to changing traditional roles. Mirasis, who occupied a crucial place from singing songs at life-cycle rituals to arranging weddings for their patrons, are now playing a marginal role in these rituals. Because of dwindling patronage, these sought-after performers saw a decline in their fortunes. In addition, these women face problems with rewards from singing at celebrations stopping slowly (Jhingan 2001). The film depicts how with acculturation and diminishing patronage, children of Mirasans struggle to survive in the current times. Without concrete steps to revive these traditions—these would soon become mere history.

III
Oppari from Tamil Nadu

Like rudaali and mirasans, oppari is a tradition of singing to express grief and lament, performed primarily by women from lower caste communities in Tamil Nadu. However, high caste communities also hire oppari singers to sing at their homes during mourning. The performance involves singing, beating the chest and wailing to the sounds of a parai (drum). It is believed that oppari brings out the depth of sorrow—pushing the aggrieved to cry their hearts out (Deces 2005, 1).

I wanted to interview a practising oppari. Since I don't know the Tamil language, I sought someone's help from the Tamil music industry to interview. Without his support, this section would have missed the crucial narrative of an oppari artist.

Muthamma, who is fifty-eight years old, has been performing oppari for the last forty years. A Dalit, hailing from the Kadapakkam village of Thiruvananthapuram district of Tamil Nadu, Muthamma lost her parents at the young age of eight years. After their demise, she migrated to Chennai to live with her relatives. In her initial years in the city, she worked on construction sites. However, when visiting her native village, she observed women singing oppari. She was mesmerized by their singing. Recognizing her talent—they started informally initiating her into this folk tradition. She used to practice oppari while working on the fields, Muthamma developed a keen interest and learned the craft.

While addressing the dead person through oppari performances, the popular expressions are oppari of a wife for her husband—oppari of a daughter for her father—oppari of a mother for her daughter—oppari of a daughter for her mother. Professionals commonly combine these oppari forms in their performances—addressing the deceased alternatively as a father, son, uncle, mother, daughter, and cousin. Besides, the songs are improvised by borrowing words and phrases from other oppari performances (Deces 2005, 29-49).

According to Hemant from the Tamil music industry, 'Oppari is a learned craft—wherein the singers sing praises of the dead person on behalf of the family. However, not everyone can be a talented performer.' This Tamil lament constitutes a particular language—the performers identify the deceased in terms of who they were and what they meant to them. Therefore, the mourning daughter might continue her song by praising her mother for what she did for her. Likewise, a lament for a husband centres around the woman's dread around the social and existential changes she will have to experience as a widow. Since the transition to widowhood is one of the most dramatic events in Tamil society, the women express their pain and suffering through oppari (Deces 2005, 29-49).

Like other communities, in Tamil society, each caste and sex has specific roles and responsibilities at funerals. The gender-based division of funeral roles stems from notions of intrinsic difference between the sexes—men being stronger and women being weaker. Although most of the functions are performed by men—mourning/crying is mainly reserved for women. Based on these expectations, the open display of grief by the men is deemed inappropriate—often interpreted as a sign of weakness. Interestingly even when men perform oppari, it is a performance of women's emotions (Greene 2000).

There is also a caste dimension to oppari—generally reserved for lower-caste communities. For instance, Paul Greene observed opparis predominantly performed by Dalits. In contrast, opparis performed by brahmin women were rare (Greene 2000).

Interestingly, women who are otherwise prevented from publicly expressing their voices communicate themselves through this public ritual. Women's oppari can be seen as a vehicle of their agency. For example, as women perform oppari at the funeral, they express their fears, concerns and suffering. Against this backdrop, singing oppari is viewed as cathartic—an outlet for women to express anguish and agony in an otherwise oppressive society (Greene 2000).

Although oppari is most commonly performed at funerals, it is also staged in other contexts with varied cultural meanings and functions. For example, women perform oppari at home, lamenting their problems and injustices. However, such forms are rare and ritually looked down upon in the community (Greene 2000).

With changing societies and urbanization, collective mourning is becoming scarce, resulting in singing laments dying gradually. According to Isabelle Clark Deces, funeral discourses are waning because gender and social experiences have changed. In addition, her informants mentioned that girls' education and resulting empowerment have slowly made these discourses embedded in gender inequality less attractive (Deces 2005, 165).

When I spoke to Hemant, a musical coordinator from Chennai, he told me, 'Efforts are being made to revive these folk traditions. In 2007, these artists were invited to a music festival called Chennai Sangamam.' He said it was a large annual open Tamil cultural festival to revive the old village art and artists organized in Chennai, covering public places like beaches, parks, corporation grounds, colleges and schools.

Gradually, some artists started showcasing their work at public events. For example, the Delhi-based artist community, Khoj, showcased oppari at an event. Besides, it is interesting to see how these performers entertain and educate the international audience.

For instance, Jayalakshmi Gopalan, an oppari performer, was showcased in Switzerland at the Belluard Bollwerk International Festival (Chandrasekhar 2016).

According to Hemant, some talented and famed artists have even started performing in films and music albums. For example, Muthamma was recently invited to record an oppari performance where she was paid ten thousand rupees for a recording.

Muthamma used to get paid ₹2000 to ₹2500 per funeral performance. But, due to Corona, the mourning performances have become scant—so have been their earnings. Like other folk performers, she finds it challenging to make ends meet in the current scenario.

These funeral performances served a particular purpose. They attracted people to the site of death. And large gatherings attested that the deceased was not alone in the world but rich in social relations. However, it is exciting to see how the style of lamentations overlaps in so many ways despite being performed in different geographical regions of the country. These mourning traditions embedded in caste and class hierarchy may become history with changing times.

21

When There is No One to Conduct the Last Rites: Funerals of Unclaimed Bodies

This section is about the unclaimed bodies that pile up in the mortuaries without anyone to care for them. These bodies belong to people who lose their lives in accidents or are pilgrims, migrants and abandoned older people who die away from home. Other than these, some impoverished patients leave this world in hospitals without anyone to conduct their funerals.

But what happens to these corpses? Who conducts their last rites? These are the compelling questions with which I started researching this section.

Till the 1990s, many districts in India didn't even have a mortuary facility. As a result, it was standard to get rid of unclaimed bodies quickly. However, these days, most corpses are cremated or buried after getting a nod from the investigating officer.

'Usually, the unclaimed bodies are kept in a morgue of the government hospital for seventy-two hours during the investigation. Subsequently, if there is no claimant, it is handed over to the police,' confirmed an NGO worker.

As soon as the police gets information about any unidentified dead body, the Thana in charge immediately deputes an officer to file the panchnama—the inquest. Based on the injury marks found during inquest, a police officer ascertains whether it's a case of a suicide or a murder. Followed by this, they send the body for post-mortem. Then, if a suicide case is confirmed—the case is filed under an Unnatural Death (UD) case number. But, for a murder case, FIR under section 302 of Indian Penal Code (IPC) is filed. However, after the postmortem, they wait for seventy-two hours. Then, in the interim, they try to gather information about the body within and around the neighbouring districts. Then, suppose they don't receive any updates within seventy-two hours, and there are no claimants, then, after conducting the proper documentation work—like taking pictures and seizing the clothes and the other belongings, they go ahead with the funeral.

The authorities try to identify the belief and follow the last rites accordingly. But, if the faith is unidentifiable, they usually cremate the bodies by handing them over to the Doms who perform the last rituals from the police department's designated funds.

I also spoke to the funeral staff to understand how these unknown corpses are cremated.

'Police authorities bring the lapata (unclaimed bodies). But, since we do not know these people's religion or the gotra—we pile them together on one stretcher and push them into the CNG furnaces without reciting any mantras. Sometimes we cremate two-three bodies together. In the end, we immerse the ashes in the Yamuna,' a funeral worker from the Nigambodh crematorium confirmed. However, a pandit in Varanasi told me that they take the name of Brahma,

Vishnu, and Mahesh if they are unaware of the gotra of the deceased and cremate the body.

Since it is considered virtuous to conduct the last rites of unclaimed bodies, Kabristan committees perform the rituals respectfully. 'We receive unclaimed bodies in this kabristan. So we perform their mitti (funeral) as per Muslim religion free of charge,' said Jawadul Hasan, a kabristan committee president.

However, besides police authorities, individuals and the Non-Government-Organizations (NGOs) also support performing a dignified funeral of the unidentified bodies.

'The department has limitations too. Sometimes, they don't have an ambulance service, and funds are limited. Then they seek our help, and we assist the police authorities wherever needed. For instance during Covid we had permanently stationed one ambulance at Delhi AIIMS hospital to transfer the bodies to the crematoriums,' said Veena Mehra from The Earth Saviours Foundation, an NGO in Gurugram.

In Cuttack, Orissa, Sabitri Jana Seva Health Helpline volunteers perform funerals of unacclaimed bodies. The organization has been doing the last rites with the local police authorities for many years. Since he was a little boy, the founder secretary of the organization, Bibhuti Kumar Ray, has been involved in social work. 'Sometimes, we find bodies of suicide victims floating in the water. Then there are unidentified bodies in the hospitals with no claimants,' he explained. So his organization handed over the bodies for cremation seventy-two hours after the postmortem.

Likewise, a non-profit organization, The Earth Saviours Foundation (TESF), is involved in cremating the unidentified bodies in Gurugram. Their project, Karmic Seva, aims at ritually cremating unclaimed and unidentified dead bodies, ensuring dignified last rites.

'These departed souls don't have a family to care for their last rites. So late Ravi Kalra, our founder member, started providing a respectful farewell focusing on environmentally friendly cremations,' Veena Mehra told me.

With the police authorities' help, the organization brings hundreds of dead bodies to the cremation centres and performs their last rites with the utmost respect. 'Police contact us, and we assist them financially and logistically in the last rituals of abandoned and poor deceased individuals,' she told me.

Not just the organizations, sometimes individuals also take up this daunting task. For instance, Jai Prakash, fondly known as Kalu Bhagat, from Dehradun, has been doing this extraordinary work for the last four decades. What started as respectfully performing the funerals for the departed became his life mission. For him, it was painful to see someone not getting the proper last rites, disrespecting an individual's soul. So in the previous forty years, he has performed the last rites for 2000 unclaimed bodies. Besides, caste, religion, or other socio-economic rigidities are no bar for him.

After the post-mortem, the body is handed over to the organizations for final rites—it's not simple. Bibhuti told me they sometimes have to use handkerchiefs to lift corpses without any safety equipment to handle the bodies. In addition, he said, there are times when refrigeration is faulty and the corpse starts to decompose, emitting a foul smell. Moreover, he feels disappointed that sometimes things get derailed because of administrative lapses. Nevertheless, he still believes in serving humanity.

Sometimes finding space in the graveyards or kabristan is tedious without identity proof. Moreover, the organizations have to seek written permission from the underprivileged families before conducting the final rites of their members. 'Our focus is ritually performing the last rituals of the deceased, like saying prayers. We also carry the flowers along,' Veena told me.

She recounted how sometimes, the bodies are in bad shape, disfigured or rotten. She recalled a twenty-four-year-old HIV patient from Uganda whose body rotted in the mortuary for over a year because of the delayed correspondence between the embassies. In the end, they received a permission letter to conduct the last rites of the lady. 'It was in a terrible shape—body *gal gayi thi* (it had started decomposing),' she remembered.

Even during the second wave of the pandemic, these organizations conducted the last rituals of unclaimed Covid patients' bodies. Sabitri Jana Seva Health Helpline volunteers were actively involved in completing the final ceremonies of the deceased during the Covid and cyclones in Orissa.

These organizations claim to perform the final rites for people as though they are their family members, irrespective of caste and religion. 'I don't differentiate between people. In the end, we are all humans,' said Bibhuti while quickly narrating the end-of-life ritual practices of other religions when I enquired.

Hats off to the souls passionately involved in giving a decent funeral to these unidentified bodies without expecting anything. Their unmatchable passion for serving humanity is indeed commendable. Bibhuti told me, 'Madam, there is so much that I want to do. I want to make the life of people better in both worlds.'

22

Deaths During the Pandemic: Challenges and Learnings

I
Introduction

Throughout history, intermittent outbreaks of infectious diseases with pandemic potential have wreaked havoc on human societies, causing long-term consequences that can last for centuries. These outbreaks have reshaped the socioeconomic, political, religious and cultural aspects of human civilization. Over the last two centuries, India has seen many devastating epidemics, including cholera in 1817, bubonic plague in 1896, and influenza in 1918.

Vaclav Smil, in his book, *Global Catastrophes and Trends*, argued: 'Modern hygiene, nationwide inoculation, constant monitoring of infectious outbreaks, and emergency vaccinations have eliminated or drastically reduced a number of previously lethal, deeply injurious, or widely discomforting epidemic diseases, including cholera, diphtheria pertussis, polio, smallpox, tuberculosis, and typhoid (Smil 2008).' However, according to him, the victory is not permanent. Despite medical advances, we found ourselves faced with a pandemic again.

Any natural outbreak throws numerous challenges on society ranging from medical, cultural, economic and social. It compels scientists and public health specialists to understand the transmission pathway of the novel pathogen, identify high-risk groups and design adequate measures and steps to contain the spread of infection.

However, despite best efforts to control a pandemic, the cases grow exponentially over weeks and months, leading to shortages of medical supplies, and personnel and conventional spaces for storage of the deceased, raising additional public health concerns. Furthermore, with an increase in fatalities, people across geographies face problems managing the dead, like lack of places to bury and absence of death care personnel.

Another big challenge is not performing the last rites according to deeply held customs and traditions amidst restrictions and coping with the unprecedented departure of loved ones—causing enormous distress and exacerbating the grief of the bereaved.

I started working on this book right after the devastating second wave in India. The idea was to capture the struggles of people involved in death care work and the aggrieved families' sentiments before it is forgotten. The personal stories and narratives featured here are very close to me, shared passionately by people impacted by the tragedy. But, more compelling was to document the humane work that happened amidst the apda (catastrophe)—how good samaritans came forward, risking their own lives to save humanity. Apda is the word many people I spoke to used to describe the catastrophe.

II
Challenges in Managing the Dead—Indian Scenario

'*Aisa time to Bhagwan kisi ko na dikhaye* (I hope no one has to witness such horrid scenes),' said a death worker at Nigambodh Ghat.

Pandemics evolve and come in multiple waves overwhelming local resources and capabilities. During deadly Covid-19 waves, we heard horror stories of medical staff shortages, essential supplies deficiencies and the scarcity of death care personnel. Along with this, funeral spaces shrank. Besides, due to the higher death fatality during the ongoing pandemic, managing dead bodies and administering the proper last rites for the deceased became a source of concern across the globe.

In India, the enormous death toll and lack of preparedness led to the mishandling of the dead bodies, denying dignified last rites to the deceased. As a result, corpses were decaying in the hospitals without proper storage and transportation facilities.

I spoke to various volunteers, death care staff and pandits after the deadly second wave to better understand the situation. Nilesh Dhayarkar, a social worker from Pune, told me, 'Many unclaimed dead bodies were rotting in Sassoon Hospital in Pune. The bodies would stink. It was unbearable. Besides, the paperwork to release them was taking a very long time. Moreover, the family members were clueless about the procedure. Some had to wait for hours before they collected the dead bodies of their loved ones.'

There were instances where the dead bodies were lying in homes without transportation and funeral facilities. Moreover, during the second wave, the spaces to cremate the dead had shrunk, due to which the bodies were piling up faster than workers could cremate/bury. Besides, there were reports regarding scarcity of resources to cremate the dead. Furthermore, in many places, the stock of firewood was running low.

Many people even took advantage of the situation, like overcharging money for the ambulance service from the families, an NGO staff told me. 'Many shamshans faced a scarcity of wood—the black market was prevailing. So to curb the situation, the government fixed the rates. Finally, however, we had enough stocks,' said Sultan Singh, in charge of the Panchkuian Road crematorium in Delhi.

Across India, there were designated shamshans for conducting Covid funerals. For instance, in Delhi, there were ten such crematoriums. Although the families were issued tokens to streamline the process as soon they arrived, there was still chaos.

Sultan Singh described the scene, 'I have worked here for eighteen years. But I have never witnessed such frightful scenes in my lifetime— bodies stacked up since morning with family members queuing outside. Sometimes we had to refuse the cremations and shut the gates. What could we do? The capacity is to cremate twenty bodies, but we managed over fifty daily.'

The scenes were no different in non-metro cities. Laalu Chaudhury, who works at the Harishchandra crematorium in Varanasi, said, 'There were many bodies to cremate. Since the death toll was high, the queues were long. Besides, there are only two active furnaces. I was overworked because I was the only one well-versed with the workings of the machines. However, there was no shortage of staff in Varanasi. Because the unemployment was high during lockdowns, people were willing to do any work, even the cremation work.'

The scene was no different at kabristans. 'The main challenge we faced during the second pandemic wave was the shortage of space as the graveyard spaces are shrinking due to the heavy encroachment on graveyard lands. The other challenge was the scarcity of trained staff to manage the burial of Covid-related deaths,' said Mehfooz Mohammad, section officer at Delhi Wakf Board.

'I have never seen so much khauf (fear) among people. Since people were scared to touch their family members, we had to employ extra staff to dig the graves and assist the families. In order to ease the process, we had divided the kabristan for Covid and non-Covid burials,' said Jawadul Hasan, a kabristan committee president.

Due to high demand during the second wave, some crematoriums expanded their facilities. As a result, many parks and open spaces were converted into makeshift crematoriums.

For instance, the Seemapuri crematorium in Delhi expanded into its parking lot, where workers constructed cremation platforms using bricks and mortar. When I visited these sites, I saw these makeshift cremation platforms in Nigambodh Ghat and Green Park crematorium.

'We can conduct 215 cremations in a day at Nigambodh Ghat. Therefore, we segregated the ghat for Covid and Non-Covid deaths with separate entry gates. Since there was a shortage of pyres, we constructed additional thirty-five to forty platforms to accommodate the open-air pyre cremations—which were also not sufficient,' said Avdhesh Sharma, the supervisor of Nigambodh Ghat.

Even staff was scarce. Sometimes workers wanted to quit because they were burnt out. It was a tough for the supervisors to keep the team motivated. Like Sharma from Nigambodh Ghat said, 'Especially during the second wave, people were not ready to work. They were overworked. By evening workers said, 'We want to go home. We can't manage this anymore.'

Due to scarcity of space and resources, there were instances when bodies were dumped in the Ganga river in Bihar and Uttar Pradesh, while others were buried in the sand. There were many cases where the departed were denied a dignified death due to the fear and stigma attached to coronavirus. During the first wave, I heard stories where the staff was scared of touching the corpse because of the fear of the unknown.

This is not a phenomenon new to the human race. Humankind has witnessed such frightful scenes in history as well. Arnold's extensive work on the history of funerals in India reveals more: 'During famines and epidemics, when firewood was scarce and the number of dead immense, or even in more normal times when cremation costs were too high for the poor to afford, bodies might simply be dumped in rivers or abandoned on their banks' (Arnold 2017, 397).

As dignity and respect for the individuals and their families are two essential aspects of death across all cultures, concerns were raised by international bodies and human rights groups regarding the violation of these rights during the second pandemic wave in India. Responding to these violations regarding the mishandling of bodies, the National Human Rights Commission (NHRC) issued an advisory to the central and state governments, instructing the protection of the dignity and rights of the dead (NHRC 2021). Besides, it underscored that the bodies should not be piled up during transportation or at any other point. Furthermore, the advisory disallowed mass burials or cremations that violated the right to dignity of the dead. Moreover, it even instructed the state authorities to pay attention to the deceased and missing persons. Again, looking at the dismal situation, even the Supreme Court of India directed the government to properly manage the unclaimed dead bodies found in public places.

III
Safety of the Death Care Staff—Issues and Challenges

During epidemics and devastations due to natural disasters, the work of managing death comes to the centrestage. But, more so, the people involved in the dead disposal come to the centre.

There was a workforce shortage at several crematoria and burial grounds in the country, leading to a higher burden on the limited death staff. Therefore, I decided to interview those warriors who worked tirelessly during the second wave, risking their own lives. In this subsection, I elucidate the struggles of the superheroes who fearlessly contributed during the pandemic.

During the second wave of Covid, the death load was exceptionally high. Rajesh, a staff member at a crematorium in Delhi, recounted the scenes. He said, 'We worked day and night. It was a tough time. Sometimes, families had to wait for hours for their turn. We generally received four to five bodies daily, while sixty-seventy bodies were cremated during the Covid second wave. We were working nonstop from 6 a.m. to 12 p.m. There was no time to breathe. We fought like an Army fight on the battlefield.' I found it very interesting how the workers took pride in working like a military force.

Similar stories were shared by workers and staff of other crematoriums. 'We worked overtime from six in the morning to six in the evening during those days. Some staff members didn't even go home—they served here day and night. But, we did everything from a distance—we were also concerned about our safety,' said a funeral pandit from Green Park crematorium.

Moreover, there was widespread reporting on the overburdening of the crematorium staff during the pandemic. The death-care team struggled hard to maintain sanity while witnessing the tragedy day in and day out. Therefore, human rights groups raised concerns about these workers' mental health. As a result, the NHRC issued an advisory for the staff's safety. It mentioned that since the team at crematoria, burial grounds and mortuaries were working round the clock during this pandemic wave, they must be paid fair wages to compensate for their hard work. Besides, they should be vaccinated on a priority basis, considering the risk they are exposed to (NHRC 2021).

Some funeral places pushed hard to arrange for fair remuneration for the staff. 'One needs encouragement, honesty and courage during these situations. The workers were working overtime. So I informed the family members to pay extra money for their khidmat (assistance). They were the ones handling the corpse. Who will look after the families if something goes wrong? Besides, we made sure that the staff wore safety equipment,' said Jawadul Hasan, a kabristan committee president.

However, many worked without fair compensation. But, challanges of death care staff is nothing new. During past epidemics, official archival reports on mortuary workers revealed the state's dependency and neglect. For example, in the 1860s, during the cholera epidemic, the Calcutta municipality expected the mortuary workers to work overtime to dispose of the bodies of cholera victims without any additional compensation. But, Calcutta's workers engaged in death care work refused to work until their salaries were raised (Chattopadhyay 2020).

There were similar instances during the bubonic plague epidemic at the turn of the 19th century. Again, the buriers in present-day Latur refused to dig graves, complaining of the increased number of bodies due to the plague. Again, however, colonial sources were vague on whether local municipalities provided safety equipment to the workers (Chattopadhyay 2020).

Like other times, during the recent pandemic, despite the challenges, the death care staff worked day and night diligently, considering it their moral responsibility. I spoke to the supervisors of two crematoriums to understand the challenges. For instance, In charge of the Panchkuian Road crematorium in Delhi, Sultan Singh closely supervised funeral work during Covid, handling dead bodies for the past eighteen years. He narrated terrifying scenes when I spoke to him after the second wave in India. 'Those twenty days were terrible—we were sleep-deprived and overworked. Being the manager, I had to oversee everything. *Din-raat ka chain nahin tha* (I did not have a moment's respite). My phone was ringing off the hook—I would receive frantic calls in the middle of the night from bereaved families requesting the funeral of their loved ones. Besides, I got requests from ministers and senior administrative officers—I had to oblige. But, despite the pressure, I never turned my face from the responsibility. If God has chosen me to fulfil this task, I must perform it well. In many instances, I even conducted the cremations of poor people and unclaimed bodies (*jinka koi nahin hota*) free of charge,' said Singh. This is the spirit with which the staff worked.

Nigambodh Ghat, the largest ghat in Delhi, was particularly crowded during the second pandemic wave. There were many problems that the staff faced. Avdhesh Sharma said:

> The challenges were different during the second wave—we were under tremendous pressure. I contributed fifteen to seventeen hours daily in April and May of 2021. *Pata nahin kahan se itni himmat aa gayi* ? (I don't know where all the strength came from?). The bereaved were completely harried—pushing us to work faster. These things can't be done in haste. Bodies kept coming, and sometimes we had to shut the gates. The staff would get tired by evening and leave. Then maali (gardeners) and safai karamchari had to pitch in. It was getting impossible for us. Therefore, on my request, the authorities redirected the load to other crematoriums.

While the staff members were working tirelessly, there was a risk of contracting the virus. Besides, during the first wave, knowledge about handling the dead safely was minimal. Therefore, in some instances, the safety of the staff's family members was compromised. 'During the first wave, I contracted Covid. After that, even my family was down with Coronavirus. There was a lack of awareness regarding safety protocols during the first wave—everyone was clueless. As a result, I was down for almost fifteen days,' said Sharma from Nigambodh Ghat.

Since people who deal with dead bodies at higher risk, the World Health Organisation (WHO) recommended the trained staff wear personal protective suits and follow preventive measures while handling dead bodies: 'Personnel should use appropriate PPE (Personal Protective Equipment) including respiratory and eye protection and using the disinfecting solution' (WHO 2020). However, despite these guidelines, there were challenges. For example, there was widespread reportage of how death care workers were denied protective gear. However, there were other problems.

The crematorium sites in Delhi and the rest of the country are mainly managed by Non-Governmental-Organizations. These organizations provided food and safety equipment to the staff members. For instance, the kabristan committee member shared that they arranged personal protective equipment for the burial workers and staff.

However, many reported difficulties using personal protective gear, thus putting them at risk. Many cremation workers could not wear protective suits due to excessive heat around the funeral pyres. 'We were wearing masks and gloves. However, being closer to fire, it was impossible to wear the PPE suits,' said Sharma from Nigambodh Ghat.

'Our sanstha had arranged everything like masks, sanitizers, protective gear. The organization even catered the food to the staff. However, we couldn't wear the protective suit—it would stick to our skin because of heat. Besides, many of us were not immunized. Only 60 per cent of the staff members were immunized against Covid—but none of us contracted Corona by God's grace (*Bhagwan ki kripa se*),' said Singh. However, in most cases, the staff members didn't acquire Covid. The crematorium and kabristan supervisors I spoke to confirmed this.

India's handling of this immediate threat was tenuous—it presented pertinent questions on the authorities' role in effective planning and management during the pandemic. But, the death care staff came to our rescue during the catastrophe, risking their mental and physical well-being. Besides, one overarching theme that guided their work during the apda was the relevance of dharam that kept them going. Unfortunately, however, we continue to ignore their vital contribution. I hope we learn from our mistakes and consider sanitation work crucial.

IV

Good Samaritans: Ensuring a Dignified Send-Off to the Covid Dead

My grandmother used to say, '*Kuch log raab ke bande hote hain jo musibat ke time pe kaam aate hain* (there are some godsend people who come forward to help during the time of need/crisis).' Mummyji's words echoed in my ears while I conducted the interviews with the Covid warriors.

Over the past two years, since the Covid-19 pandemic hit us, several groups had worked tirelessly on the ground. These volunteer groups pitched in where the state found it challenging. The interventions by these individuals and groups included setting up helplines, supporting the death care workers and ensuring dignified last rites to persons succumbing to Coronavirus. Besides, people from diverse religious backgrounds helped cremate or bury the dead respectfully, blurring the binaries of class and religion. How these individuals and organizations worked amidst the raging crisis was awe-inspiring.

Initiatives such as Cremation Project in Pune, assisted hospitals in managing the dead bodies and streamlining the process. 'The death toll in Pune city was enormous, ranging between sixty to hundred and twenty deaths per day—there was chaos. The hospitals were flooded with patients from Pune and adjoining districts. Even the hospital staff was overworked. So, the mayor approached us to extend support. Soon after, a help centre was set up at the city hospital to restructure the process. We hired and trained the team on safety protocols. In the beginning, people were reluctant. However, many young volunteers joined us later,' said Naresh Karpe, leading the project.

Cremation Project supported the families in cremating the deceased when families could not step out of home isolation or were overseas. Besides, there were also times when families were reluctant to step out because of fear. The team members ensured that the corpses were taken quickly to the mortuary and transferred to the crematoriums. The team even assisted in collecting the ashes from the crematorium and delivering them to the respective families. The members worked for eight days and were then sent into quarantine. Ultimately, the government honoured the workers for their crucial contribution during Covid.

The team faced many challenges—there were days when the volunteers cremated thirty to forty bodies daily, witnessing deaths day and night. In most cases, family members were not allowed to accompany the patients. Therefore, the entire burden fell on the volunteers. Besides, sometimes, paperwork took hours. Naresh recounted one instance when a disabled minor from Mumbai succumbed to Covid in Sassoon Hospital, Pune while her family was in Mumbai. Since there was no identification proof, Naresh had to run from pillar to post to get a signed letter from her family to conduct cremation. 'It was a very emotional time for everyone. I can't even describe some moments. However, I can't forget how a seventy-year-old man begged me to cremate his son—it was a touching moment,' Karpe told me.

In Cuttack, Orissa, Sabitri Jana Seva Health Helpline volunteers performed funerals at the Satichaura crematorium. The organization has been involved in fulfilling the last rites of unclaimed bodies, assisting the Commissionerate Police for many years. 'During Covid, many homeless people died due to scarcity of food. So my team members and I performed the last rites of these people,' said the founder secretary of the organization, Bibhuti Kumar Ray.

During the second wave, the volunteers didn't take a break—most of them remained in the crematorium round the clock to cremate the corpses, despite numerous challenges and lack of access to protective gear. 'When the victim's relatives were reluctant to enter the crematorium, fearing the infection, we ensured a dignified farewell to everyone,' Bibhuti said. The members did everything from arranging firewood to managing paperwork and lighting the pyre. The wood had to be appropriately positioned for the cremation. He added that the volunteers even recited mantras for the mukti of the soul in the absence of family members. In the end, the team even collected the asthis of the deceased members. Unfortunately, many families didn't even turn up to claim the remains the following day. 'Not only Hindus, but we even conducted last rites of people from other religious groups like Muslims and Christians—I don't differentiate between people from different faiths,' he said while elaborating on other religions' funerary practices and rituals.

Bibhuti is passionate about his work. I could sense his excitement over the telephonic conversation. Besides, he goes a long way. He has conducted the last rites of unclaimed bodies for many years. Yet, he feels disappointed that sometimes things get derailed because of administrative lapses. Nevertheless, he still believes in serving humanity.

Amongst those helping people say their final farewells were women volunteers from the NGO, Swaroop Wardhinee. Despite the resistance, these women volunteers seamlessly carried out the cremation work. 'In the beginning, only four women joined the team, but slowly, thirty came forward. It was encouraging. Besides, we rejected the patriarchal norms by ensuring women's involvement,' said Nilesh Dhayarkar, a social worker from the NGO.

During Covid, Swaroop Wardhinee registered the dead bodies in a Pune municipal hospital. Dhayarkar told me that there was chaos all around. So, the organization streamlined the entire process from registration to transportation of the bodies. Also, the team assisted families in conducting the last rites ritually, according to Hindu traditions. The volunteers even provided psychological support to the bereaved. 'The families were broken. But, the team helped the bereaved overcome the grief to some extent—they were contented in the end that their loved ones were respectfully cremated,' said Nilesh. Besides, when the entire family was Covid-infected, the organization even delivered the ashes to their doorstep.

Amid the catastrophic wave of Covid, United Sikhs, a United Nations-affiliated human rights and advocacy organization, helped people cremate their loved ones with dignity in India's capital. United Sikhs was the last resort for the families after calls to the local authorities and hospitals for ambulances went unanswered. The organization initially supplied food to the hospitals, arranged langar for the migrant workers, and sanitized the churches and Jama Masjid in Delhi. Unfortunately, three team members got infected by the deadly virus during the first wave. But the work continued. The team took on cremating the Covid-dead when others were reluctant. When I spoke to Pritam Singh, the director of United Sikhs, he had something interesting to share. 'During the first wave, while recovering from Covid, I received a call from Fateh Nagar in Delhi. A man had passed away ten hours ago, and no one was willing to collect the body for cremation. Unfortunately, we had no means to collect and transport the dead either. We felt helpless. At that point, a volunteer, Manjeet Singh, decided to convert his car into a makeshift ambulance, and our journey began. After converting the car, we collected and cremated the deceased person, following the Covid protocols,' he said.

After that, there was no stopping—the families who lost family members to Covid-19 contacted United Sikhs. 'Our contact number circulated across the hospitals and crematoriums, and we continuously received calls from families. Initially, it was challenging since the team had to single-handedly manage everything like wrapping, transporting and ritually cremating the bodies. However, later it became manageable with more hands joining. I remember one day we cremated twenty-two bodies in a day during the second wave of Covid. It was terrible. Besides not just Hindus and Sikhs, we were also approached by Christian and Muslim families. Although, initially, we were clueless about the funeral rites of other religions—we eventually figured out everything. We helped families in distress irrespective of their faith and caste—ensuring respectful funerals based on their religion. Not only this, but we also offered financial assistance to the needy,' said Pritam Singh.

The families who approached United Sikhs could not arrange for a funeral because they were sick, afraid or too weak to leave their homes. Yet, despite many challenges, the team managed to perform the last rites of more than three hundred and fifty individuals succumbing to the deadly virus. In the end, they were assisted by twenty-two team members covering three shamshans of Delhi.

He narrated one challenging instance when the team had to carry a heavyweight body from the third floor without an elevator, wearing PPE suits. 'Cremating the dead while wearing PPE suits is tough, especially when the temperatures rise and summers are setting in. The team members were breathless and faintish. Yet, the courage and inspiration from within kept guiding us,' he said.

Can any of us think of doing this in the scorching sun wearing PPE suits? When I inquired about his motivation, he said something profound, 'During Harmandir Sahib's construction, Punjab faced an epidemic. Subsequently, guru sahib halted the construction and diverted the funds to relief work. I feel the teachings of the Sikh gurus steered us all along—our gurus taught us to contribute selflessly towards humanity.'

It was reassuring to hear such stories during these dark times. Besides, the surroundings would have been a breeding ground for infection without their crucial contribution. Yet, before talking to these people, I wondered what kept them going. Finally, however,

I realized the deep desire to help humanity was something that motivated them.

V
Funeral and Post-Funeral Practices During the Pandemic: Challenges

Funeral practices vary widely between groups across geographies. During the pandemic, different faith and cultural groups have been affected by current restrictions. For example, washing the body of the deceased—an essential ritual in Islam, Zoroastrianism, Hinduism and Sikhism—was restricted in India. While I feel every individual will be affected differently by restrictions on their mourning process, these losses are a source of communal and individual distress.

While talking to a Sikh Granthi, he said something profound, 'The rituals don't matter during an apda. The scale of deaths is huge, and it's impossible to perform the last rites and rituals as per the scriptures. So instead, one should just recite Ardas in the name of the dead.' Through this conversation, I understood how the meanings attached to last rites change during a catastrophe. What matters is giving a respectful send-off to the deceased members, even if that means just saying prayers for the departed souls. In the next part, based on my conversations with the ritual specialists and staff, I discuss how we had to forgo the funeral rituals based on deeply held customs and beliefs.

1.   The Hindu Tradition

According to Hindu tradition, one must follow elaborate funeral ceremonies to attain moksha. Death is the last sanskaar of all the life cycle rituals among Hindus. While elaborating on the pre-cremation rituals that Hindus follow after the death of their loved ones, Parry writes: 'When a person expires, the corpse must be washed, anointed with ghee, wrapped in a white cloth, perfumed and decked with garlands. A piece of gold should be placed into the mouth and nostrils through which the body may be worshipped' (Parry 2014). Besides, Hindus worship the deceased before cremation, called 'shava pujan'. However, the pandemic changed the meanings of the customs and rituals prescribed in Hindu scriptures. Many who witnessed their loved ones going would agree.

Besides, the Hindu religion distinguishes between a good death and a bad one. According to scriptures, death on a purified ground and cremation of the body done in the open air near a riverbank is believed to be good. In addition, hearing or chanting the name of God at the time of his death is considered a good death as per Hindu scriptures. On the other hand, a bad death is commonly expressed as untimely where the deceased could not prepare themselves for death. For instance, the passing away caused by violence, accidents, epidemics or chronic illnesses are categorized as bad (Parry 2014, 163).

According to the categorization, pandemic deaths would fall under the above category—denied a ceremonial death due to the infectious nature of the virus and the constraints in performing the end-life rituals. Furthermore, there are mandatory guidelines issued by the government and international bodies to control the pandemic. For instance, the World Health Organisation (WHO) recommends wrapping the corpses in leak-proof plastic body bags and advises against washing or embalming the bodies. As a result, many crucial cremation rituals like site purification, ritual bath, kapal-kriya, and appropriate recital of mantras had to be compromised. Moreover, the families had to forgo many post-cremation rituals like pind daan and asthi visarjan.

The antim yatra to the crematorium is considered a critical end-of-life ritual we had to sacrifice. In Hindu tradition, the loved ones carry the bier to the crematorium, accompanied by neighbours and friends. During the pandemic, I learned that even though ten people were permitted to accompany the dead, two or three people came forward because of the scare of spreading infection. And in some cases, none.

In many instances, I found how staff members were shocked at the families' apathy during the Covid pandemic. A crematorium-in-charge had something interesting to share. 'Madam, rituals lost their meaning during Covid. Due to the pandemic, the highly respectful ceremony of cremating the deceased member changed. The family members insisted that the staff members or volunteers complete the cremation (*tum hi kar do sanskaar*) because of the fear of contracting the infection. There are instances where members even refused to enter the crematorium. Instead, they waited in the parking areas,' added Sultan Singh.

Similarly, Avdhesh Sharma, a supervisor at Nigam Bodh Ghat, said that the cremations previously performed with utmost respect became a burden for many families during the pandemic. *'Pehle insaan kandhe par aata tha* (the deceased was once carried on the shoulders). During Covid, the corpses came wrapped in white plastic sacks instead of kafan. Furthermore, the plastic-wrapped bodies were lifted straight from the ambulances and placed on the pyre—the arthi was missing. The only recognition of the person was the labels—their lone identity,' he said. Bound by the government protocols, the staff had to sacrifice many rituals.

Some of them reported how everything was done in haste. The workers compared the cremations done in normal circumstances to those during the pandemic. 'We conducted over 200 funerals daily during the second wave, so things were hurried up. Earlier, cremations were performed with vidhi-vidhan (ceremonially)—the dead bodies were given a ritual bath. Besides, the family could touch the person's feet and face—put honey or sesame seeds in the deceased's mouth during the ceremony. Whereas during Covid, all one could do was sprinkle the ghee and recite mantras in the name of tradition,' said Ramesh, a funeral pandit.

Even bereaved family members were not permitted the deceased's darshan (auspicious viewing), considered crucial during Hindu last rites. So the rituals that help provide much-needed closure to the family members had to be sacrificed. 'Since there was a scare of spreading infection, we had to be careful—what if the family member got bhavuk (emotional) and touched the dead person's face during the darshan? Then we will be blamed,' said Avdhesh Sharma.

During the second wave, there was a severe staff shortage. Sometimes, other staff members doubled as pandits in reciting mantras—the ritual usually confined to a funeral priest. However, many things were done differently during Covid. For instance, in Pune, hospitals permitted the family members to perform rituals like reciting mantras and flower arpan before leaving the hospital premises. 'Once the body reached the site, there was no time to do anything. The queues were long—the staff issued tokens to the families to ease the load,' said Naresh Karpe during a conversation.

While some families were fine missing the rituals, others relied on online mediums like Zoom to perform the end-of-life rituals. 'We had circulated the copy of mantras for antim sanskaar, making it accessible for the funeral staff and the family members. However, in some instances, I recited the *dah sanskaar mantras* online on the families' insistence,' said Dr Manisha Shete, a practising Hindu priest.

Among Hindus, the post-cremation rituals are equally important. However, in many cases, families had to forgo these rituals. But, some insisted on performing the post-funeral rites like the shraddh ceremony online. Initially, there were hiccups, but the pandits soon learned the new skill amidst the catastrophe. While talking to Dr Manisha Shete, she recounted, 'Online sanskaar became very common during the pandemic. However, we informed the families that certain post-cremation rituals could be postponed. But, some insisted, so we proceeded with the online mode like Zoom. Initially, I wasn't very well-versed with these mediums myself—I had to learn to use them. Moreover, there was hesitation—even the families weren't confident about the online mode. For instance, there were concerns like: what if a network glitch interrupts the ceremony? So we had to assure them and acquaint them with the online mode. In the end, I conducted 150 ceremonies online during the pandemic lockdowns. Later, as things eased, we reverted to the physical rituals while following the restrictions and precautions.'

While talking to other pandits, I learned about other issues. For example, some said that they had to cut short the rituals. For example, some sanskars spread over three days had to be wrapped up in just one day. In addition, sometimes, the samagri wasn't available due to Covid-induced lockdowns—so they had to look for alternatives.

Another crucial aspect of Hindu funerals is immersing ashes in the flowing river. The families were told to collect the remains the following day. However, Singh said that some didn't turn up to collect the asthi due to quarantine and fear. So the management had to arrange for the asthi visarjan in the holy river. According to Sharma, a bus leaves every month on the purnima (full moon) for asthi visarjan of the abandoned ashes at Haridwar, the holy city for Hindus. During Covid, however, the remains were immersed in the Yamuna river. But, people managed to visit Haridwar by getting the special passes issued in exceptional cases.

During those unprecedented times, what was essential is to perform the last rites and ensure respectful goodbyes than elaborate rituals.

2.   The Islamic Tradition

Some kabristans were busier during the pandemic compared to others. However, a Maulana, who supervises a kabristan in Uttar Pradesh said they were well-prepared for the emergency. According to him, they didn't receive many bodies due to the smaller Muslim population in the city.

He said, discussing the preparations, 'We couldn't have delayed the funerals since there was a scare of spreading the infection. Therefore, we had kept ready two to four kabrs and kafans. Moreover, we had staffed three to four extra labourers who handled the bodies. We usually don't dig the graves beforehand, but we were helpless during the apda. Furthermore, I kept my phone switched on, anticipating an emergency. Since this is a government kabristan, we often receive unidentified bodies. However, I usually start the arrangements only after receiving a call from the police department. It was different during the pandemic.'

Some followed the pandemic guidelines, and others questioned the pre-preparations based on the scriptural prescriptions. There was a dilemma in forgoing the ritual prescriptions. 'In the beginning, we kept the kabr ready beforehand. Then we questioned ourselves—*hum kahin gunhegaar to nahin ho rahe* (are we becoming sinners)? Therefore, we followed the standard procedure after a few days. But we were digging the graves deeper than the usual for safety,' recounted Jawadul.

Just like other times, the work divisions were clearly defined. For example, labour handled the corpses by lifting them from the ambulances and laying them in the graves, whereas he looked after the ceremonial part. 'I am the supervisor, and, therefore, I kept away from touching the bodies. That's not my job,' Maulana insisted.

Due to Covid-related restrictions, the families had to forgo some rituals. For instance, washing the body is a vital death ritual that had to be skipped. Usually, the body is first washed clean of all impurities, especially those that typically nullify prayers. 'We followed the rest of the rites appropriately. But unfortunately, giving a ghusl wasn't permissible, so we had to skip that. What to do? We had to follow the guidelines. Even the viewing of the body was forbidden during the pandemic. However, some families insisted on viewing the body—I didn't stop them. It was their decision, after all,' recounted a supervisor. Similarly, Jawadul said that some families begged the didaar of their deceased members, so we permitted.

Other rituals like shrouding and funeral procession were missed in the wake of the Covid protocols. Furthermore, during the pandemic, the staff saw a lack of community support and apathy because of the scare of infection. Close family members came forward to support the bier, while the rest were reluctant to help. 'In usual times when one hosts a funeral feast, many people join the funeral procession, but during these troubled times, no one was forthcoming. Some people could have at least entered the kabristan and paid their last tributes while following the protocols. But, unfortunately, there were instances where both the parents went away—and no one else was available to honour the deceased except the son. I understand large gatherings were not permitted, but some could still join. I was managing the show here, but by Allah's grace, no one contracted Covid,' he recalled. Similarly, Jawadul recalled instances where sons hesitated to honour their dead parents. He said, '*Beta baap ko kabr main utarne se dar raha tha* (even the son was hesitant in performing the rituals*)*. Some would stand and wait outside.'

3. The Parsi Tradition

During the pandemic, the Parsi community had to forgo their traditional laying of dead at the Towers of Silence. Instead, the government guidelines only permitted the burial or cremation of the dead. Therefore the gates of Doongerwadi in Mumbai and other cities were closed for funerals.

'I had performed four to five funerals in a day during the second wave without carrying the body inside the prayer hall. Instead, the deceased body remained inside the ambulance—we said the funeral prayers outside the vehicle. Afterwards, we carefully carried the deceased for the cremation without touching or opening the wrapped body. At Doongerwadi, we need to perform elaborate rituals like bathing the body, which can lead to the infection spreading,' recounted Framroze Mirza, one of the only Parsi priest priests assisting the families in conducting the funeral rites for the Covid victims. However, it must have been difficult for the Parsi community to forgo their age-old tradition of sky burials based on ancient scriptures.

There are deeper meanings attached to last rites and rituals, which we had to forgo because of Covid protocols. However, we missed human touch the most—giving a ritual bath, combing the hair one last time, tying a sacred thread, or giving that last hug. But, more than anything else, the absence of distant or sick family members and the lack of collective mourning during the pandemic left the bereaved confused, helpless and guilty. However, unlike other outbreaks, technology bridged the gap to some extent—if not physically, but the families could at least be part of the rituals virtually.

VI
Women Volunteers Performing the Pandemic Funerals: Breaking Gender Stereotypes

A crematorium is an inauspicious place, and even though women are not expressly banned from attending funerals, they have always been discouraged from being present during the cremations. The explanation is that women are perceived as softer and weaker and may get traumatized seeing the death rituals.

But during the pandemic, let alone entering the crematoriums, women even conducted the last rites of the deceased. Besides, the women volunteers assisted in carrying the dead bodies from the ambulances, lighting the pyres and collecting the funeral remains. Despite the resistance, the women volunteers carried out the task of serving humanity. I wanted to capture these experiences here before they were lost.

Sometimes, these unprecedented situations bring changes unimaginable during normal circumstances. As soon as I read about these women, I contacted the organization and enquired if I could interview them. I instantly received an overwhelming response from these warriors. This section is my attempt to document the unthinkable, demonstrating how crises change gender stereotypes in end-of-life rituals.

Nikita, 19, initially worked with a Covid care Centre in Pune, assisting the doctors in taking the patient's vitals. While doing this, she witnessed pain and distress around her. Then, an NGO approached her during the Delta wave to conduct the funerals. She was initially reluctant since girls were traditionally restricted from entering the crematoriums. 'My aai was terrified. She told me working with an NGO is fine, but this work is unacceptable for girls. Even my friends discouraged me. They warned me that I would get nightmares. I, nevertheless, took the plunge and joined the team. In the beginning, it was challenging to carry the bodies from the ambulances. *Bahut baas aati thi* (the smell was too strong)—the entire atmosphere was gloomy. But, eventually, I got used to it,' Nikita said.

She takes pride in completing the last rites dignifiedly. Nikita recollected how the volunteers recited mantras while reading the posters on the walls. She recounted an instance of conducting the funeral of a senior citizen, and the family thanked her in the end. 'Our father always wanted a proper funeral—you made it possible. You did everything with love and affection—just like his grandchild,' said the daughters.

Nikita joined without informing her family members. 'None of my extended family members were aware. I knew they wouldn't be forthcoming. But, when the organizations felicitated our efforts, everything suddenly changed. They started appreciating the work. They understood that girls could do everything—even performing the last rites. Moreover, I feel good about inspiring others to come forward,' she told me.

What was initially seen as a nightmare turned into a great learning experience for her. Finally, she could overcome her fears and inhibitions.

However, she hopes that humanity doesn't have to witness such horrid scenes again in the future.

Similarly, nineteeen-year-old Payal, pursuing her Bachelor of Science (BSc) degree, volunteered during Covid. Initially, she volunteered with a Covid centre, which gave her the strength to pursue work at the shamshan when the time came.

'There was chaos around us. Ambulances would queue up—but there was no single soul to attend to the dead. That's when NGOs started streamlining the process. In the beginning, only boys volunteered since it was inappropriate for the girls. Then, we received a message from the group that they needed more hands. Moreover, the previous group needed a break. So, they approached us for the morning and evening shifts. But, my family wasn't too keen on me working at the shamshan. Besides, I was terrified of death. I would change my route if I learned about a death in the neighbourhood. Not only this, I was even scared of the ambulance siren. So, my parents were worried for me,' she said. 'But later on, father agreed and said, "if you are so keen, go ahead and do this work,"' Payal recounted.

In the beginning, she wasn't aware of the nature of work. She was under the impression that she would be managing the paperwork. Later, she realized that the work involved lifting the dead bodies and performing the last rites. 'We even collected the asthi and handed them over to the families with the support of our team members,' she said.

Since she was already working with the Covid centre, she wasn't paranoid about contracting the infection. However, besides being a biology student, Payal knew working with living infected persons involved more risk than the dead.

'My family wasn't aware of the true nature of the work. I hadn't informed them. Then one day, a police officer arrived at my house. My grandmother was petrified to see the police officer. But, when he told her he was there to felicitate my work—she understood what I was doing,' Payal said excitedly.

There were many instances and stories to share. However, Payal recounted one where the team cremated a nine-year-old. Her body was swollen because it kept lying in the hospital for a long time. Payal told me she was terrified for a moment and even stepped back. That incident taught her a lot. At that moment, she realized how crucial this work was. Not only this, the experience taught her the significance of delivering dignified last rites in the absence of families.

It was a life-changing experience for Payal at a young age—she learned many essential lessons. For example, she told me that she understood the concept of impermanence through this experience. 'We give so much attention to our physical body that is bound to perish someday,' said Payal. Moreover, she also learned about the body's anatomy while collecting and segregating the bones, which will help her in her future work. She said, 'I learned how to live my life meaningfully while contributing to society. I want people to remember me for my good deeds.'

Women performed the last rites for the deceased during the pandemic, leading the show. However, of course, the context is different in a catastrophic situation—created by the scale of deaths. Unfortunately, these changing hands are sometimes transitory, more situation-specific, and not permanent. But, I hope these changes become everyday phenomena. Permanent or transitory, these were nevertheless path-breaking experiences for these young women—understanding life during death.

Women's participation in funeral work might be new in India. However, women have been involved in funeral work in the West. While writing this section, I was reminded of my conversation with Dr Ravi Nandan Singh, a sociologist. 'Many women funeral workers involved in the industry in Denmark and Italy have college degrees. However, the emotional component of grief attracts women to funeral work. In Europe, women primarily take care of the emotional bit while men handle the bodies physically.' said Dr Ravi.

VII
Professional Funeral Services: Aiding During the Pandemic

In India, when the families struggled with the surge in cases during the second wave, funeral organizers saw a rise in requests from family members either infected by the virus, residing abroad or currently stuck in other cities.

Although new in India, these professional funeral services came to the rescue by assisting families in making the arrangements but, in most cases, performing the rituals in the absence of the family members. In addition, research from the western world highlights the crucial role of funeral organizers and officiants in helping the bereaved create funerals that are personal, meaningful and expressive of collective grief despite the restrictions associated with Covid.

The task was challenging since managing a funeral in this context required sensitivity and skill, especially in the absence of family members. Therefore, I spoke to a few directors to understand their role in India during the second wave of the pandemic. It was overwhelming to hear their stories of service.

'Before the pandemic, things were smooth. I didn't have to rush three different ambulances or hearses, but the situation was terrible during the pandemic. There were tonnes of calls that we were unable to attend. I was contacted by people who had relatives in India needing funeral services,' recalled Cyril Joseph from JCJ Funerals, a funeral director from New Delhi.

Similarly, the owner of Noble Sparrows, Jatin, a service provider in Gurugram, said his phone was ringing off the hook during the second wave. He was concerned about ensuring a dignified funeral for the families. So his team took over when families were reluctant to enter the crematorium.

During Covid, there was a scare of contracting the infection. Therefore, these funeral directors were summoned when the aggrieved were fearful. 'In many instances, no one was practically willing to perform the funeral. It was terrible—families announced that they wouldn't be exposing themselves. I recall one instance when the son was present at the cremation ground but was unwilling to light the funeral pyre. Not just this, families wouldn't even come to collect the ashes—such was the scare. Therefore I would go the following day and ritually immerse the ashes,' recounted Cyril.

Despite challenges, these service providers worked tirelessly amidst crisis. JCJ funerals repatriated over 200 bodies and ashes to India. Besides, there were close to seventy to eighty funerals that Cyril Joseph conducted personally. Similarly, Jatin performed cremations while the families stayed back in the parking area. 'There were around 300 cases wherein I independently did everything without the family members,' recalled Jatin.

Sometimes, the Covid infected families could not step out due to quarantine. Then these professionals were summoned. These service providers recalled instances when harried families contacted them for help. 'I got a call from the family, and they said their mother had died of Covid and needed help with the funeral because the entire family was down with Covid infection. So I reached the place along with two helpers. We not only performed the cremation but dispersed the ashes in Haridwar, as per family's wish,' Jatin told me.

These funeral directors managed everything with empathy and respect when no one else was available. Cyril recounts one instance, 'The children were in the USA, and the parents were here in Chitranjan Park, New Delhi. It was heartbreaking. The wife could not dress the deceased husband. Can you imagine the situation? I went there, cleaned his body and sanitized him. Then I packed the body according to the protocols and performed the cremation.'

Moreover, the technology bridged the gap when the families were not physically present to perform the rituals. There was high demand for live streaming through Zoom. In many cases, the service providers live-streamed the ceremony to the children or the extended family members. 'The situation was heartbreaking and upsetting. We received requests for online asthi visarjan and pind daan. Besides, we received courier asthi packages ten times more than the regular days. We subsequently performed the online pujan (prayers) and live-streamed the rituals for the families. We handled everything seamlessly with our IT team's assistance,' said Pallavi from Kashi Moksha, a registered society in Varanasi. 'The requests for live streaming had become very common during the pandemic. So we had to set up tripods. Then, I went in front of the camera to conduct the funeral,' recalled Cyril. Funeral directors recounted many stories.

For instance, Jatin recounted, 'The daughter was in Australia. At her request, we arranged for video streaming. Finally, they insisted that the ashes be dispersed in Haridwar, the holy Ganga, since their ancestors' ashes were immersed in the same waters. Thus, one needs to respect the sentiments of the families. Moreover, the prayer meetings were not conducted during the second wave. Therefore, the other rituals had to be done properly.'

However, it wasn't easy—these directors faced many challenges. It was overwhelming for the funeral organizers since the caseload was very high. But, these funeral directors worked diligently. According to them, the rates for the materials had increased manifold. In addition, the funeral staff demanded money from the families in the name of an emergency. Besides, there were long hours of waiting after reaching the facility. Sometimes, there was waiting for twelve to fourteen hours to conduct a funeral. Things were out of control. Besides, there were three to four days of waiting at the burial grounds of cemeteries in Delhi.

Moreover, there were times when families couldn't afford funerals since many had lost their jobs. The funeral directors had to make a tough choice between profits and social service. 'This year was devastating. I felt helpless at times. Even if I waived my fees, I had to pay my staff and labour. So, I introduced a minimal package wherein the essential services were provided at ₹15000. I was making a bare minimum profit,' recalled Cyril.

It was interesting how the funeral directors looked after the needs of people from all faiths and backgrounds with love and care. For instance, Jatin recounted, 'One day, I got a call from a Muslim family at five in the morning. Unfortunately, the family was helpless because there was no one to collect the deceased from the hospital and perform the last rites. Although I wasn't well-versed with the Muslim last rites, I nevertheless took the plunge and went ahead. First, I dashed to the hospital and cleared the bills. Then I contacted the Maulana and arranged everything. After that, there was no looking back.'

These funeral organizers did everything while putting their own lives at risk. I wondered what made them carry on with the task when it was life-threatening. The directors confided that they trusted God, that helped them sail, all through. 'I remember going to DRDO Hospital, which was the hub of infections. We picked around fifty to sixty bodies from the hospital and never got infected, by the grace of God,' Cyril told me.

These warriors risked not only their physical but also their mental well-being while performing their duties. 'It was a tough time for everyone. I didn't see my family for days—I decided to stay back in my office to ensure their safety,' said Jatin. They shared how the aggrieved families would cry, and the phone rang continuously. 'My day started early. I picked up the ashes from the crematoriums to be delivered. My day ended at 10 or 11 p.m. But, I could hardly sleep. Then, one day, I had to cremate six different members of the same family—which was devastating,' remembered Joseph.

VIII
Covid Good-Bye: Tales from the Families

The bereaved families were severely hit by the Covid crisis. Through my heartbreaking conversations, I gathered how the loved ones dealt with grief. Besides, many family members could not physically attend the last rites due to travel restrictions. Moreover, constraints on the number of mourners permitted to participate in funerals further impacted the bereaved during the crisis. Even worse, some could not retrieve the corpses or the remains of their loved ones from the hospital due to strict Covid protocols and mismanagement of dead bodies.

In this context, a friend said something interesting that I thought would be worthwhile sharing. 'My paternal aunt passed away after meeting with a terrible train accident a few years back. Naturally, my entire family was traumatized by this accident. But, my grandmother was particularly impacted by her sudden loss. Whenever someone visited our house, she would repeatedly cry and narrate the entire incident. At that time, I was getting agitated by the repeated details. However, later I realised how these thirteen days of mourning rituals provided us with the space to grieve, which was lacking during the pandemic,' said Roopal Kewalya, a friend. Perhaps, this is why communal grieving is embedded in our last rites and rituals—providing a safe place to mourn and grieve.

I feel the customs around death have been meaningfully incorporated into nearly all cultures serving many functions for bereaved persons. For example, there is a widespread belief that participating in body disposal-related ceremonies in the company of family members helps deal with grief. On the other hand, minimal or no observance of funeral rites could harm adjustment to the loss of loved ones.

1. Dealing with Guilt and Grief: When They Died, I Could Not Be There

It was challenging to ask families to speak, especially when dealing with grief. However, Rohini and Asha were courageous to share their stories here.

In the summer of 2020, Rohini's parents succumbed to the deadly Coronavirus. She was in Hyderabad while her parents were in Bokaro, Jharkhand. As a result, she couldn't attend her parent's funeral. So she participated in the funeral rites through video calls instead.

'A tsunami hit our lives in 2020—I lost my parents to Coronavirus. They were gone—the two most-loved people were now numbers— the official count of Covid deaths. My father tested positive when we were still dealing with my mother's loss. We immediately started his treatment under home isolation. From thousands of miles away, I monitored his vitals daily. When his oxygen levels dropped, we rushed him to a private hospital in Ranchi. However, his condition fluctuated every day. Unlike for my mother, we could procure everything possible—plasma for plasma therapy, superior antibiotics and other resources. After a long struggle, my father succumbed too. I feel guilty that I couldn't take care of my parents. I couldn't be there for them when they needed me the most,' said Rohini.

Many were confronted with questions like: would they get to cremate their loved ones? Families had heard horror stories about Covid patients being denied dignified funerals. Nevertheless, some found solace that they could at least see their loved ones leave. But lack of physical touch left the aggrieved family members in pain and suffering.

In some instances, the risk of infection necessitated the disposal of the body without the family members. However, being unable to see the deceased and perform cremation rites was painful. For instance, during the second deadly pandemic wave, Asha Mehta lost her thirty-six-year-old brother within four days of hospitalization. 'I was in the USA, and my seventy-two-year-old mother managed everything alone in Vadodara, India. There was chaos everywhere. First, arranging a hospital bed was challenging. Then, organizing the emergency medication and plasma therapy was a hurricane task. I, nevertheless, did everything I could. I was in touch with Rahul through video calls. He was getting better, but suddenly, his oxygen levels dropped, and his vitals went haywire after he was administered an emergency injection. When I received a call at 3 a.m., I went completely numb. I couldn't believe he was gone. Besides, Rahul was a perfectly healthy person without any comorbidities,' she told me.

Mourning and performing rituals is a cultural defence that aids in healing. Unfortunately, that was not done during the pandemic and resulted in minimal ceremonies, like face-to-face mourning, potentially leading to guilt and lack of closure. In addition, the grief may worsen with the guilt of surviving the illness, unlike the deceased member. While talking to therapists, I understood that many survivors experienced survivor guilt'. Rohini told me:

I was suggested to stay away from their last rites for the sake of my toddler daughter. I attended the funerals through video calls—I saw my brother performing the rituals wearing a personal protective suit—how we wished to hug Ma and Papa and touch them the last time. But there he was, performing everything alone under strict protocols from a distance. We witnessed the brutality of losing a loved one to this deadly virus. I haven't been able to deal with my parents' death. Perhaps because I was deprived of the closure that the end-life rituals provide—like physically seeing off the departed. The families of patients with non-infectious illnesses at least get the opportunity to cry and laugh together.

While Rohini's family could conduct the last rites of her parents, it was different for Asha. Asha's family couldn't retrieve the body from the hospital due to the negligence of the hospital authorities. Even the remains were not handed over to the family. So all they were left with were his memories and the pain of losing him. 'It was the most traumatizing experience for my family. My mother was shocked—she didn't speak for two days. I felt helpless sitting here in the USA. I still feel numb so many times,' said Asha with a heavy heart.

2.   Coping with Grief

While some continue to suffer in silence, others have found solace in mourning with the entire universe. In the absence of traditional mourning, it is interesting to see how individuals find ways to deal with their grief.

According to Smita, a therapist, there was an upsurge in grief. As a result, people didn't know how to deal with their survivor guilt. 'One of my clients felt guilty because she could not attend her parents' funeral,' Smita told me.

'It was initially very tough to deal with the loss of my brothers. I lost my two brothers within one month. I couldn't come to India because of travel restrictions. Besides, my mother is alone as my father died many years ago. Grief keeps coming back like waves. But, I find strength in meditation and yoga—I am a Jain. In Jainism, we believe in the immortality of the soul. Death is not the end but the beginning of a new life,' Asha told me. However, Asha came to India in July 2020 when the restrictions were lifted. She plans to move back to India to be with her mother. Asha regularly volunteers with NGOs in India to find meaning in her life. Her spiritual disposition and optimistic character is her strength. Also, facing numerous emergencies from a very young age gave her the power to deal with this crisis.

Some families find solace in spiritual activities, while others find peace in fulfilling the last wish of their loved ones. 'We were not a typically religious family. For instance, we celebrated festivals, but rituals were not of paramount importance. Celebrations mostly centred around food and clothes. Thus, the traditional Hindu practices for my immediate family were not as crucial even after death. Even though a born Hindu, my father desired to be buried. So we tried fulfilling his wish. But, he had to be cremated for logistical reasons,' Rohini told me.

Rohini ritually dispersed her mother's ashes in water. Because her father had a philosophical disposition, she thought he would appreciate some unusual ritual. He introduced her to the concept of sohum, to identify oneself with the universe/ultimate reality. His teaching of sohum is helping her relate to all the bereaved families whose loved ones are now sheer numbers in the Covid death tally.

Studies emphasize the importance of meaningful and supportive funerals for the bereaved, enabling relatives to achieve a sense of control and social support. Many experts suspected mental health conditions would exacerbate after the Covid pandemic because of the limited social support available to the bereaved. Besides, research highlights how social isolation may exacerbate psychological morbidity in bereavement. Therefore, those who lost a family member were at particular risk of distress.

IX
Online Platforms: Aiding in Healing

As discussed before, during the pandemic, the absence of traditional rituals and condolence practices was challenging for the loved ones. The families had to choose between the emotional trauma of grieving alone and the risk of spreading the virus by opening their doors to family and friends. However, humans discovered newer/novel platforms for grieving during the crisis. Online initiatives were started by people from different walks of life. These initiatives enabled people to express sorrow, loss and pain without avenues for families to attend funerals or express grief. Besides, these online initiatives helped honour the dead and assist the families in healing.

1.   Online Covid Memorial

While families were struggling to provide a proper tribute to their loved ones, the National Covid Memorial, an online memorial to commemorate Indians who have lost their lives to Covid-19, was launched by doctors and social workers. The virtual memorial allows family members and friends of the victims to pay their tributes by posting eulogies online.

The memorial is run by social workers helped by doctors, health workers and journalists. The National Covid Memorial was launched by the Covid Care Network, a non-governmental organization led by doctors in Kolkata. One can see the painfully touching tributes posted on the site—families have to upload the death certificates of their loved ones or provide their phone numbers for verification.

2.   Coping with Loss and Grief: Online Sessions

When there was a lack of avenues for sharing grief through communal rituals, the online sessions were used to support the individuals in dealing with grief. For instance, Living Earth Trust started online sessions 'Coping with Loss and Grief' to help the aggrieved family members remember their loved ones and cope with their loss. They used online platforms like Zoom meetings and Google Hangouts to conduct sessions and webinars. 'There is an enormous outpouring of emotions. During the sessions, the expressing time usually exceeded the allocated time. A lady from Bangalore said that she was always perceived as strong. Therefore she never got a chance to express her grief after losing her husband. However, she could empty herself during these sessions while maintaining her anonymity. It was a good starting point for her.' …Technology has its challenges, sometimes my dogs bark, and there is a disturbance in the participants' background sometimes. Nevertheless, the technology comes in handy during these unprecedented times,' said Andrea Jacob, founder.

Andrea comes from a musical family. Their family sang at the funerals when no one showed up. However, she did not realize its importance until her dad explained the significance of attending funerals. Also, her father regularly read obituaries in the newspaper to honour the dead in his own way. Even she picked up this habit from her father. These childhood experiences inspired her to conceive this online initiative.

Andrea had many exciting things to share. For instance, she met a lady who lost her parents to Covid-19. Her grief was immense, and she could not get up from the bed. However, Andrea saw a massive change in her after their first online meeting. That made her realize the power of expressing grief, sometimes in words and sometimes in silence.

Andrea's sessions included dance movements, music and numerous other mediums. She has received an exhilarating response from the community, getting constant enquiries on social media about her sessions. She is constantly innovating since she believes in no one-size-fits-all approach. Andrea was busy prepping for her upcoming event, Care Circles, another online event, when I spoke to her.

Similarly, Smita Rajan started The Katha Club to help grief-stricken and depressed people during the pandemic. According to Smita, there has been a surge of grief in the last two years. This is because people are experiencing loss during the pandemic. In addition, people are facing stigma attached to Covid. 'I was also handling my grief at that time. Moreover, I was concerned about what was happening around me. Usually, when death occurs, there is a considerable grieving process that humans go through. But unfortunately, this was not happening during Covid. So, people were carrying the grief with them. I understood that people needed help. They wanted to talk and vent. This is why I started The Katha Club,' said Smita, a Mumbai based dance and movement therapist and personal counsellor.

The Katha Club, an online platform, helped people deal with these issues. She has conducted five sessions to demonstrate self-care practices like breathing and practising subtle movements. In addition, she taught them how to stimulate polyvagal nerves. Slowly, the tribe grew bigger and bigger. 'It was a superhit,' she said.

'It was not easy conducting sessions online. There were times when I got overwhelmed. There is so much more one can do in physical sessions. I am a dance and body movement therapist. For me, healing starts with the body. I believe body-based experiences open doorways towards enhanced living,' said Smita. She is also associated with Thunai, an organization that helps survivors of trauma recover and build resilience. However, these days Smita is conducting more one-to-one sessions.

In the end, I would say the dead have important stories to tell—about humanity, neglect, and mismanagement—if we care to listen. In the end, if nothing else, this global catastrophe has changed how we view life and death from a new perspective.

Afterword

As I mentioned in the beginning, writing a book is a journey. It was indeed an incredible one with highs and lows. For example, I remember someone asking me what it is like to write a book on last rites and rituals. It was exciting and thought-provoking but never dull, I would say.

However, in the end, one must tie the loose strands. Now, I feel betterequipped to answer the questions I confronted initially or while performing my father's last rites. Yet, I am sure there is much more to unravel.

My conversations with experts, priests, workers, individuals and filmmakers made it more enriching and my visits to shamshan ghats and kabristans broadened my perspective. It helped me disentangle many strands and discover exciting facets. Therefore, I attempt to elucidate the similarities in last rites, underscore the changes and highlight the challenges in laying the dead across religions. Besides,

I dwell on how humans had to forgo many crucial rituals during the pandemic, impacting us in myriad ways.

First and foremost, the last rite is a process of bidding goodbyes to loved ones. Just like in other parts of the world, I was intrigued by how funerals are accompanied by music in some cultures in India. For instance, parai and gaana in Tamil Nadu. However, these traditions entrenched in caste discrimination are fading from the funeral scene and transforming into new avatars, finding space in Tamil films and music festivals.

Similarly, it is refreshing to see how death is not mourned in Varanasi. It is celebrated. Here Shiva, the bestower of salvation, whispers the taraka mantra in the ear of the corpse to help the soul sail. Therefore, people travel to this land of the Ganges from far and across to attain moksha. Besides, how people joyously play Mashaan Holi with cremation ashes on the Manikarnika Ghat of Varanasi, celebrating life and death with zeal, is fascinating.

I feel India's rich diversity can be experienced in life and death— some bury their dead, some cremate and others expose them to nature in Towers of Silence. Moreover, scriptures or religious rule books in every religion specify how to approach death and perform end-of-life rituals. Yet, despite differences, I found interesting facts and fascinating parallels in end-of-life rituals throughout faiths in India. Therefore, I want to highlight these unifying aspects of end-of-life rituals here.

Death is seen as the separation of the soul from the gross body across religions. Besides, death in Hinduism and Sikhism is seen as a new beginning, not to be mourned excessively. Moreover, extreme mourning is discouraged in every faith. In contrast, accepting the inevitable with equanimity is valued everywhere. Furthermore, I found exciting inferences about ways of approaching death in different faiths. For instance, in the Sikh religion, death is seen as an opportunity for the individual soul to unite with the Supreme—not a moment for lament.

Furthermore, in each religion, family members have predetermined roles in end-of-life rituals, carefully demarcating who participates in which ritual. For instance, among Hindus, the eldest son lights the funeral pyre. Moreover, in funeral rituals, gender roles are clearly defined, with men actively performing the rituals except mourning, a domain exclusively reserved for women. However, with changing times, Hindu and Sikh women have slowly started performing end-of-life rituals other than mourning. During the pandemic, there were instances of women volunteers actively participating in lighting the funeral pyre or carrying the dead.

Furthermore, the ritual aspect is crucial in last rites across religions. For instance, there are references to how the deceased's body should be washed or wrapped. Besides, there are specifications on the length and colour of a shroud. In addition, although specific to every religion, funeral prayers are recited in every religion.

I feel that end-of-life rituals and embedded traditions in different religions offer enough space for the families to grieve. For instance, a pre-funeral ritual bath conducted lovingly to the deceased, and subsequent dressing by close family members is a common custom followed across religions. Besides, among Hindus, the shava before being offered to agni is decorated with flowers.

Above everything, these rituals give family members a purpose—helping mourners grieve and heal while doing these rituals. But unfortunately, these intimate pre-funeral and post-funeral rituals were missed during the pandemic—making it alienating for the bereaved. Moreover, we had to forgo prayer meetings and collective grieving. But, in the absence of traditional mourning avenues, it was interesting how technology came in handy during the pandemic. The online grieving platforms became common, accessed by members from far and across. However, these online mediums couldn't replace the physical presence and comfort of humans.

During a conversation, a friend narrated an exciting experience worth mentioning here. Through the second pandemic wave, he saw a Muslim man helping a Hindu family retrieve the ashes scattered on the road, joined by other people. This is how we understand the significance of last rites in India across faiths. It doesn't matter even if the remains belong to a stranger from another religion.

Furthermore, when the State found it challenging, it was heartwarming to witness how community-led initiatives and individuals from diverse faiths helped during the pandemic waves to perform the funerals of strangers in the absence of families—reinstating the belief in humanity—blurring the binaries of religion and caste. Unlike dogmatics, many anthropologists point out death rituals' unifying function within and across religions. However, this aspect manifested more starkly during the pandemic.

In India, preparations for last rites are a community-led affair throughout religions, making it less isolating. Although, with changing patterns and urbanization, things are slowly altering. For instance, professional funeral services are gradually penetrating the urban landscape, especially the metros. With the Covid-19 scenario, these services have gained momentum in India, but time will tell what the future holds. How comfortable will Indians be in leaving their loved ones in the hands of strangers?

During the last rites, ritual specialists have an indispensable role in every religion. But, these professions are transitioning too. For instance, Hindu women have joined the priestly work in the previous decade, rejecting the status quo. Moreover, many ritualists acquired new skills during the pandemic, performing rituals online. While working on the book, I had fascinating conversations with the ritualists. However, some exchanges left me wondering. Like, a Parsi priest telling me he didn't want to be reborn as a priest in his next life. Besides, the Sikh Granthi confessed that his children were not keen on joining the priestly work. With other professions perhaps luring the current generations, I wonder how many would be keen on joining this work in future. In the absence of ritualists, I suppose we would have to rely on technology to attain salvation in future. Therefore, I think these professionals warrant adequate attention in safeguarding the future of last rites in India.

The task of carrying and managing the corpse is entrusted to the lower caste workers in every religion. For instance, in Varanasi, there are Doms. While visiting kabristans and shamshans, I witnessed how the death care workers seamlessly assisted families during funerals. Besides, I understood the crucial contribution of Doms, safai karamcharis, and burial workers across religions in delivering respectful funerals. Moreover, through my conversations, I realized how enduring the stench and witnessing the tragedy every day without proper remuneration impacted workers' well-being—sometimes even bringing about intoxication among workers like Shambu. Unfortunately, their contribution has been primarily ignored throughout history. However, the Covid-pandemic has perhaps put things back into perspective, reminding humanity of the cruciality of death work in controlling the spread of deadly infections. Besides, their accounts of selfless work were incredible when families were quarantined or scared to step out. Therefore, we must recognize their contribution to death care work and give them adequate attention.

Last but not least, I have elaborated on how traditional funeral methods have an environmental impact. With the looming ecological crises, I can't predict whether enough wood will be left for future generations or if there will be adequate space to bury the dead. Besides, we have already seen how the Parsi community is struggling with the environmental problem impacting the age-old funerary practice. Who had imagined or anticipated this crisis a few decades back? Therefore, we must take this looming crisis seriously and explore the options before the situation is beyond control. World over, people are looking at more environmentally friendly alternatives. Moreover, with limited spaces and resources, I cannot imagine how challenging it would be for the Dalits, the poor or transgender people to bury or cremate their departed members in future.

I don't know the future of last rites in India, but history suggests that death rituals are the last to change. No one wants to meddle in this sensitive territory with underlying religious sentiments and emotions at stake. But, I think we should strive to take the Covid pandemic's learnings forward to avert mistakes in the future.

I faced many questions before I embarked on this beautiful and challenging journey. Through this book, I could answer some. Ultimately, I would say there are no easy answers to others. However, through this volume, I have attempted to present the last rites and rituals and the actors involved while raising pertinent questions which need collective attention and exploration from various sections and stakeholders in India.

Glossary

- *Agni sanskar*   open pyre cremation followed by Hindu
- *Ahura Mazda*   God/The Supreme Being of the Zoroastrian
- *Akhand Path*   unbroken reading of the Guru Granth Sahib
- *Akhanda Jyothi*   eternal light
- *Anand*   bliss
- *Anand Sahib*   'Hymn of Bliss' in Guru Granth Sahib
- *Ardas*   Sikh prayer
- *Arthi*   bier
- *Asthi*   mortal remains
- *Asthi Visarjan*   immersion of ashes/remains after cremation
- *Ashram*   hermitage or retreat
- *Atma*   soul
- *Avesta*   the holy scriptures of Zoroastrianism

- *Bhog*   end/conclude
- *Bhagavad Gita*   the 'Song of the Lord', forms part of the sixth book of Mahabharata
- *Bhagwan*   God
- *Bhakti*   devotion
- *Brahmin*   traditionally brahmins were priests and teachers.
- *Chandan*   sandalwood
- *Celas*   disciples of a hijra guru
- *Chinvat*   a bridge which souls of the dead cross
- *Daan*   ritual donations/gifts
- *Dakhma*   a tower-like structure on which dead bodies are exposed
- *Dakshina*   fees
- *Dalits*   Untouchable, belonging to the lowest stratum castes in India
- *Dharmsalas*   pilgrim lodge
- *Dharam*   religious or moral duty
- *Dhoti*   a loin garment
- *Diya*   a small oil lamp
- *Doaba*   the plain tract of central Punjab in between the Beas and Sutlej rivers
- *Gaddi*   throne
- *Galli*   lane
- *Ganda*   ritually polluting/dirty
- *Ganga Jal*   Ganges water
- *Gatha*   the five sacred hymns of Zarathushtra
- *Gayatri Mantra*   a recital of mantra among Hindus
- *Gehan*   iron bier
- *Ghat*   a segment of river frontage
- *Ghusl*   bath
- *Granthi*   a reader of Guru Granth Sahib
- *Gurmukh*   God-fearing

- *Gurmat*   wisdom of the Guru
- *Gurbani*   compositions by the Sikh Gurus in Guru Granth Sahib
- *Guru*   a religious teacher
- *Guru Granth Sahib*   sacred scripture of Sikhism
- *Hadiths*   pronouncements made by Prophet Mohammed
- *Hafez*   a title for a person who knows the Koran by heart.
- *Hijra*   transvestites who sing and dance at the birth of a son
- *Hukam*   divine order
- *Imam*   the prayer leader
- *Jajman*   client of a Brahmin priest
- *Japuji Sahib*   Sikh thesis that appears at the beginning of the Guru Granth Sahib
- *Kabr*   grave
- *Kabristan*   Muslim graveyard
- *Kaccha*   cotton underwear worn by Sikhs
- *Kafan*   shrouds or traditional white cloth
- *Kapal-Kriya*   the rite of breaking open the skull of the deceased on the cremation pyre
- *Kara*   unadorned iron bracelet worn by Sikhs
- *Karma*   deeds
- *Karam-kandi*   a brahmin ritual priest
- *Karah prasad*   sacred pudding
- *Kashi*   Kashi is the spiritual name of the northern Indian city of Varanasi
- *Kashi labh*   the profit of Kashi
- *Kathavachak*   Sikh narrator/storyteller
- *Kirpan*   a short sword or knife with a curved blade
- *Kirtan*   devotional singing
- *Krim Kund*   holy tank

- *Kusti*   sacred cord worn around the waist by Zoroastrians
- *Majha*   the area of central Punjab lying between the Beas and Ravi rivers
- *Malwa*   The plain tract extending south and south-east of the Sutlej river, more precisely the area covered by the districts of Ludhiana, Ferozepore and the princely states of Patiala and Nabha
- *Manmukh*   material being
- *Mantra*   a sacred formula
- *Martak*   dead
- *Moksha*   salvation or liberation from the cycle of rebirth
- *Mukti*   salvation or liberation from the cycle of rebirth
- *Nahn*   ablution/a ritual washing of the entire body
- *Paap*   moral imperfections
- *Panda*   pilgrimage priest
- *Patet*   prayer of penance
- *Phul chugna*   collecting funeral remains
- *Pind daan*   a gift of pinds to the departed
- *Pitr*   an ancestor
- *Pravah*   immersion
- *Pret*   an incorporated ghost
- *Puja*   worship
- *Purvej*   ancestor
- *Qiblah*   it is the fixed direction towards the Ka'bah in the Grand Mosque in Makkah
- *Quran*   central religious text of Islam
- *Rahit*   The code of discipline of the Khalsa

- *Resurrection*   all the people who have ever lived will be raised from the dead and will face judgement by Allah
- *Sadhus*   ascetics
- *Safai karamchari*   cleaning workers
- *Sagdid*   dog-sight during funerals
- *Sagri*   prayer hall/a small building near dakhma where a fire is kept alight
- *Sangat*   Sikh community
- *Sanskar*   auspicious rite/one of the sixteen lifecycle rituals
- *Shamshan bhoomi*   crematorium
- *Samadhi*   time at which union with the divine is reached before or at death/the tomb of an ascetic
- *Sapinda*   kin with whom one shares the same body particles
- *Sapindikarna*   rite performed on the twelfth day
- *Sevadars*   workers
- *Shav Pujan*   praying the dead body
- *Shava*   corpse
- *Shraddh*   rites performed for the dead
- *Shubh karya*   auspicious work
- *Swarg*   heaven
- *Taro*   bull's urine
- *Taraka mantra*   ferryboat hymn
- *Tirath*   pilgrimage
- *Tirath priest*   pilgrimage priest
- *Tulsi*   holy basil
- *Vibhuti*   holy ashes
- *Yasna*   one of the books of Avesta, the holy scriptures

References

Antam Sanskar in Sikh Tradition

1. Gulshan Gurbax Singh 2015. *Understanding Sikh Rehat Maryada*. UK: Khalsa Pracharak Jatha.
2. McMullen, C.O.1989. *Religious Beliefs and Practices of the Sikhs in Rural Punjab*. Delhi: Manohar.
3. McLeod, W.H. 2003. *Sikhs of the Khalsa: a History of the Khalsa Rahit*. New Delhi: Oxford India Paperbacks.
4. Oberoi, Harjot.1994. *The Construction of Religious Boundaries: Culture, Identity and Diversity in the Sikh Religion*. Chicago: The University of Chicago Press.

Islamic Last Rites and Rituals

1. Gatrad, AR. 1994. Muslim Customs Surrounding Death, Bereavement, Postmortem Examinations, and Organ transplants. *British Medical Journal* 309: 521-23.

2. Halevi, Leor. 2007. 'The Torture of the Grave Islam and Afterlife.' *The New York Times*, May 4. https://www.nytimes.com/2007/05/04/opinion/04iht-edhalevi.1.5565834.html. (accessed July 21, 2022).

3. Halevi, Leor. 2007. *Muhammad's Grave: Death Rites and the Making of Islamic Society*. New York: Columbia University Press.

4. Smith, Jane Idleman and Yvonne Yazbeck Haddad. 1981. *The Islamic Understanding of Death and Resurrection*, Albany: State University of New York Press.

5. Sultan, Dawood H. 2003. 'The Muslim Way of Death.' In *Handbook of Death and Dying*, ed. Clifton D. Bryant pp. 649-655. California: Sage.

6. Taylor, Richard P. 2000. *Death and the Afterlife: A Cultural Encyclopedia*. Santa Barbara, CA: ABC-CLIO.

Last Rites in Zoroastrianism

1. Zykov, Anton. 2016. Zoroastrian Funeral Practices: Transition in Conduct. In *Threads of Continuity: Zoroastrian Life and Culture*, ed. Cama Shernaz, pp. 287-305. New Delhi: Parzor Foundation.

2. Chaubey, Gyaneshwar et al. 2017. "Like sugar in milk": Reconstructing the genetic history of the Parsi population. *Genome Biology*. 18: 110. https://genomebiology.biomedcentral.com/articles/10.1186/s13059-017-1244-9 (accessed August 11, 2023).

3. Daruwalla, Kerman. 2016-2017. Evolution of the Zoroastrian Priestly Rituals in Iran. *The SOAS Journal of Postgraduate Research*. 10: 100-110.

4. Lasania, Yunus Y. 2015. 'With No Vultures, a Parsis Ritual on the Brink.' *The Hindu*. September 7. https://www.thehindu.

com/news/national/with-no-vultures-a-parsis-ritual-on-the-brink/article7622310.ece (accessed July 5, 2022).

5. Mahapatra, Dhananjay. 2021. "Can Parsi community be denied customary last rites during pandemic." *Times of India.* December 7. https://timesofindia.indiatimes. com/india/can-parsi-community-be-denied-customary-last-rites-during-pandemic/articleshow/88136485.cms (accessed August 11, 2023).

6. Modi, Jivanji Jamshedji. 1928. The Funeral Ceremonies of the Parsees: Their Origin and Explanation. Avesta Zoroastrian archives. Fourth Edition. http://www.avesta. org/ritual/funeral.htm (accessed July 5, 2022).

7. Subramanian Samanth. 2020. 'Vultures'. *Granta.* November 19. https://granta.com/vultures/ (accessed July 5, 2022).

8. Stepaniants, Marietta. 2002. The Encounter of Zoroastrianism with Islam. *Philosophy East and West.* Vol. 52, 2: 159-172. https://www.jstor.org/stable/1399963. (accessed August 9, 2023).

9. Taylor, Richard P. 2000. *Death and the Afterlife: A Cultural Encyclopedia.* Santa Barbara, CA: ABC-CLIO.

10. Walker Shaun. 2020. 'The Last of the Zoroastrians'. *The Guardian.* August 6. https://www.theguardian. com/world/2020/aug/06/last-of-the-zoroastrians-parsis-mumbai-india-ancient-religion (accessed July 5, 2022).

Funerary Customs Among Christians

1. Joo, Tan L. 2020. A Christian Theology of Life and Death. *Trinity Theological College,* pp. 1-15.

2. Taylor, Richard P. 2000. *Death and the Afterlife: A Cultural Encyclopedia.* Santa Barbara, CA: ABC-CLIO.

Antim Sanskar in Hindus

1. Eck Diana. 2015. *The Banaras City of Light*. Gurugram: Penguin Random House India.
2. Knipe, David M. 2019. *The Hindu Rite of Entry into Heaven and Other Essays on Death and Ancestors in Hinduism*. New Delhi: MLBD Publishers.
3. Lamb, Sarah. 2000. *White Saris and Sweet Mangoes: Aging, Gender, and Body in North India*. California: University of California Press.
4. Parry, Jonathan. 1994. *Death in Benares*. Cambridge: Cambridge University Press.
5. Rambachan Anantanand. 2003. 'The Hindu Way of Death'. In *Handbook of Death and Dying*, ed. Clifton D. Bryant, pp. 640-648. Thousand Oaks: Sage.

Ritual Specialists Among Hindus

1. Knipe, David M. 2019. *The Hindu Rite of Entry into Heaven and Other Essays on Death and Ancestors in Hinduism*. New Delhi: MLBD Publishers.
2. Kundalia, Nidhi Dugar 2015. *The Lost Generation, Chronicling India's Dying Professions*. Gurgaon: Penguin Random House India.
3. Parry, Jonathan. 1994. *Death in Benares*. Cambridge: Cambridge University Press.

Women Performing the Last Rites: The Hindu and Sikh Faith

1. Pandey, Geeta. 'Mandira Bedi: What Hindu Scriptures Say About Women at Cremations.' *BBC News*. July 21. https://www.bbc.com/news/world-asia-india-57894855 (accessed June 9, 2022).

Ritual Technicians

1. Devi, Mahasweta, and Usha Ganguli. 1997. *Rudali.* Trans. Anjum Katyal. Calcutta: Seagull Books.
2. Kundalia, Nidhi Dugar 2015. *The Lost Generation, Chronicling India's Dying Professions.* Gurgaon: Penguin Random House India.
3. Parry, Jonathan. 1994. *Death in Benares.* Cambridge: Cambridge University Press.

People Involved in Laying the Dead to Rest–Cremation Workers and Mortuary Staff

1. Anton Zykov. 2016. Zoroastrian Funeral Practices: Transition in Conduct. In *Threads of Continuity: Zoroastrian Life and* Culture, Cama Shernaz, pp. 287-305. New Delhi: Parzor Foundation.
2. Baria, Farah. 1995. 'Parsi Pallbearers Battle Social Exclusion, Dwindling Numbers to Eck Out a Living.' *India Today.* November 30. https://www.indiatoday.in/magazine/offtrack/story/19951130-parsi-pallbearers-battle-social-exclusion-dwindling-numbers-to-eke-out-a-living-808016-1995-11-30 (accessed June 23, 2022).
3. Chattopadhyay, Sohini. 2020. What Researching Cremations of the Dead in Colonial India Taught Me About Life in Our Cities Today. *Scroll.* August 23. https://scroll.in/article/971096/what-researching-cremations-of-the-dead-in-colonial-india-taught-me-about-life-in-our-cities-today (accessed June 23, 2022).
4. Chattopadhyay, Sohini. 2020. 'Do Mortuary Workers Come Last in the Covid-19 Fight?' May 8. http://sohinichattopadhyay.com/2020/05/do-mortuary-workers-come-last-in-the-covid19- fight/ (accessed June 23, 2022).

5. Chattopadhyay, Sohini. 2020. 'The Silence of the Archives: Why the Grave Diggers of the Bubonic Plague are Unremembered.' May 14. http://sohinichattopadhyay. com/2020/05/the-silence-of-the-archives-why-the-grave-diggers-of-the-bubonic-plague-are-unremembered/ (accessed June 23, 2022).

6. Communist Party of India. 2021. 'DIGNITY DISPOSED: AICCTU Report on Crematorium and Burial Groundworkers in Bengaluru during the COVID-19 pandemic.' https://www.aicctu.org/article/2021/05/ dignity-disposed-report-crematorium-and-burial-ground-workers-bengaluru-during-covid-19-pandemic (accessed June 23, 2022).

7. Ghaywan, Neeraj, director. 2015. *Masaan*. Drishyam Films, Phantom Films, Macassar Productions, Sikhya Entertainment, Phate, Arte France Cinema. 109 minutes. https://www.hotstar.com/in/movies/masaan/1000087441/ watch.

8. Kumari, Sarita. 2019. "The City of Death: Capturing The Landscape of Hindu Cremation Rituals in Varanasi." *Youth Ki Awaaz*. June 8. https://www.youthkiawaaz. com/2019/06/review-of-city-of-death-varanasi/. (accessed August 11, 2023).

9. Iyengar, Radhika. 2017. 'A Day in the Life of a Corpse Burner.' *Mint Lounge*. November 24. https://www. livemint.com/Leisure/rbcQ3K5FhR8fTddOmV8UGM/A-day-in-the-life-of-a-corpseburner.html (accessed June 23, 2022).

10. Laxmaiah, Mallepalli. 2021. 'Crematorium Workers Deserve a Life of Dignity.' *The Tribune*. May 12. https:// www.tribuneindia.com/news/comment/crematorium-

workers-deserve-a-life-of-dignity-251586 (assessed June 23, 2022).

11. National Human Rights Commission India. 2021. NHRC issues Advisory to the Centre and States to ensure dignity and the rights of the dead. 14th May. https://nhrc.nic. in/media/press-release/nhrc-issues-advisory-centre-and-states-ensure-dignity-and-rights-dead-14052021. (accessed August 11, 2023).

12. Parry, Jonathan. 1994. *Death in Benares*. Cambridge: Cambridge University Press.

13. Patturaja, Selvaraj, and Srinath Jagannathan. 2013. Exploring the Work & Lives of Crematorium Workers. *Indian Journal of Industrial Relations* 49: 54-49.

14. Sengupta, Avipsha. 2017. 'For Morgue Workers Dealing with Dead Bodies is Easier Than the "Other" Problems'. *Youth ki Awaaz*. April 18. https://www.youthkiawaaz. com/2017/04/where-dead-teach-the-living/ (accessed June 23, 2022).

15. Srinivasan, Meera. 2011. 'For Mortuary Assistants, a Thankless Job.' *The Hindu*. March 17. https://www. thehindu.com/news/cities/chennai/For-mortuary-assistants-a-thankless-job/article14949801.ece (accessed June 23, 2022).

16. The Times of India Network. 2021. "SDMC Fixes Rates for Last Rites at Crematoria." *The Times of India*. June 13. https://timesofindia.indiatimes.com/city/delhi/sdmc-fixes-rates-for-last-rites-at-crematoria/articleshow/83471225. cms. (accessed August 11, 2023).

17. Zykov, Anton. 2012. Corpse-bearers (Nasusalars) in the Zoroastrian Communities of India and Iran: Origins and Transformation. *Hamazor* 4: 33-37.

18. Zykov, Anton. 2012. Cyrus Mistry's '*Chronicle of a Corpse Bearer*'. *Hamazor* 4: 38-40.

Last Rites and Rituals: Spending

1. Census of India. 2011. Hindu Muslim Population in India. Government of India. https://www.census2011.co.in/religion.php. (accessed August 11, 2023).
2. Devi, Mahasweta, and Usha Ganguli. 1997. *Rudali*. Trans. Anjum Katyal. Calcutta: Seagull Books.
3. Kaushik, Archana. 2018. Can You Afford to Die? Estimates of Expenditure on Rituals and Impact on Ecology. *Economic and Political Weekly* 53, no. 3 (20 January 2018), https://www.epw.in/node/150846/pdf (accessed 13 June 2022).

Professional Funeral Services in India

1. Thomas, Mathews Prince. 2015. 'Death Inc.' *The Hindu Business Line*. March 2. https://www.thehindubusinessline.com/news/variety/death-inc/article6952117.ece (accessed June 8, 2022).

Varanasi: A Site of Death Tourism

1. Barrett, Ron. 2008. *Aghor Medicine: Pollution, Death, and Healing in Northern India*. California: University of California Press.
2. Cuskelly, Claudia. 2016. 'Why Tourists Can't Get Enough of This Real-life Land of the DEAD.' *Express*. July 31. https://www.express.co.uk/travel/articles/695071/tourists-can-t-get-enough-real-life-land-of-dead-varanasi-india-holy-site (accessed July 2, 2022).

3. Eck, Diana. 2015. *The Banaras City of Light*. Gurugram: Penguin Random House India.

4. Jindal, Aditi. 2019. 'That's Strange in India: Varanasi's Manikarnika Ghat.' *Make My Trip*. September 24. https://www.makemytrip.com/tripideas/blog/thats-strange-manikarnika-ghat-varanasi (accessed July 2, 2022).

5. Mishra, Geetanjali Joshi. 2016. From Manhattan to Manikarnika: A Study of the Aghori Cult and Its Influence on the Life of Allen Ginsberg. *International Journal of Linguistics, Literature and Culture* 2: 91-100.

6. Mitton, George. 2012. *Sacred Branches, and Other Indian Memories*. London: George Mitton.

7. Parry, Jonathan. 1994. *Death in Benares*. Cambridge: Cambridge University Press.

8. Sharma, Natasha. 2016. Beyond the Shades of Darkness: A Case Study of Varanasi, India. *Teoros* 1: 35.

Funeral Methods: Challenges and Way Forward

1. Arnold, David. 2017. Burning Issues: Cremation and Incineration in Modern India. *Springer*, 24: 393-419.

2. Davies, Douglas J. 2003. 'Cremation'. In *Handbook of Death and Dying*, ed. Clifton D. Bryant, pp 767-74. Thousand Oaks: Sage.

3. Kalia, Ammar. 2019. 'A Greener Way to Go: What's the Most Eco-friendly Way to Dispose of a Body?' *The Guardian*. July 9. https://www.theguardian.com/lifeandstyle/2019/jul/09/greener-way-to-go-eco-friendly-way-dispose-of-body-burial-cremation (accessed June 26, 2022).

4. Kaushik, Archana. 2018. 'Can You Afford to Die? Estimates of Expenditure on Rituals and Impact on Ecology. *Economic and Political Weekly* 53, no. 3 (January

20) https://www.epw.in/node/150846/pdf (accessed June 26, 2022).

5. Khandekar, Nivedita. 2020. 'By Using Agro-Waste to Cremate Bodies, This Indian Man Has Saved 35,000 Trees.' *Vice.* October 21. https://www.vice.com/en/article/n7vjgz/by-using-agro-waste-to-cremate-bodies-this-indian-man-has-saved-35000-trees (accessed June 10, 2022).

6. Knight, Helen. 2010. Depart This World with a Green Conscience. *New Scientist* 206: 8.

7. Lasania, Yunus Y. 2015. 'With No Vultures, a Parsis Ritual on the Brink.' *The Hindu.* September 7. https://www.thehindu.com/news/national/with-no-vultures-a-parsis-ritual-on-the-brink/article7622310.ece (accessed June 26, 2022).

8. Little, Becky. 2019. 'The Environmental Toll of Cremating the Dead'. *National Geographic.* November 5. https://www.nationalgeographic.com/science/article/is-cremation-environmentally-friendly-heres-the-science (accessed June 26, 2022).

9. Minhaz, Ayesha. 2015. 'Crematoria Lack Basic Facilities.' *Deccan Chronicle.* August 17. https://www.deccanchronicle.com/150817/nation-current-affairs/article/crematoria-lack-basic-facilities (accessed June 10, 2022).

10. Parry, Jonathan. 1994. *Death in Benares.* Cambridge: Cambridge University Press.

11. Sharma, Manoj. 2014. 'Fighting for Space: Delhi's Grave Problem.' *The Hindustan Times.* March 2. https://www.hindustantimes.com/delhi/fighting-for-space-delhi-s-grave-problem/story-M3QnwbsMp9n1qOyYnSNJ6I.html (accessed June 10, 2022).

12. Taylor, Richard P. 2000. *Death and the Afterlife: A Cultural Encyclopedia.* Santa Barbara, CA: ABC-CLIO.

13. Thomas, Mathews Prince. 2015. 'Death Inc'. *The Hindu Business Line*. March 2. https://www.thehindubusinessline. com/news/variety/death-inc/article6952117.ece (accessed June 8, 2022).

14. Vishwambhar, Nath Prajapati, and Saradindu Bhaduri. 2019. Human Values in Disposing the Dead: An Inquiry into Cremation Technology. *Journal of Human Values* 25, no. 1. https://journals.sagepub.com/doi/ pdf/10.1177/0971685818806416 (accessed June 26, 2022).

State of Cremation and Burial Spaces in India

1. Eck, L. Diana. 2015. *Banaras City of Light*. Gurugram: Penguin Books.

2. Mathur, Anisha. 2016. 'Hard look—RIP: Ground Reality in the City.' *The Indian Express*. January 25. https:// indianexpress.com/article/cities/delhi/hardlook-rip-ground-reality-in-the-city/ (accessed June 10, 2022).

3. Minhaz, Ayesha. 2015. 'Crematoria Lack Basic Facilities.' *Deccan Chronicle*. August 17. https://www.deccanchronicle. com/150817/nation-current-affairs/article/crematoria-lack-basic-facilities (accessed June 10, 2022).

4. 'Where do We Take Our Dead?' *The Indian Express*. February 26, 2014. https://indianexpress.com/article/ cities/mumbai/where-do-we-take-our-dead/ (accessed June 25, 2022).

5. 'Those Pyres at Nigambodh Ghat'. *The Hindu*. March 18, 2002. https://web.archive.org/web/20101227005356/ http://www.hinduonnet.com/mp/2002/03/18/ stories/2002031800310200.htm (accessed June 25, 2022).

Caste Discrimination in Last Rites

1. Chandran, Rina. 2020. 'Denied in life, India's lower-caste Dalits fight for land in death.' *Reuters*. March 6. https://www.reuters.com/article/us-india-landrights-caste-trfn-idUSKBN20T0T1. (accessed June 14, 2022).

2. Gokhale, Nihar. 2020. "For Dalits, a landless tryst with destiny." *The Hindu Business Line*. November 13. https://www.thehindubusinessline.com/blink/know/for-dalits-a-landless-tryst-with-destiny/article33090534.ece. (accessed August 16, 2023).

3. Goyal, Divya. 2020. 'How Patiala Villages Ended the Practice of Separate Cremation Grounds for Dalits.' *The Indian Express*. March 15. https://indianexpress.com/article/india/how-patiala-villages-ended-practice-of-separate-cremation-grounds-for-dalits-5772529/. (accessed June 14, 2022).

4. Kummil, Sanu, director. 2019. *Six Feet Under*. 35 min. https://idsffk.in/2019/06/20/six-feet-under/. (accessed June 17, 2022).

5. K, Stalin, director. 2007. *India Untouched: Stories of a People Apart*. Drishti Media, Arts & Human Rights. 108 min. https://www.youtube.com/watch?v=fvke6ycgkL4. (accessed June 14, 2022).

6. Murali, Poornima. 2019. 'Dalits in a Tamil Nadu Village Carry Funeral Procession Through Sewers After Villagers Deny Passage to Crematorium.' *News18*. November 1. https://www.news18.com/news/india/dalits-in-tamil-nadu-wade-through-sewer-to-reach-crematorium-after-upper-caste-community-denies-passage-2370169.html. (accessed June 14, 2022).

7. Pawar, Yogesh. 2015. 'Dalit, Death and the Fight for Dignity.' *DNA.* July 21. https://www.dnaindia.com/india/report-dalits-death-and-the-fight-for-dignity-1961535 (accessed 14 June 2022).

8. Shah, Ghanshyam, Harsh Mander, Sukhdeo Thorat, Satish Deshpande, Amita Baviskar. 2006. *Untouchability in Rural India.* New Delhi: Sage.

Last Rites Among the Kinnar: A Neglected Group

1. Goel, Ina. 2019. 'India's Third Gender Rises Again'. *Sapiens.* September 26. https://www.sapiens.org/biology/hijra-india-third-gender/. (accessed June 12, 2022).

2. Jaffrey, Zia. 1997. *The Invisibles: A Tale of the Eunuchs of India.* London: Weidenfeld & Nicholson.

3. The Indian Express. 2016. "Eunuchs And Transgenders Perform 'Pind-Daan' For Departed Soul in Varanasi." *The Indian Express.* September 24. https://indianexpress.com/article/india/india-news-india/eunuchs-transgenders-perform-pind-daan-for-departed-soul/. (accessed August 11, 2023).

4. KV. Maulika. 2019. 'Death No Great Leveller for Transgender Community.' *The Times of India.* July 24. https://timesofindia.indiatimes.com/city/hyderabad/death-no-great-leveller-for-transgender-community/articleshow/70353569.cms (accessed August 1, 2022).

5. Malhotra, Nishi. 2016. 'For the First Time, 151 Priests in Varanasi Will Perform Post-Death Rituals for Transgenders'. *The Better India.* August 16. https://www.thebetterindia.com/64904/transgenders-cremation-pind-daan-death-rituals-india/. (accessed June 12, 2022).

6. Reddy, Gayatri. 2005. *With Respect to Sex: Negotiating Hijra Identity in South India.* Chicago: University of Chicago Press.

7. Roade, Vaishali. 2013. 'Lakshmi's Story.' *Words Without Borders.* June 1. https://www.wordswithoutborders.org/article/lakshmis-story. (accessed June 12, 2022).

8. Williams, Victoria. 2017. *Celebrating Life Customs Around the World: From Baby Showers to Funerals.* Santa Barbara, CA: ABC-CLIO.

Gender Discrimination in Last Rites

1. Devi, Mahasweta, and Usha Ganguli. 1997. *Rudali.* Trans. Anjum Katyal. Calcutta: Seagull Books.

2. Global Gender Gap Report. 2022. Benchmarking Gender Gaps 2022. World Economic Forum. July 2022. https://www3.weforum.org/docs/WEF_GGGR_2022.pdf. (accessed August 1, 2023).

3. Lamb, Sarah. 2000. *White Saris and Sweet Mangoes: Aging, Gender, and Body in North India.* California: University of California Press.

4. Parry, Jonathan. 1994. *Death in Benares.* Cambridge: Cambridge University Press.

The Funeral Performances: Parai and Gaana from Tamil Nadu

1. Deces, Isabelle Clark. 2005. *No One Cries for the Dead: Tamil Dirges, Rowdy Songs, Graveyard Petitions.* Berkeley and Los Angeles: University of California Press.

2. Kumar, J. Vijay Ratna. 2016. 'A Culture of Transition: A study of Gaana Singers in Chennai.' PhD diss., Manonmaniam Sundaranar University.

3. Srinivasan, Anil. 2018. 'Funeral Songs from Across the World.' *The Hindu*, July 5. https://www.thehindu.com/entertainment/music/funeral-songs-from-across-the-world/article56837137.ece (accessed June 7, 2022).

Grieving Widows in Hindi Cinema

1. Bist, Umesh, director. 2021. *Pagglait.* Balaji Motion Pictures and Sikhya Entertainment. 1 hr., 54 min. https://www.netflix.com/in/title/81242571.
2. Pahwa, Seema, director. 2019. *Ramprasad ki Tehrvi.* Jio Studios. 1 hr., 52 min. https://www.netflix.com/in/title/81113922.
3. Sibal, Vatika. 2018. Stereotyping Women in Indian Cinema. *Scholarly Research Journal for Interdisciplinary Studies* 43, No. 5, https://www.researchgate.net/publication/323786469_STEREOTYPING_WOMEN_IN_INDIAN_CINEMA (accessed June 12, 2021).
4. Srivastava, Soumya. 2021. 'Pagglait Movie Review: Sanya Malhotra is Anything But Crazy in This Tale of Family, Death and Rebirth.' *Hindustan Times.* March 26. https://www.hindustantimes.com/entertainment/bollywood/pagglait-movie-review-sanya-malhotra-is-anything-but-crazy-in-this-tale-of-family-death-and-rebirth-101616741326668.html (accessed June 12, 2021).

Gendered Mourning: Rudaalis, Mirasans and Oppari

1. Chandrasekar, Anand. 2016. 'The Dying Art of Professional Mourning.' *SWI.* July 19. *https://www.swissinfo.ch/eng/from-india-to-switzerland_the-dying-art-of-professional-mourning-/42290112.* (accessed June 17, 2022).

2. Das Reetamoni and Nath Debarshi Prasad. 2014. Rudaali in Film Narrative: Looking Through the Feminist Lens. *Cinej Cinema Journal.* 3.2. https://pdfs.semanticscholar. org/5e58/9c867294c6fde00c7bd1eb97030c53ad9441. pdf?_ga=2.200475310.1405006402.1625819227-2021192368.1625819227 (accessed August 11, 2023).

3. Deces, Isabelle Clark. 2005. *No One Cries for the Dead: Tamil Dirges, Rowdy Songs, Graveyard Petitions.* Berkeley and Los Angeles: University of California Press.

4. Devi, Mahasweta, and Usha Ganguli. 1997. *Rudali.* Trans. Anjum Katyal. Calcutta: Seagull Books.

5. Greene, Paul D. 2000. Professional Weeping: Music, Affect, and Hierarchy in a South Indian Folk Performance Art. *Ethnomusicology,* no 5, (January 10), https://www2.umbc. edu/eol/5/greene/Greene_2.htm (accessed June 18, 2022).

6. Jhingan, Shikha, director. 2001. *Mirasans of Punjab.* 49 minutes. IGNCA. https://archive.org/details/dli.Mirasans. Of.Punjab. (accessed June 17, 2022).

7. Kohli, Namita. 2016. 'Songs of Experience: The Mirasi Women of Punjab.' *Hindustan Times.* April 27. https:// www.hindustantimes.com/art-and-culture/songs-of-experience-the-mirasi-women-of-punjab/story-olsROIl9BtaPMoBOfVqUbJ.html. (accessed June 17, 2022).

8. Kundalia, Nidhi Dugar. 2015. *The Lost Generation, Chronicling India's Dying Professions.* Gurgaon: Penguin Random House India.

9. Lajmi, Kalpana, director. 1993. *Rudaali.* NDFC. 115 minutes. https://www.amazon.com/Rudaali-Rakhee-Gulzar/dp/B09CFW7RDZ.

10. Parry, Jonathan. 1994. *Death in Benares.* Cambridge: Cambridge University Press.

11. Schreffler, Gibb. 2011. Music and Musicians in Punjab: An Introduction to the Special Issue. *Journal of Punjab Studies* 18: 1-48.

12. Singh, Surjeet. 2016. *Oral Traditions and Cultural Heritage of Punjab*. Patiala: Punjabi University.

Deaths during the Pandemic: Challenges and Learnings

1. Arnold, David. 2017. Burning Issues: Cremation and Incineration in Modern India. *Springer* 24: 393-419.

2. Chattopadhyay, Sohini. 2020. What Researching Cremations of the Dead in Colonial India Taught Me About Life in Our Cities Today. *Scroll.* August 23. https://scroll.in/article/971096/what-researching-cremations-of-the-dead-in-colonial-india-taught-me-about-life-in-our-cities-today (accessed June 23, 2022).

3. National Human Rights Commission India. 2021. NHRC issues Advisory to the Centre and States to ensure dignity and the rights of the dead. NHRC. 14th May. https://nhrc.nic.in/media/press-release/nhrc-issues-advisory-centre-and-states-ensure-dignity-and-rights-dead-14052021. (accessed August 11 2023).

4. Parry, Jonathan. 1994. *Death in Benares*. Cambridge: Cambridge University Press.

5. Smil, Vaclav. 2008. *Global Catastrophes and Trends: The Next Fifty Years*. Massachusetts: MIT Press.

6. WHO. 2020. 'Infection Prevention and Control for the Safe Management of a Dead Body in the Context of COVID-19: Interim Guidance.' https://www.who.int/publications/i/item/infection-prevention-and-control-for-the-safe-management-of-a-dead-body-in-the-context-of-covid-19-interim-guidance (accessed June 29, 2022).

Acknowledgements

Writing acknowledgements is the best part of writing a book. At the onset, I want to thank my husband Sourabh for believing in me and being my best critic. You are a great listener! My seamless writing wouldn't have been possible without your unwavering support.

My heartfelt thanks to my daughter Kaavya for curiously enquiring about my book progress and sacrificing our time together. You are my ultimate cheerleader, Kaavi.

Thanks, Papa, for blessing me from heaven—I know you have been watching after me. How I wish you were here to hold the copy. I sincerely thank my mummy for her unconditional love and deep respect for my work. I thank my sister, Sakshi, for her support even though she dreads discussing death. Thanks, mom and dad, for worrying about my deadline and encouraging me. I wish my grandparents, mummyji and papaji were here to bless me in person.

I sincerely thank my publisher HarperCollins for giving space to this title. I deeply thank my editor, Prerna Gill, for her helping me conceptualize and envision the book. This book wouldn't have become as exciting without your involvement.

I thank Amrit for taking me around and deepening my understanding of Varanasi. Finally, I sincerely thank Dr Ravi Nandan Singh for deepening my knowledge of the subject with his insights.

My immense gratitude to all my friends. Thanks, Neha Bhat, for helping me. I want to thank my friend, Anupreet, for being my cheerleader. Vibhav Nuwal, thanks for showing excitement about the subject. Sharique, thanks for clearing my doubts on Muslim last rites and rituals. My colleagues and friends from my alma mater, JNU, have been a great help. Thanks for helping me download relevant books and academic articles. Thanks, Naveen, for helping me get in touch with the activists. Gunjan Arora, a big thanks for retrieving the relevant articles and materials. I thank Aarti Kapoor for making my section on personal stories livelier.

I sincerely thank all the people who have made this book possible and whose voices I feature in the volume. I hope I have done justice to your narratives. But, ultimately, I want to thank the entire universe that came together to help me write this book. It's been an incredible journey, I must say.